A Blueprint for Humanity

Prof. Paul Tillich, c. 1935.
(Paul Tillich Archives, Harvard Divinity School Library.)

A Blueprint for Humanity

Paul Tillich's Theology
of Culture

Raymond F. Bulman

Lewisburg
Bucknell University Press
London and Toronto: Associated University Presses

© 1981 by Associated University Presses, Inc.

Associated University Presses, Inc.
4 Cornwall Drive
East Brunswick, New Jersey 08816

Associated University Presses
69 Fleet Street
London EC4Y 1EU, England

Associated University Presses
Toronto M5E 1A7, Canada

Library of Congress Cataloging in Publication Data

Bulman, Raymond F   1933-
   A blueprint for humanity.

   Bibliography: p.
   Includes index.
   1. Christianity and culture.   2. Tillich, Paul,
1886-1965.   I. Title.
BR115.C8B84   230   78-75208
ISBN 0-8387-5000-1

Printed in the United States of America

To My Wife

As wings to bird,
water to fish,
life to the living—
so you to me.
But tell me,
Madhava, beloved,
who are you?
Who are you really?

Vidyapāti says, they are one another.
Songs from the Bengali

Contents

Foreword

James Luther Adams

Paul Tillich's theology of culture was intended not only to provide a fresh conceptualization of the ground and meaning of human existence but also to relate them to the various spheres of culture, to individual and institutional behavior, to daily life and its anxieties, to politics, economics, and technology, to the arts and the sciences, to education and worship. What with the continuing interest in his writings, it is important for us to recognize that it is his theology of culture that constitutes the most embracing approach to the understanding (and criticism) of his whole outlook and effort. We are therefore fortunate to have here available Dr. Bulman's lucid, comprehensive exposition.

The first lecture Tillich published after his four years of field service as chaplain in the German army in the First World War was entitled "On the Idea of a Theology of Culture," delivered before the Kant Society in Berlin in April 1919. He was thirty-two years of age. We may take it as a sign of his reputation that he was at this age invited to speak before that prestigious body. Even more striking is that in this lecture he set forth what turned out to be his conception of his life-vocation as a theologian.

Although the lecture reads like a typical academic performance, it was forged in the teeth of the cultural disaster of 1914–1919. It did come as from a Hotspur

. . . perfumed like a milliner
And 'twixt his finger and his thumb holding
A pouncet-box, which ever and anon
He gave his nose and took 't away again.

During the war he had experienced the agony of carrion
struggle leading to national defeat; he had conducted the
burial of scores of soldiers. At one period in the war he was
compelled by the strain to repair to a hospital for recupera-
tion. After the war he adopted for a time a Bohemian style of
life.

Following upon the war the German economy was practically in chaos. By reason of the daily and rapid decrease in the
value of the German mark, the middle class saw itself being
virtually wiped out. Moreover, workers on receiving their
paychecks would run frantically to the bank to cash them at
the earliest possible moment. Revolutionary groups had been
formed at the right and the left. On 9 November 1918, Kaiser
Wilhelm had fled to the Netherlands, and the Armistice had
been declared on 11 November. On 29 December Gustav
Noske, a Majority Socialist, organized a volunteer corps with
which to defeat revolution from the left, and on 11 January
1919, in the midst of heavy street-fighting, these volunteers
entered Berlin. On the evening of 15 January the two Sparta-
cist leaders, Karl Liebknecht and Rosa Luxemburg, were
arrested and murdered by the volunteer officers. On 19
January elections for a national assembly were held. This
assembly met on 6 February in Weimar and eventually prom-
ulgated the Constitution. On 1 January Tillich had been
released from army service. On 16 April he delivered the Kant
Society lecture.

Many of the forces that surrounded him at this time were
evident throughout his life. A quarter of a century after the
First World War he said, "We did not feel it in its horrible
depth and its incredible thoroughness." The triumph of
Nazism in Germany leading to the Second World War
confirmed this feeling of the "horrible depth" of the crisis.
The whole period of his lifetime he spoke of as "our disinte-

grating world," "the end of the Protestant era." After the Second World War he characterized the cultural situation as "a sacred void."

Between 1910 and 1915 he had published three books, two on the philosopher Schelling, and one a critique of the concept of the supernatural. Before the end of the war he sensed the collapse of philosophical idealism, and came to believe that the regnant ideologies of the nineteenth century, including those of the churches, had lost their relevance and power.

During the year 1919, in addition to the Kant Society lecture, two publications came from Tillich's pen, showing the stance he took in face of the political situation. One was a brochure on "Socialism as a Question for the Church" and the other an article on "Christianity and Socialism." The latter was a speech he gave less than a month after the delivery of his lecture before the Kant Society. To the shock of many of his fellow churchmen, this speech was given at a meeting of a left-wing group, the Independent Socialist Party. Because of this he was reprimanded by a representative of the conservative Protestant Consistory of Brandenberg of which his father was a member. A few years later he became one of the first theological protesters against the burgeoning Nazi Party. Just before Hitler came into power he published his book entitled *The Socialist Decision*, a critique of the regnant socialist ideology and an exposition of religious socialism. During the 1920's he published articles on a great variety of topics belonging to his theology of culture as well as a book on the system of the sciences, a *Philosophy of Religion*, a book on mass culture in relation to the plastic arts, and his best-seller, *The Religious Situation* (later to be translated by H. Richard Niebuhr). Beside all this he published critical essays on a number of philosophical and theological figures from Augustine to Troeltsch, Otto and Barth.

In these writings Tillich devised the concepts that became the coinage that for the rest of his life would be associated with his name—in effect a new language to provide self-transcending clues to the human condition. In his view, much of the familiar language had been frayed by routine usage. He wanted a language that even in the midst of meaninglessness would effectively point to the Majesty of God, allowing it, as Gerard Manley Hopkins would say, to "flame out, like shining from shook foil."

Although this coinage was in the main adapted from Biblical sources—for example, such concepts as kairos, the demonic, the Kingdom of God—it was also drawn from philosophical sources—such concepts as theonomy, meaning, the Unconditional, ecstasy, import (or substance), ground and abyss, the Protestant principle, the Gestalt of grace, the manifest and the latent church, and religion as "ultimate concern." Thus his theology of culture must be seen in the context of historic humanism as well as of Biblical literature. The figures of this historic humanism, screened through Tillich's apperception and serving often as critics of religion, are as varied as those that appear in Raphael's *The School of Athens*.

But in order to sense the thrust of Tillich's theology of culture one must not forget that the coinage, his linguistic cachet, was minted for the purpose of discerning meaning—significant interrelatedness in religion and culture—in order to identify latent promise and creativity as well as distortion and destruction.

The recognition of the turmoil and the bewilderment and of the universal involvement in them Tillich did not find in the churches. They were content in the main to proclaim the Word from on high in self-righteous aloofness. Nor did he find an adequate recognition in the thunderings of Karl Barth who in this early period placed everything under indiscriminate judgment in the name of the Word—Barth saw in the present culture only "judgment without grace." Idealism with its idols (which had crumbled in face of disaster) wanted to see "grace without judgment." The "religious" tendency was to make a sharp distinction between religion and culture, forgetting that the moment religion finds expression it is itself a part of culture. Tillich, recognizing ambiguity in both religious and cultural expression, indeed perceiving the positive as well as the negative in both, came to the formulation, "Culture is the form of religion, and religion is the substance of culture." Religion and culture are thus "mutually immanent." In differing ways both are motivated by "ultimate concern."

What one needs therefore is a sort of X-ray detector not only to find the religious elements that somehow inform every aspect of culture and, to identify substitute or distorted forms of religion but also to discover that which goes beyond both culture and religion breaking through their self-enclosed idols to provide both judgment and grace. The theologian of culture must understand history in these terms.

What Tillich saw in history (past and present) with its grace and its disgrace, with its freedom and fate, may perhaps be symbolized by the "action painting" of Jackson Pollock. Viewing his paintings at first blush, some of the critics were reminded of Ruskin's charge that Whistler had only flung a pot of paint at a canvas and "in the public's face." Pollock saw in paint not a passive substance to be manipulated but a storehouse of pent-up forces for the painter to release; and he intended to release them by pouring and spattering his colors on a large canvas instead of transmitting the paint from the tip of the brush. The consequence is that the billowing and surging of shapes and lines on the immense canvas reveal the internal dynamics of his material and of the process releasing energy, so to speak, in a field of combat.

In Tillich's theology of culture the historical process is somewhat similar to what one sees in an "action painting"—continuities and conflicts, unities and contradictions, affinities and disjunctions, revealing the energies of the power of being and its distortions—all in a field of combat. Fundamental for Tillich here is the presupposition that conditioned beings participate ambiguously in unconditioned Being. Dr. Bulman expounds in detail this ontological interpretation of the human condition and of history, showing the pervasiveness of the coincidence of opposites.

The task of Tillich's theology of culture is also to discriminate the shadings between the overt and the covert, the explicit and the implicit, the esoteric and the exoteric, the authentic and the idolatrous, even finding the religious hidden in the secular—discerning, as Tillich would say, the temptations and the seductions but also the creativity. Important to note here is Tillich's rejection of the notion that the religious stands alongside the secular, indeed the notion that the divine is a Being, a Supreme Being, alongside or above other entities. Rather, the divine "flames out, like shining from shook foil," revealing "the paradoxical immanence of the transcendent" in and through *concrete* phenomena in all spheres of existence, to be observed most crucially in the total historical situation of turmoil and bewilderment. Critical response to this Power engenders "the courage to be" and to become.

Before we consider some of the concepts Tillich employed to identify the differentiations in culture and religion, we should note two things. First, the distinctions employed (in great number) do not obtain only between the religions and cultures but also within them. They are not vertical so much as they are horizontal, reaching across the religions and cultures. To be sure, Tillich initially drew (and modified) differentiations from the traditions with which he was more directly familiar. The second thing to note is the fact that from the beginning of his career, indeed even in his youth, he was confronted by and felt oppressed by authoritarianism, at first in the sphere of religion and later in the political and economic spheres. Early in life he came into conflict with his father as the representative of orthodoxy; at the same time he felt that by resistance for the sake of independence he incurred guilt in the violating of tabus. In time he gained freedom by means of philosophical perspectives available to him from his training in the German *gymnasium* and the university. Only a little later he was captured by Schelling's Romantic philosophy of freedom.

Out of this and analogous conflicts he early developed the distinction between autonomy and heteronomy, the "law" from within and the alien "law" from without. But both of these authorities were to be seen as provisional, for he recognized a sublation of the autonomous and the mandatory in a theonomy transcending them both. Accordingly, the "law" from within the individual or the culture is not properly to be abrogated; it is rather to be fulfilled or deepened. Theonomy, viewed in its broadest dimensions, is a "culture in which the ultimate meaning of existence shines through all finite forms of thought and action." To be sure, theonomy in this broad sense is rarely, if ever, to be found. Indeed, the three terms are to be interpreted as types. In this typological sense one or other of the three attitudes may dominate a period in the history of religion and culture. The high Middle Ages were in the main theonomous in contrast on the one hand to the heteronomy of the later Middle Ages and on the other to the complacent autonomy or "self-sufficient finitude" of modern humanism and of bourgeois society, a finitude which, if not deepened by theonomy, is on the way to emptiness or to heteronomy. By means of such concepts as these (and others) Tillich was able to formulate a conception of different philosophies of history and also to delineate his own. Here his procedure is somewhat analogous to, though not dependent on, the dynamic philosophy of history coming from Max Weber who distinguished between traditional, legal-rational, and charismatic authorities.

The conceptualizations devised or adapted by Tillich are more or less familiar. It may be instructive, however, if we briefly note the historical provenance of some of these concepts. For example, the distinctions between autonomy, heteronomy and theonomy had been successively delineated by Immanuel Kant, Richard Rothe, and Ernst Troeltsch. Indeed, the relation between autonomy and theonomy defined by Tillich was indicated by Troeltsch in his term *Autotheonomie*. For Tillich, moreover, there may be a hidden theonomy in secularism.

All of these concepts are interrelated and find explication in "the Protestant principle" (implicit in the doctrine of justification through faith) which negates every claim to finality or absoluteness (idolatry), negating also every relativistic nihilism, by affirming "all genuine creativity and discovery," including openness to criticism from the realm of the secular, an indispensable source. The concept of "the Protestant principle" was over a century ago employed by Friedrich Julius Stahl, the shaper of the Throne-and-Altar ideology, who made the doctrine of justification by faith the ground for authoritarian, antidemocratic monarchism. "Authority, not Majority" was his slogan.

Tillich often speaks of the distinction between content and import (or substance). Initially, he applied the distinction to painting, the import being a sense of the transcendent—of spiritual depth. A painting may have a spiritual depth or import that has little to do with the content, the subject, or the picture, for an ultimate meaning may "shine through." This distinction between content and import involves in German a play upon sounds, *Inhalt* and *Gehalt,* a formulation used by Hegel in his *Lectures on Aesthetics,* though the meaning of *Gehalt* is different for Tillich from what it was for Hegel.

The concept of *meaning* may be traced also to German philosophical idealism which employed it to cut across religion and culture, in order to find in them various relationships between the finite and the infinite. Schelling, for example, finds this variety of relatedness *successively* in polytheism, radical dualism, exclusive monotheism, and Christology. Polytheism possesses the virtue of concreteness but it idolatrously identifies a concrete-finite sphere with the infinite; Christology combines concreteness with the idea of judgment and the universality of exclusive monotheism. Here we see the ingredients of a dynamic philosophy of history. Most prominent among the later philosophical idealists who used the concept of meaning in a fundamental way were Wilhelm Dilthey and Rudolf Eucken. Reinhold Niebuhr understood religion to be concerned with "the source of meaning" in "a total scheme of meaning." We should note here that Schelling's philosophy of history (an evolutionary cosmology) attracted Charles S. Peirce who at one time referred to his own philosophy as "Schellingian"; John Dewey, like Tillich, was impressed by Schelling's view regarding the pervasiveness of the aesthetic experience. Tillich saw Schelling, along with

Kierkegaard and Marx, as among the first of the existentialists, all serving as his mentors (not, to be sure, without critical scrutiny).

The concept of *kairos* ("fulfilled time") is historically of early vintage, to be traced to ancient Greek thought as well as to the New Testament. In the latter it refers to the fulfillment of time in the appearance of Jesus as the Christ after a long period of preparation.

> *Kairos* implies that the central event—the appearance of the Christ—is not an isolated happening falling, so to speak, from heaven; but that it is an event which is prepared for by history and by the "timing" of historical providence. One can express this by saying that "the great *kairos*" presupposes many smaller *kairoi* within the historical development by which it was prepared. From this statement one can derive the other; that in order for "the great *kairos*" to be received many smaller *kairoi* are required in the historical development following it.

"The great *kairos*" provides the universal criteria for decision and opportunity. For Tillich the concept bespeaks a decisive relationship between theonomy and the concrete, dynamic historical situation; it bespeaks also a theology of history that takes history seriously as the arena of responsible decision. Tillich radicalized this idea of *kairos* to make it applicable to the historical process anywhere, also in other religions and cultures.

The concept was given contemporary relevance when the Tillichian Religious Socialism attempted to come to terms with the crisis situation at the end of the First World War, a situation that gave occasion for this group to delineate what was held to be a religious interpretation of history. From Tillich's point of view the concept points to the critical transcendence of the divine over against pessimism or conservatism on the one hand and against utopianism on the other. At the same time it recognizes concrete personal and social demonries which must be struggled against.

Probably the concept of the demonic has been given wider currency in our time by Tillich than by any other writer.

Again we encounter here an ancient concept. Demonology has been a venerable concern in all cultures. In the New Testament, a demonic possession was viewed as a psychological phenomenon of numinous origin, understood to be ambiguous in that deranged persons may have special insight. In subsequent Christian history it tended as a concept to lose its ambiguous character. This ambiguity was recovered by Schelling and before him by the seventeenth-century Lutheran mystic who saw in Lucifer the demonic as participating in being, also as expressing autonomous freedom, and yet bloated with self-seeking—and thus representing a radical tension between the universal and the self-isolating will *(der eigene Will)*. Especially significant is the adaptation given by the Lutheran pastor Christoph Blumhardt (the younger) at the end of the nineteenth century. With him, as with Augustine, the concept of the demonic is expanded from the psychological to the social-institutional sphere. He suggested that demonic powers had invaded the bourgeois churches, and were rightly being attacked by the (Marxist) Social Democrats. A generation later Tillich referred to Blumhardt in his defence for having made a speech at a meeting of the Independent Socialists (noted earlier in this Preface). With Tillich, however, the concept recovers its earlier ambiguity. The demonic may be creative as well as destructive (though it is defined as dominantly destructive). This ambiguity is interpreted ontologically by Tillich. If the demonic did not offer promise of meaningful fulfillment, it could not be seductive, it could not offer temptation to the abuse of freedom. If on the other hand it did not in some measure participate in the structures of reality (and in the power of Being) it would become Satanic, that is, non-existent. By reason of its primeval power, however, it is not to be overcome by good will or moral resolution but only by a *Gestalt of grace* which, like the demonic itself, is "holy" and ultimately not under human control. Therefore, one may only prepare for it. As in the New Testament, then, history is seen as a struggle between the divine and the demonic.

These are only a limited number of the concepts devised by

Tillich to deal with the phenomena of religion and culture. I have not at all considered his conceptualization of the doctrine of the church. I have done no more than merely to mention his analysis of current political and economic structures, their demonries and needed changes. Nor have I even mentioned his ontological categories, essence, existence, and estrangement. These categories, along with the concepts already discussed here, he employs in one of the most elaborate documents of its kind, his memorandum on "Christian and Marxist Views of Human Nature," prepared for the 1937 World Conference of Churches at Oxford. Four and five years later in essays on "Protestant Principles" and on "War Aims" he set forth a program for economic and political organization, including "Application to the Churches"—"in order to anticipate a united world." In all of this we see the dialectical character of Tillich's theology of culture, its pathos for the concrete, and its relation to a kairotic interpretation of history. These are the features Dr. Bulman takes into account in his substantial presentation of Tillich's theology of culture as an intellectual discipline relating culture to theology.

There are so many facets to Tillich's theology of culture, ranging far and wide as it does boldly and with considerable specificity, and finding utterance in a massive literary output, that occasions for criticism are legion.

Perhaps one of the most radical of the criticisms of Tillich is the claim that his fundamental approach is phenomenological and that his explication of theological-ethical criteria "precede and determine his Christology rather than being determined by it." This claim is made possible by the relative lack of Biblical exegesis in his writings, except perhaps in his sermons.

For some theologians his orientation to a doctrine of being (ontology) represents a diversion of attention from a Biblical foundation. One way of evaluating this claim is to assert that the Christian perspective is only one dimension of his outlook, albeit a pervasive one. Moreover, he saw no reason for failing to explore the ontological implications of Biblical thought.

An analogous criticism is the claim that his conception of culture with its sometimes hidden theonomy takes the sharp edge from his critique of culture and of its characteristically "self-sufficient finitude." This criticism is the sort that becomes almost inevitable for an apologetic theologian addressing himself as apostle to the Gentiles and especially to what Schleiermacher called "the cultured despisers of religion." The charge becomes all the more plausible in the light of Tillich's sharp criticisms of the churches. When we consider the reductions effected by some of his admirers we must say that "the hardest knife ill-used doth lose his edge." We of course have not heard the last of these criticisms.

They will appear to be confirmed by Tillich's views as set forth in the last lecture he gave, the lecture on "The History of Religions and the Systematic Theologian" (1965). Here he uses his characteristic concepts to arrive at a critical appreciation of the great world religions. Accordingly, he asserts that

> Revelatory experiences are universally human. Religions are based on something that is given to a man wherever he lives. He is given a revelation, a particular kind of experience which always implies saving powers. There are revealing and saving powers in all religions. God has not left himself unwitnessed.

In a tribute to Tillich written after his death, Mircea Eliade stated, "In the course of that superb and moving lecture, Professor Tillich declared that, had he had time he would write a new *Systematic Theology* oriented toward, and in dialogue with, the whole history of religions . . . a theology taking into consideration not only the existential crisis and the religious vacuum of contemporary Western societies, but also the religious traditions of Asia and the primitive world, together with their recent crises and traumatic transformations." Professor Eliade concludes by saying, "One of the dominant characteristics of his thought was the capacity for renewing itself after an encounter with a radically different, and even inimical, ideology or historical situation."

Tillich began to develop his theology of culture in face of

the crisis of 1919 in Germany, and it finds its culmination as he confronts the global crisis of our time, recognizing the threat of destruction and yet looking for seeds of renewal. In this situation and in the spirit of his theology of culture Tillich, eschewing both despair and dogmatism, both cynicism and utopianism, declared that "a system should be not only a point of arrival but a point of departure as well. It should be like a station at which preliminary truth is crystallized on the endless road toward truth."

Preface

Contemporary society continues to undergo radical changes, both institutional and psychological, that have a profound effect on our culture and on human self-understanding. The rapidity and extent of these changes tend to produce confusion and uncertainty in values and a loss of a sense of purpose. The traditional religious answers that satisfied our forefathers appear outdated and irrelevant in light of our new cultural situation. The persistence of the churches in simply repeating these antiquated formulas, reflecting questions of a past age, has succeeded in alienating countless numbers of modern people from the option of a religious world view and driven them to a purely secular interpretation of human existence.

Philosopher-theologian Paul Tillich, one of the greatest religious thinkers of our century, showed a profound and sympathetic understanding of this disenchantment with religious dogmas and institutions that seemed fast on their way toward becoming quaint souvenirs of the past. Tillich saw contemporary secularism as a necessary protest against the authoritarian entrenchment of religion at the expense of human autonomy and real spiritual advancement.

Tillich was convinced, on the other hand, that this protest had taken the form of an overreaction that would eventually rob modern man of his own religious or depth dimension, thereby creating a spiritual void and a loss of meaning. In his theology of culture, he offers us the vision of a fully human and truly progressive society in which the most creative human achievements will be intimately united to their own

25

religious depth. The following pages deal with an exposition and critique of this *Blueprint for Humanity* which Tillich left us as his theological legacy.

Raymond F. Bulman

St. John's University

Acknowledgments

To Professors John H. Randall, Jr., the late Horace L. Friess, Joseph L. Blau, and James A. Martin, Jr. of Columbia University for their valuable insights and suggestions.

To Professor A. J. Ayer of Oxford University for generously sharing his views on humanism and to H. J. Blackham, former director of the British Humanist Association, for his helpful clarifications as well as living exemplification of the best in the humanist spirit.

Especially to Dr. John Macquarrie, the Lady Margaret Professor of Divinity at Christ Church, Oxford, who guided me through the initial stages of this study, which resulted in a doctoral dissertation presented to Columbia University. This book is an adaptation, updating and revision of that earlier work. That my research visit at Oxford was as pleasant as it was fruitful I also owe to Dr. Macquarrie.

To St. John's University for their support in granting me time for research. To Dr. David B. Evans of St. John's University and Dr. Minna Cardoza of Queens College for their helpful criticism of the manuscript. And to Mary Bowen and James Annarelli for their competent help in preparing the manuscript for publication.

To Chicago University Press for permission to quote from *Systematic Theology* and from *The Protestant Era*, both by Paul Tillich.

To Professor James Luther Adams, President Emeritus of the North American Paul Tillich Society, for his many helpful suggestions and especially for his willingness to enhance the book with his preface.

Finally, to the late Professor Charles Frankel of Columbia University, who contributed a number of important ideas to this study, and whose tragic and untimely death was a great loss to the American academic community.

A Blueprint for Humanity

1
Introduction

The work of Paul Tillich scarcely needs an introduction, especially in this country, where he won his greatest fame as a theologian, philosopher, and religious interpreter of culture. Indeed, Paul Tillich, who had already established himself academically in a very productive career before coming to the United States at the age of forty-seven, has been widely proclaimed as the greatest American theologian of this century. He is also considered by some notable historians to have made a significant contribution to the current revival of metaphysical thought, and to have possessed, in general, "a first-rate philosophical mind."[1] On the other hand, serious objections have been raised against various aspects of Tillich's thought, by his fellow theologians, as well as by philosophers and secular critics of his system.

This work deals with Paul Tillich's theology of culture and with his interpretation of contemporary secular humanism within that context. In the course of analyzing and evaluating Tillich's theological reflections on the human and divine in our culture today, we also hope to respond to a major objection that has been growing in frequency and strength among critics of Tillich's thought. This objection consists essentially in the claim that Tillich is not really a Christian theologian at all, and that he only serves to bring confusion to important issues by using religious symbols in a way that is substantially different from their ordinary use, and, in general, by masquerading as something other than he really is. At heart, these critics maintain, Tillich was really a humanist, a nontheist, for whom the Christian symbols merely served to keep him within the community and tradition to which he had deep emotional attachment. In short, Tillich is said to be a Christian in name only, or, as has been sometimes stated, Tillich was a "humanist in disguise."[2]

Tillich and Humanism

Before examining Tillich's understanding of secular humanism it would be of value to clarify the nature of this objection, insofar as the issue it raises has important bearing on this study. A careful examination of the relevant literature reveals that there are, in fact, two principal variations on the objection. The first variation maintains that Tillich's philosophical and humanistic presuppositions render his thought intrinsically incompatible with the Christian faith, despite Tillich's attestations that he explicitly intended to take his stance from within the framework of the Christian tradition, or as he expresses it sometimes, within the "theological circle." The second variation is less flattering than the first, in that it attributes to Tillich an *intentional* plan of deception. Ordinarily, this second approach takes the form of an accusation of "double-speak," in which Tillich is said to have had separate messages for different audiences, and to have tried to preserve his loyalty to the Christian tradition, as well as to his own philosophical system, through this kind of intellectual maneuvering. This form of the objection assumes that without such a device Tillich's thought is incompatible with Christian faith. At times, however, this second variation has taken an even harsher turn, as in the case of a recent work by Leonard Wheat,[3] who presents Tillich as the great theological impostor of our times. Tillich, according to Wheat, has by way of a very clever hoax managed to undermine the Christian faith from within, while successfully winning from his peers universal acclaim as a leading theologian.

philosophical and theological expertise to the interpretation of an astounding variety of cultural phenomena, including such issues as types of art, movements in history, schools of psychoanalysis, modern architecture, and current economic and political thought. Understandably, the works of this genre are usually gathered under the heading of "theology of culture." It is unfortunate and even misleading that commentators on Tillich only rarely seem aware that he saw his *entire* theological enterprise as a theology of culture. The student of Tillich would make a serious mistake to think that these apparently autonomous pieces represent the substance of his theology of culture. Indeed, it is a central task of this book to vindicate the view that the essential core and inner *Geist* of Tillich's entire theological system is precisely the theology of culture.

Beyond this, it must also be shown that what the theology of culture is to Tillich's theological work in general, the concept of "theonomy" is to the theology of culture, i.e., its keystone and nucleus. In the course of tracing the growth and development of the theology of culture, we are attempting to substantiate the central role of the notion of theonomy and to point out its function and impact on Tillich's interpretation of secular humanism.

In our judgment, Tillich occupies a unique place among theologians who have addressed themselves to reading the signs of our times, so that Paul Lehmann is guilty of no exaggeration when he writes:

> No theologian . . . in the tradition of the Reformation has addressed himself to the tremendous responsibility for culture, for the life of man as it is actually lived in time and space, with the passion and persistence, the consecration and learning that marks Paul Tillich's life-long work.[4]

According to Tillich's multifaceted yet intricately systematic analysis of culture, the current characteristic world view is the spirit of *secularity,* or, as he sometimes called it in more dramatic terms, the spirit of "self-sufficient finitude." It is not by chance or arbitrary decision, therefore, that Tillich's

Despite the various forms of this objection, a co
theme runs through them all, namely, the convictio
beneath the protective covering of the traditional Ch
symbols, combined with a clever mixture of idealist, ex
tialist, and psychoanalytic terms, Tillich's authentic me
is essentially a kind of ecstatic, naturalistic humanism, th
quite irreconcilable with Christian belief.

The goals of the present work Our main purpose in t
investigation is to explore the background, development, a
structure of the theology of culture and to discover the preci
location of secular humanism on the dynamic map that Tillic
has drawn of contemporary technological culture. The worl
outlook we are describing by the term *secular humanism* i
more than a movement or school of thought (though it
certainly includes a number of noteworthy and effective
organizations, with particularly strong impact among the
more intellectual sectors of society); it is rather a comprehensive *Weltanschauung* that permeates the attitudes and fashions
the temper of modern Western society. Not only does it offer
an alternative sense of meaning and purpose for people who
no longer find biblical faith a viable option but it also makes a
significant impact on the thought and feelings of those who
remain loyal to their church and religious traditions. To a
great extent, for the believing Christian or Jew, to reflect on
secular humanism is at the same time a form of self-
examination.

Tillich's work as a theologian is widely known among
scholars of varied disciplines, among atheists as well as believers, and can even boast a substantial popular audience. Tillich
has, doubtlessly, won his greatest fame as a systematic
theologian and his three-volumed *Systematic Theology* is
considered his greatest intellectual achievement. Tillich is also
frequently referred to as a philosopher-theologian, and
fittingly so, for he has not only produced a number of
significant philosophical works but his theological thought is
thoroughly immersed in a complex philosophical framework.

In addition to these works, Tillich has directed both his

apologetic or dialectical theology was directed to a specifically "secular" cultural situation: "Most of my writings," declared Tillich in the 1959 preface to his *Theology of Culture,* "including the two volumes of *Systematic Theology*—try to define the way in which Christianity is related to secular culture."[5]

The meaning of the term secular   The word *secular* is currently understood in a variety of ways, and religious writers express a marked diversity of reactions to the reality this term is meant to indicate. Ordinarily, for more traditional theologians, for example, the term *secular* connotes a very negative, antireligious attitude, often equivalent to "loss of faith." For liberal theologians, especially of the 1960s, the term has a very positive significance, such as in Harvey Cox's idea of the religious "celebration of the secular." For still a third group, in which we will locate Tillich, although the "secular" is taken very seriously, and where possible, positively, it has a rather ambiguous value, insofar as it can easily yield to exaggerations and distortions that are incompatible with biblical faith.[6]

In this last view, the "secular" is treated as a factual element of our culture—neutral in itself, but capable of both destructive and creative possibilities. This dialectical relationship of theology to the secular has certain unexpected affinities to the social sciences, which, since the time of Max Weber, have attempted to rescue the term *secular* from its acquired ideological and controversial connotations and restore it, if possible, to its more fundamental meaning, which hopefully can be simply descriptive or neutral.

The etymological history of the term immediately offers some justification for this approach, for the word *secular* (Lat. *secularis, saeculum*) was used in pre-Christian, classical Rome simply as a "temporal" term to describe the world. It was the counterpart of *mundus,* which signified the world in its "spatial" aspect. Thus, at the time of the emperor Augustus, the *ludi saeculares* ("secular games") were celebrated every one hundred and twenty years. During these games, which had an unmistakably religious character, hymns called *carmina saecularia* ("secular hymns") were sung. Obviously, the term was not then antithetical to religion.

Under the impact of Christian eschatology, with its sharp contrast between "this world" *(hoc saeculum)* and "the world to come" *(vita venturi saeculi),* a gradual change of connotation and valuation in the term begins to be noticeable. For example, by the end of the fourth century we find Saint Jerome translating in the Latin Vulgate the term *this world* (aiōn toūto) of Romans 12:2—which signified the world under the power of Satan—by the phrase *hoc saeculum: "et nolite conformari huic saeculo."*[7] In the Middle Ages the word began to mean "nonspiritual"—belonging to this transitory existence, as in the expressions *secular clergy* and *secular arm.* Thus, canon law forbade a woman to dress in a secular or worldly fashion in sacred places: *"mulierem saeculariter ornari."*[8]

Once the secular realm actually began to achieve some significant autonomy during the late Middle Ages and the Renaissance it began to threaten the church, which had reluctantly to yield its absolute control over such vital areas as education, politics, science, and the arts. Understandably, under such circumstances, the concept of the secular became more negative and the term began to be used more frequently with derogatory and negative connotations. Church lands confiscated by civil authorities during the Reformation were referred to as "secularized," so that by this time, in church usage, the term has acquired an unmistakably negative significance.

The nineteenth-century struggles in England between freethinkers and the established church further contributed to the antireligious implications of the term *secular,* especially in the English-speaking world. Under the leadership of H. J. Holyoake, the Secular Society was founded to protect the political rights of the freethinkers and atheists from infringements of church authority. Holyoake coined the term *secularism* to describe his program, defining it as "a practical philosophy for the people intended to interpret and organize life without recourse to the supernatural."⁹ He later joined forces with the more polemical and outspoken Charles Bradlaugh, a self-declared atheist. Significantly, despite this alliance, Holyoake staunchly disassociated himself from atheism, which like theism, he considered to be an overbelief. His attitude was rather practical: "modern man finds neither time nor sufficient motivation for concerning himself with these questions belonging to the "unknown world." Modern man, according to Holyoake, has more than enough to do in attempting to improve his lot and to advance his happiness in the "known world"—the world that could be approached with material means and secular or scientific knowledge.¹⁰

This is the essence of the spirit or temper of modern secularism—it is more agnostic than atheistic; it does not even do the religious questions the honor of taking them seriously. It prefers to ignore religion rather than attempt to deny it. The church historian Martin Marty describes this attitude as "mere secularity" in contrast to the continental mood of "utter secularity," epitomized in Nietzsche's famous proclamation that "God is dead."¹¹ Contemporary secularism, especially the Anglo-Saxon brand, conflicts with religious dogma and authority only when the latter seems to militate against human dignity or to undermine human potential and autonomy. This kind of secularism is the major concern in this study. Oddly enough, however, as a result of the bitter contest that raged in nineteenth- and early twentieth-century England between the secularists and the established church, the term *secular* has assumed in that country an unmistakably antireligious connotation.¹²

In the American context, on the other hand, the secular was never so sharply opposed to the religious or ecclesiastical sphere as it was in England. Having a constitutional safeguard against an established church, Americans have never had so clearly definable a target that presented itself as *the* religious authority. Although there have been and still are individual churches that attempt to foist their views on legislation and public life, most Americans have not found it necessary to encourage an overt secularism. In the New World the secular spirit was more often absorbed into radically transformed religious symbols.[13] These transformed symbols served to legitimize the secular trends and interests, thereby forming a kind of "civil religion,"[14] which could adjust to the rapidly changing social, economic, and cultural situation. Religion in America, apart from some striking exceptional cases, has shown a remarkable adaptability to the dynamics of a secularized, technological, and industrial society. In this way, the "American dream" was given full religious sanction. Under these special circumstances, it is not surprising that from the earliest days of American nationhood there developed a tradition of "religious secularity"—frequently divorced from the churches, but always religious in temper, as exemplified in the thought of Franklin, Jefferson, Emerson, Thoreau, Santayana, and Dewey. The appearance of a radical "Death of God" theology in America in the 1960s was a continuation of a long line of nonconformist religious expression.

Other key terms connected with the "secular"   The kind of ambiguity that surrounds the term *secular* carries over to the other derivative expressions used in contemporary social theory: *secularization, secularity,* and *secularism.* This is particularly true of the first of these, the process of secularization. The aim of this work, as described previously, clearly demands that we should have from the beginning an accurate meaning of the way these terms are being used. Although we are not unaware of the complex polemic connected with the use and meaning of these terms, it seems, for our purposes in this study, that it is both permissible and desirable to move immediately toward a responsible definition of the key terms involved, without going into the history and details of the discussion. Such detailed information is also readily available to the interested reader.[15]

Secularization   will be understood in the way it is used by sociologist Peter Berger, namely, as "the process by which sectors of society are removed from the domination of religious institutions and symbols."[16] Berger's definition entails both social-structural and cultural-intellectual change. Following a number of reputable authors, it will be assumed here that of the two, the cultural-intellectual or transformation of consciousness is the most fundamental.[17] The nature of this transformation, we believe, is correctly indicated by British sociologist of religion Peter McCaffery, who maintains that secularization is essentially an epistemological attitude: "a form of empiricism which is never content merely to accept inherited legitimations, but always asks, is this or that institution or opinion viable or valid for us now?"[18]

For the same reasons cited in relation to the term *secular,* no antireligious connotation is assigned to *secularization* or to the process it signifies. On the other hand, it would seem to be less than realistic to overlook the cultural and religious crisis occasioned by the process of secularization for so many people in contemporary society.[19] Whether this spiritual crisis or "loss of meaning," as it has also been called, is the result of a radical irreconcilability between the resulting secular mentality and the traditional creeds, or whether the conflict is caused by the outmoded categories in which these latter are expressed, is one of our major questions, which can be left as an open issue for the present.

Secularity will be understood as the general outlook and temper that is effected by the secularization of consciousness. With Oxford theologian John Macquarrie, we assume that this attitude is "almost universal in civilized countries"[20] and that it is characterized by a serious concern for concrete, practical affairs of this world, with a high appraisal of the value of human autonomy in both thought and ethics. As an attitude, it is found both within and without the churches, and is not necessarily opposed even to institutional and creedal religion. A variety of convincing analyses by prominent authors[21] have drawn attention to the following elements as constituting the essence of the secular attitude: *temporality,* or concern with this historical existence in the here and now; *this-worldliness,* or emphasis on the everyday, concrete, social, and political realities; *empiricism,* or confidence in human intelligence and scientific method; and *autonomy,* or sense of independence and responsibility for one's life and actions.

To these four we must add a fifth and unique element—one that is really implicit in all the other four and thoroughly grounded in the great faith and confidence that the secular spirit places in the resources and potential of man. Following theologian Roger Shinn, we might call this all-pervasive element "a new humanism":[22] "humanism," because it *cherishes* humanity in all its diversity, its strengths and weaknesses; and "new," because it is not based on the grandeur of the human spirit, as we find in classical humanism, but rather on the post-Darwinian and scientific image of man—earthbound, in his relation to the humbler forms of life, and at the same time, mighty in his scientific and technological achievements and potential. Any secularity that lacked this last element would be a crass materialism and would not merit a place among the contemporary candidates for a new source of meaning and purpose in modern culture.

Finally, as secularity signifies a very generalized attitude, which is present in all sectors of society, religious or not, it must be carefully distinguished from the more rigid and unmitigated expression of the secular spirit, which we call "secularism."

Secularism   Once again we consider the efforts of John Macquarrie, who in an attempt to distinguish these closely related yet clearly different views, defined *secularism* as the position that "*only* through science can trustworthy knowledge be attained and that *only* the tangible and human affairs of this world are worthy of attention."[23] Macquarrie's emphasis on the word "only" in either part of the definition draws attention to the more rigid nature and more specified stance that this position entails. The definition, on the other hand, although having the merit of distinguishing a more unqualified and full-fledged "secular philosophy" from the more general and indeterminate attitude he describes as "secularity," runs the risk of an oversimplifying caricature. For we would be hard pressed to find today serious secular thinkers who would feel comfortable with this description of their thought. This is particularly true of the first part of the definition, for contemporary secular writers show at least an equal sensitivity to the limitations of scientific and technological solutions as do the proponents of religion.

Though it could be quite misleading to leave Macquarrie's definition precisely as it stands (one could rightly assume therefrom, for example, that all secularists must be logical positivists of a sort), this fact should not conceal the truth and insight contained in the definition. From the context of Macquarrie's work it becomes evident that it is his contention that the secularist recognizes no source of knowledge or insight having priority over human intelligence, and considers the time that the religious man spends in prayer, worship, and other such specifically religious pursuits as but distractions and deviations from the pressing problems of a this-worldly nature upon whose solution the real betterment of the human condition depends.[24] The radical theology of the 1960s, however, has made it clear that even the religious believer today frequently shares at least a great deal of sympathy for this view. The distinctive feature of pure secularism consists finally in something more specific, namely a clear-cut and unambiguous denial of biblical revelation and all that is entailed in the Judaeo-Christian creeds. The basic reason for this denial is that all such revelation is considered either illusory or at least totally irrelevant to authentic human concerns.[25]

Our understanding of secularism is thus as an essentially negative term. By this we in no way intend a value judgment, but rather a simple statement of fact. History supports this position in that secularism arose primarily as a reaction to clericalism. It was a rejection of the absolute hegemony of ecclesiastical institutions in such vital cultural areas as politics, education, science, and law. Secularism zealously tried to avoid involvement in theological and religious questions, seeing these as the occasions of political and social intolerance, as well as the principal source of the destructive religious wars that marred European history in the sixteenth and seventeenth centuries.[26] In short, secularism from its beginnings consisted in a negation of church control over society and over man's mind in the name of reason and autonomy.

Accordingly, secularism is not a positive world view, but rather involves a discarding of one way of seeing the world—the way traditionally taught by the church or the synagogue. For this reason it is compatible with a number of world views or philosophies, but does not specifically determine any particular outlook. Strictly speaking, secularism is not even necessarily humanistic, as humanism would be only one possible world view open to the secularist attitude.[27]

Finally—and in one of its most enigmatic aspects— secularism, although denying the "religions," is not incompatible with what might be called "the religious attitude." This could already have been inferred from the consideration of the peculiarly American brand of secularity. Indeed, some of the most significant secular humanist writers in this country have been staunch proponents of the "religious quality" or "sacred dimension" of life.[28]

This brings us to the last and most important (in terms of our proposed aims) term connected with the notion of the secular: "secular humanism." A clear and precise understanding of the meaning of this compound term is vital to our thesis, for otherwise historical ambiguities and ideological connotations surrounding the term might too easily distort an objective appraisal of Tillich's analysis.

Secular Humanism and "Humanistic Theology"

The elements that have been proposed as constituting the essence of the secular consciousness all tend to produce a man-centered or anthropocentric attitude. This is not meant to imply any direct logical connection between secularity and anthropocentrism. In fact, the very evidence of modern science and the resulting scientific world view requires that man be removed from the position of centrality and be regarded "as having happened in a universe no more made for him than for any other of its teeming infinitudes of existences, and no more precious or significant than any other to the universal economy."[29] The centrality, however, which was taken away from man in one way was returned in another. The outstanding successes of science and the accompanying prestige of scientific method in this century have produced in our culture a very high level of confidence and trust in the potential of the human mind and human resources in general.

This new man-centeredness, therefore, although not grounded in modern science, is to a very great extent occasioned by it. It is occasioned, furthermore, not only by the positive achievements and opportunities deriving from scientific and technological development but also by the ill uses and dehumanizing side effects of these same successes. Contemporary literature is filled with protests against the ever-growing urbanization, destruction of the environment, routinization of life, shattering of traditional family patterns, and dangers of social engineering—all phenomena that depend upon modern technology and, ultimately, upon the recent advances of science. The very threat to humanity occasioned by these negative effects of scientific progress doubtlessly can also account for the growing concern over man and the force behind the new humanism.[30]

This new humanism that emerges from our contemporary secular culture may well be considered one of its finest fruits and achievements.[31] Yet despite the rationality and empiricism that characterize our technical society, it should be evident now that present-day secular humanism is far from an intellectual or philosophical stance; it is rather one subjective option, a practical attitude for which man can *decide* within the framework of today's scientific world view. That the outlook of contemporary humanism represents a free choice rather than a logical conclusion based on scientific evidence should not be glossed over lightly. There are certainly many thoroughly secular thinkers of strong humanistic bent today whose scientific awareness makes them balk before a humanism that philosophically would relocate man at the center of the universe. When humanism becomes an organized movement or school of thought, it tends to lean in this direction and has aroused the suspicion of other secular humanists.[32]

In the practical or functional order, on the other hand, secular humanists have the same kinds of priorities, all of which center around man, so that we can identify a "secular humanist" as one whose attitude and actions are such that he *functions* "as if" human concerns are the ultimate ones and merit our greatest attention. Likewise, the secular humanist is one who *in practice* depends upon human intelligence and ethical sensitivity as the final criteria for good conduct. Quite apart, therefore, from the secularist's specific theory of man and the universe, one whose general outlook implies a functional anthropocentrism will be considered to be a humanist.

In summary, *secular humanism can be defined as a contemporary form of empiricism that sees man and human concerns as at least functionally ultimate, relies confidently on human intelligence and scientific method, to the rejection of the authority and guidance of biblical revelation and the traditional creeds.*

It is especially the last part of this definition that distinguishes a strictly *secular* humanism from the more general attitude of secularity, which is still compatible with creedal religion. For religious writers will frequently vie with their secular counterparts for the title "humanist," sharing fully with the latter an "appreciation of man and of the values, real and potential, in human life."[33] This very general humanistic attitude cuts across the frontiers of atheism, agnosticism, and religious belief, whereas the outlook of secular humanism finds religious belief to be either detrimental, distracting, irrelevant, or, at best, of very limited value in the pursuit of human happiness and fulfillment. The fact that a number of secular humanist writers are proponents of the "religious quality" of life has raised a serious question about the suitability of the term *secular* to describe their outlook. The foregoing brief review of the history of the term,[34] however, should make it clear that the "secular attitude" is not antithetical to religion; it is simply more concerned with the affairs of this world than with distinctively ecclesiastical or other-worldly interests. Regardless, therefore, of their attitude toward the sacred or religious dimension, we consider as "secular" all those humanists who reject the authority of biblical revelation as the ultimate source of wisdom and conduct.[35]

This definition of secular humanism at the same time enables us to exclude from its ranks those contemporary religious writers and theologians who stand for a kind of humanism within the biblical tradition, such as Tillich, Maritain, Rahner, Gogarten, Macquarrie, Niebuhr, Buber, Heschel, and Teilhard de Chardin. Religious humanism within the church and synagogue has a long tradition going back at least as far as the Renaissance. Understandably, many religious leaders are reluctant to surrender the term *humanism* to an exclusively secular usage. They see biblical revelation as the culmination of human hopes and expectations, fulfilling rather than denying man's greatest dignity, achievements, and potential. For this type of humanism we reserve the term *humanistic theology,* by which is meant "an intellectual and contemporary expression of traditional biblical faith, informed at the same time by a spirit that is both scientific and humanistic."[36]

Whether, in fact, Tillich's name should properly be placed on a roster of humanistic theologians, or whether, as some contend, he is really a sort of secular humanist in disguise remains one of the key questions of our investigation. An examination of Tillich's own understanding of secular humanism should obviously throw some light on this issue. Such an examination, however, requires that we first clarify the scope and nature of Tillich's theology of culture, as it is within this framework that his analysis of secular humanism is made. It should prove helpful, at this point, to outline the general plan that is followed in this book.

A- A description of the basis and systematic foundations of Tillich's humanistic theology (chap. 2).
B- An exposition of the historical beginnings, the sub-

stance, and the development of Tillich's theology of
culture from its earliest form, showing the continuity
and evolution of the original principles (chap. 3).

C-   An explanation of the meaning of the notion of
     theonomy and a demonstration of its central place in
     the whole structure of the theology of culture (chap.
     4).

D-   An analysis of Tillich's interpretation of contempo-
     rary culture in light of his principle of theonomy with
     special emphasis on his critique of secular humanism
     (chap. 5).

E-   An evaluation of Tillich's interpretation and critique
     of secular humanism in terms of his assertion that a
     purely secular cultural outlook loses the crucial
     human dimension of "depth" (chap. 6).

F-   The *conclusion* in which it is argued that, despite
     similarities, Tillich's theonomous vision of culture is
     quite distinct from that of secular humanism. The
     direction and advantages of an ongoing dialogue be-
     tween humanistic theologians and secular humanists
     are indicated (chap. 7).

A final word of introduction will clarify the method or
approach used in this book. The work is intended as a
philosophical analysis of Tillich's theology of culture, in
general, and of his interpretation of secular humanism, in
particular. Although we are dealing with the thought of a
theologian, our approach is not theological, in that it does not
draw upon the faith presuppositions of any religious tradition
but only upon generally accepted philosophical criteria, such
as coherence, evidence, and conformity to experience. Although the author also shares the Christian faith that provided the motivating force and ultimate concern of Tillich's
reflections, the philosophical approach seems preferable, insofar as the book is addressed not only to Christians and
religious believers but to all serious-minded readers who
share a human concern for the ultimate meaning and direction
of our contemporary culture.

Furthermore, as regards approach, the aim of this study,

which is primarily one of intellectual clarification and deeper understanding of an important cultural issue, would seem to preclude any unduly polemical approach. To the contrary, we assume that the more objective and detached our analysis of both the Tillichian and secular humanist views on culture, the greater will be the likelihood of successfully achieving the proposed aims of the book.

Our professed commitment to objectivity and open-minded philosophical inquiry notwithstanding, this introduction should also have made it apparent that we hold Tillich's thought in high esteem and consider his theological interpretation of culture to be worthy of a most careful scrutiny by all who are committed to the creation of a more fully human cultural situation. We share the conviction of the humanist philosopher Corliss Lamont that "philosophy has the task not only of attaining the truth, but also of showing how the truth can become operative in the affairs of men."[37]

"The unexamined life is not worth living."

(Socrates)

2

The Foundations

Humanistic Theology

The term *humanistic theology* as explained in the previous chapter, must be understood within the special context in which it was discussed. Tillich did not refer to his own theological system by this term; nevertheless his entire work is permeated with a strongly humanistic attitude. On the other hand, Tillich could never have countenanced the substitution of a "mere" humanism for theology. In the Introduction to Volume 1 of the *Systematic Theology*, he refers to this latter approach as "naturalistic" and rejects it insofar as "it derives the Christian message from man's natural state"; it envisages man's religious fulfillment as a situation in which "everything was said by man, nothing to man." As opposed to "humanistic" theology in this sense, he insisted on the reality of revelation which "is 'spoken' to man, not by man to himself."[1]

Similarly, in the 1958 Lowell Lectures that he delivered at King's Chapel in Boston, Tillich rejected what he called "man-centered theology" as a one-sided and inadequate stage of a dialectical process, insofar as it failed to recognize the self-estrangement and "demonic structures" of the human condition.[2] Evidently, therefore, there is a sense in which the term *humanistic theology* must not be applied to Tillich's system, for his theology was from beginning to end, as he maintained, "God-centered." There was for Tillich, however, no contradiction between a "God-centered" theology and a truly authentic humanism. By intention, at least, Tillich's own theology was to reflect a synthesis of God-centeredness and human concern. Typically, in a German address delivered in 1958, on the occasion of receiving the Goethe Prize for service to humanity, Tillich made it very clear that he could imagine no greater dishonor to the name of God than a theology that could proclaim the divine majesty only at the expense of human dignity.[3] In the third volume of the *Systematic Theology*, written toward the end of his career, Tillich maintained that the aim and inner *telos* of all cultural activity can best be described as "humanity" by which he meant man's personal and social fulfillment.[4] Furthermore, if we may anticipate here an issue that is later dealt with at length, the most frequent criticism brought against Tillich is a questioning of the authenticity of his Christianity rather than of his humanism.

In Tillich's early German writings much consideration was given to a doctrine that he called "belief-ful realism" *(gläubiger Realismus)*. It is sufficient to note for the present that this doctrine for Tillich signified a philosophical viewpoint which "sees the world with the sober eyes of the scientist or realistic artist, accepting it at the same time as symbolic of the eternal and unconditioned source of all meaning and ground of all being."[5] This attitude remained dominant throughout Tillich's intellectual development and gradually found precise expression in his concept of "theonomy." With theonomy as his guiding principle, Tillich endeavored to preserve the autonomy of human intelligence and creativity, as well as the fundamental dignity of human nature, within a framework that sees the true value and ultimate meaning of humanity as necessarily rooted in the divine ground. It is precisely in this way that Tillich's work can be understood as a "humanistic theology."

This chapter constitutes the first stage in an analysis of Tillich's theology of culture, in general, by showing its background and foundations. In this respect, an essential aspect of our understanding of Tillich's theology of culture is its dependence on the ontological systems of the German romantic philosopher Friedrich Wilhelm Joseph von Schelling. For this reason, a good portion of the chapter is devoted to a survey of Schelling's ontology to the extent that it provided a framework and foundation for Tillich's thought.

This analysis is continued in Chapter 3, in which we return in a more specific way to Tillich's first attempt at a theology of culture and then proceed to trace the evolution of these basic principles in the course of his later theological development.

The Background and Historical Context of the Theology of Culture

The religious socialist movement and the beginning of a theology of culture   Tillich's interpretation of culture and analysis of the human situation from its very inception was never a purely theoretical question. The absolute seriousness and deeply personal emotional force of the issue facing the young philosopher-theologian as he returned from the horrifying experiences of World War I, in which he had served four years as chaplain in the German army, are concretely revealed in a photograph taken of him at the time of his discharge.[6] Anyone who has seen this portrait will not be surprised to read from Tillich's autobiographical reflections that these war years constituted a major revolution in his life.[7] Although his study of the later works of the philosopher Schelling had brought Tillich to seriously question the German classical idealism on which he had been weaned prior to the war, it is clear that in his own view it was primarily the concrete horror and shock of the war that brought him to challenge a philosophical system that was so easily compatible with the self-satisfied optimism of the German bourgeoisie. In Hegel, in particular, and in German idealism, in general, Tillich saw no place for the acceptance of real estrangement; the injustices and ambiguities of the real life situation were smoothed over and taken up into an ideal process in which the final age of perfection was inevitably to be achieved. He saw this philosophically closed system as an intellectual reflection and support of the now apparently crumbling bourgeois class society, so intricately interwoven with the latter that he referred to this philosophy as *"bürgerlicher Idealismus."*[8] The idealistic philosophy that Tillich had begun to oppose on scholarly philosophical grounds through his reading of Kierkegaard and especially of Schelling prior to his war experience, he now began to attack even more intensely, impelled by very concrete motives of a social and political nature.

Before returning to Schelling and his profound philosophical influence on Tillich's thought, more need be said about the concrete political and social awareness that resulted from Tillich's war experience. Although Tillich had been reflecting for some time already on the importance of recognizing the fundamental ontological estrangement at the heart of the human condition, the full reality of this estrangement and the terrible power of the irrational and unconscious forces at work in man were brought home most vividly to him as a young military chaplain at the front. Already in 1912, in his thesis for Licentiate in Theology, Tillich had written that "the deeper and more absolute the awareness of guilt so much the more complete is the understanding of true Identity."[9] In this thesis Tillich had maintained that through this emphasis on the concept of guilt Schelling had corrected the tendency of idealism to reduce all reality to a unified, rational process. The question of responsibility for the war was one that could not escape such a serious thinker as Tillich, so that now on a profound personal and psychological level the significance of Schelling's *Schuldbewusstsein* for a correct understanding of the existential situation became ever more marked. Tillich's pastoral duties during the war, which brought him into close contact with soldiers from all the social classes, convinced him of the terrible class divisions in German society, and especially of the great chasm that separated the church from the industrial masses.[10] This same sense of social guilt and social responsibility inspired his intellectual efforts toward a theology of culture and his untiring political endeavors in the newly emerging religious socialist movement.

Tillich spent the years from 1919 to 1924 as a *Privatdozent* of theology at the University of Berlin. Here he joined forces with a very enthusiastic group of young religious socialists, and though he first took a very active role in the practical, political activities of the group, he soon became its principal theorist. An examination of Tillich's activities and writings from this period makes it very clear that his interest in religion and culture and the philosophy of history were by no means purely theoretical in nature. "The political problems," he writes in his "Autobiographical Reflections," "determined our whole existence; even after revolution and inflation they were matters of life and death."[11]

Tillich and his colleagues were thoroughly convinced that the growing socialist movement of postwar Germany would carry the day, and that a new social order would emerge in the nation that had suffered so devastating and humiliating a defeat. They shared an exuberant enthusiasm and deep sense of vocation to participate in a unique way in a decisive moment in history—a *kairos,* in which the Eternal would invade the temporal, bringing about a more perfect social order in the form of religious socialism.[12] At the same time, the Berlin group was equally convinced that the particular atheistic and utopian direction which the dominant secular socialism was taking was both negative and self-destructive. Like secular bourgeois society before it, the current socialist revolution was lacking in spiritual depth; it sought infinite goals within the limitations of finite history and continued to foster the gap that separated the sacred from the secular, faith from culture.

The predominant thrust in the socialist direction was, of course, from Marxist doctrine. Although Tillich had already been sympathetic to antibourgeois protest through the reading of Nietzsche and through his enthusiastic interest in revolutionary and existentialist art, his reading of Marx during this postwar period deeply influenced his own thought and inspired his involvement in the political movements of his day. Both Marx's analysis of bourgeois society and his notion of "ideology" appealed to Tillich, who pays tribute to this debt in a number of places in his writings. For example, in the autobiographical sketch, *On the Boundary,* Tillich writes:

> I owe to Marx, first of all, the insight into the ideological character not only of idealism, but of all systems of thought, religious as well as profane, which serve as power structures and thus prevent, even if unconsciously, a more just organization of social reality.[13]

Even Marx's atheism, which, as has been noted, appeared to Tillich to further human estrangement by broadening the gap between the sacred and the secular, had a certain amount of justification to Tillich. He considered Marx, just as he did Nietzsche and Freud, as a kind of secular prophet, whose atheism was a necessary protest against religious idolatry and heteronomy. The major difference between the two thinkers on this point, however, is that Tillich saw this protest as transitional and dialectical, rather than as a permanent account of reality. Tillich also recognized in Marx both a profound humanism and a strong historical realism. Both these elements of Marxist thought were of special concern to Tillich at this time, as he embarked on a campaign to construct a more fully human society, and realized that his own previous idealism could stand as an obstacle to a full understanding of the historical and existential estrangement of man. In Tillich's own philosophical terms, he learned "that man lives within existence and not in the realm of essence."[14]

As has already been indicated, there was much in Marx that Tillich also rejected and repudiated, even apart from his utopianism and atheism. In 1933, Tillich wrote an analysis of the Marxist system for the sake of distinguishing the positive and enlightening elements of Marxism from the negative and untenable ones.[15] Two years later he continued this project in a further study entitled, "Marx and the Prophetic Tradition," and periodically through the years of his long career he has directed his efforts in a number of articles toward distinguishing in Marx that which he considered of great permanent value, so that these elements might not be lost in the general condemnation of Marx by the capitalist West.[16] In light of these facts, which also correspond to Tillich's own recorded evaluation of the major influences on his thought,[17] one cannot afford to underestimate the impact of Marx on Tillich's interpretation of culture. Marx's great stress on the estrangement of the proletariat and of man in history helped to give Tillich's thought that necessary concrete grounding, which was so essential if he were to leave his system open to the impact and concerns of the political and social order. By the same token, Marxism provided for Tillich a helpful intellectual framework within which to understand the full significance of his war experience. In a recent and very controversial interpretation of Tillich's dialectical system, Leonard Wheat finds a much greater affinity to Marxist philosophy than Tillich interpreters have been wont to recognize. We return to this question and to Wheat's thesis in our conclusion; in the meantime, there is sufficient reason to accept Tillich's own word that for him the main attraction in Marx was both his historical consciousness and his emphasis on humanity.[18]

In a way that was typical of his whole life-style, Tillich was standing in 1919 "on the boundary" between two apparently rival ideologies: Christianity and Marxism. If he could successfully relate the Marxist socialist ideal to biblical prophecy and the Protestant principle, he could provide the religious socialist movement with the kind of intellectual underpinnings it needed so desperately. To seek anything less than synthesis was simply not Tillich's style, and as he saw the situation, would tend only to widen the gap that separated official religion from the actual social and political struggle. This was not the first time that Tillich had stood in such a boundary situation. Earlier in his school days he had to make a choice between the humanist ideals of the *gymnasium* and the Christian principles he met in his home and church. Characteristically, the young Tillich would not choose the one to the rejection of the other, but with the careful guidance of his father, he worked out a personal synthesis between the two.[19]

Much of Tillich's inclination and ability to synthesize rather than to contrast different points of view or even philosophical systems may have been the effect of a total intellectual immersion into the nineteenth-century German philosophical tradition. Apart from this general formal tendency to interpret thought and reality in terms of dialectical dynamics (which enable one to salvage the truth element in otherwise negated propositions), there is concrete evidence to show that he was inwardly convinced of the ultimate reconcilability between Christianity and any authentically humanistic world view.

In Tillich's school days it was the classical humanism of the *gymnasium,* in the period following World War I it was the revolutionary humanism of Marx, and, in still later stages of his career, it was the existential humanism of his artist friends and the scientific humanism of the American intelligentsia that continually urged Tillich to search for the common source of unity or point of contact *(Anknüpfungspunkt)* between Christianity and humanism. Tillich's famous doctrine of the essential unity of religion and culture is but another aspect of this same fundamental assumption. Finally, the close analogy between this personal experience in which the young Tillich chose to draw up an alliance between his Christian and humanistic tendencies and what later became his theological dialectic of "correlation" should already be apparent. These early syntheses certainly constituted in germinal form what would later become a carefully elaborated methodology. From his early years, Tillich could not tolerate in himself what he would later call a "split conscience"[20]—an impossible attitude, to be sure, for one who feels drawn to live "on the boundary." Nor was his success at synthesis a forced or artificial compromise, for as stated at the beginning of the chapter, Tillich's theology was totally imbued with a humanistic spirit, whereas conversely, his humanism was, in terms of his understanding, essentially religious at its very roots:

> The first and most enduring answer to the question of the relationship of religion and humanity, is the awareness of that which appears in the depths of every human being and of mankind in general, namely in the struggle of those powers which engage in combat over man. Here lie the religious roots of humanity; here lies the possibility of deciding for a true humanity.[21]

The Ontological Framework

Although Tillich's attempts to formulate a theology of culture and a theological analysis of the current cultural situation grew out of a concrete political and social challenge, he already possessed the philosophical or ontological frame of reference within which to construct his theory. The strong intellectual influence of the later Schelling on Tillich's thought, particularly by reason of the romantic philosopher's staunch opposition to Hegel's attempt to absorb the conflict and estrangement of life and history into an idealistic system of conceptual reconciliation, has already been mentioned.[22] We have also indicated that if Tillich's studies prior to World War I had already grafted deeply in his thinking a repulsion to the idealist temptation of undermining the reality of man's estrangement and the ambivalence of his predicament, his war experiences had reminded him in an irrevocable way of the correctness of this existential awareness, and of the full personal and social dimensions of this notion of estrangement. This awareness and conviction so thoroughly and profoundly affected his whole intellectual approach that the reality of man's existential estrangement from his essential nature can be said to be the basic starting point of all Tillichian anthropology or "doctrine of man."[23]

Tillich was also able to tie in this philosophical assumption with one of the most fundamental doctrines of his Lutheran Christian heritage, namely, the doctrine of justification through faith. He was able to do this by continuing in the direction that his own renowned professor of theology Martin Kaehler had taken earlier. The student, in this case, however, carried the logical process of that direction to a conclusion that the master could hardly have foreseen. Kaehler, like his pupil, was both Christian theologian and humanist, who saw the reformation doctrine of justification as a basis of mediation between Christian doctrine and humanistic culture. He encouraged his students at Halle to look for new contemporary meanings for this fundamental Protestant principle—the kind of meanings that would open the way of grace and redemption to modern secular man, so often estranged from the church and from formal religious practice. The uniqueness of Tillich's interpretation was that he extended the meaning of justification to the religious-intellectual realm. In other words, even he who doubts about God can be justified by God, in spite of his doubt. For as Tillich writes in the *Protestant Era:*

> There is faith in every serious doubt, namely, the faith in the truth as such, even if the only truth we can express is our lack of truth. But if this is experienced in its depth and as ultimate concern, the divine is present; and he who doubts in such an attitude is "justified" in his thinking. So the paradox got hold of me that he who seriously denies God, affirms him. . . There is, I soon realized, no place beside the divine, there is no possible atheism, there is no wall between the religious and the non-religious. The holy embraces both itself and the secular.[24]

In brief, Tillich maintained a keen and unswerving belief in the reality of man's radical estrangement from his own essential nature and was able to provide an ontological basis for this insight in the later philosophical system of Schelling. Finally, having also found a theological link for his vision through the Reformation doctrine of justification through faith, Tillich found himself in an excellent position to develop a thorough and significant "theology of culture"; an interpretation of Christian doctrine that would speak in a special way to contemporary secular man, with all his anxieties and doubts, even the most radical doubts about God himself.

In our modern, secularized, technological society, according to Tillich's analysis, which we examine in greater detail in Chapter 5, man experiences a special kind of estrangement from his true essential being. He is threatened by what Tillich termed "spiritual non-being"—the anxiety of emptiness and ultimate loss of meaning.[25] This contemporary experience of meaninglessness, which tends to lead toward existential despair, is the peculiar way that our modern cultural situation reflects man's fundamental ontological estrangement that is at the core of the human predicament throughout all changing periods in cultural history. One of the greatest strengths and overriding sources of unity in Tillich's system was that he had at his service an ontological framework that he had derived from Schelling within which his most basic doctrine of universal human estrangement could be understood and interpreted.

A correct understanding of Tillich's theology of culture, as well as an adequate response to various critics of Tillich, requires a brief survey of some of the more relevant features of these philosophical underpinnings. With this purpose in mind, we focus our remarks around three central Schellingian doctrines: the relation of the finite to the infinite, the divine principle of self-defection, and the doctrine of the Fall.

Before considering these three themes in detail, however, it will be helpful to make some general observations about the overall nature of Schelling's ontological system. We begin with an aspect of that ontology which seemed to have been the center of greatest interest and concern for Tillich, namely, the corrective that Schelling's doctrine offers to Hegel's essentialism. According to Schelling, whose critique is fully endorsed by his theological successor, Paul Tillich, Hegel's dialectic failed to take human estrangement with sufficient earnestness, insofar as by logical process he had removed all ambiguity and contradiction from life and history. Schelling, on the other hand, tried to take estrangement and conflict with full seriousness by giving due recognition to the irrational and ambiguous elements of reality, without attempting to explain them away as part of a rational dialectic. Schelling called rather for an "existential" dialectic in which thought would be forced to confront reality rather than for more abstract thought.[26] Schelling's objection to Hegel is not to his use of dialectic, but only to a certain kind of dialectic. In terms of logical system the fundamental dialectic of Schelling is quite similar to that of Hegel. The nuances that Schelling added, however, especially during his period of "positive philosophy" (the later Schelling), were deemed very important by Tillich, who adopted them into his own methodology. These nuances appear in those doctrines that have special bearing on Tillich's thought. In an examination of these basic doctrines, the dialectical nature of Tillich's thought, colored as it was by the peculiar emphases of Schelling, his philosophical master, must always be borne in mind. The reader who is familiar with Tillich's thought will not fail to detect some very familiar themes in the following Schellingian *Grundegedanken.*

The relation of the finite to the infinite   In a way that seems strange to the contemporary philosophical temper, Schelling found the notion of an infinite absolute reality a markedly more intelligible and congenial concept than that of concrete, finite existence. Nevertheless, we are at the very heart of Schelling's philosophical inquiry when we ask the question of the meaning and intelligibility of finite existence or, in his own terms: "Why should there be something rather than nothing at all?"[27] It was just this irrationality, this inner conflict and resistance to intelligibility, that Schelling refused to see absorbed by any kind of artificial, logical system.

The "non-being" that constitutes the given reality of finite existence is more than a logical contradiction *(Widerspruch)*; in fact, it consistently rejects being grasped even in logical dialectic.[28] But granted the seriousness of the philosopher's concern for "empirical rooting," how do we explain the ease with which Schelling presumes the reality of that which is expressed in the concepts "Infinite" or "Absolute"? In Schelling's mind there was no contradiction here at all, for though conceding to Kant that we discern nothing but what is in experience, Schelling does not fail to add: "but what alone is in experience is just the living, the eternal or God."[29] This is for Schelling *the* empirical fact, the ground of all experience—the infinite Truth that is self-evident and presupposed in all thought and meaning. The Augustinian, the Neoplatonic, and the mystical (Boehme) sources of Schelling's thought are apparent; upon further reflection it also becomes clear that such a position or understanding of the infinite places it outside the realm of things or beings, beyond the subject-object dichotomy—the Ground of all being (the

Urgrund), the presupposed absolute in all man's creative and spiritual acts.[30] Schelling's absolute is not to be identified with any being, but is present in everything that exists. Tillich continued this ontological perspective and, like his philosophical teacher, spoke of God as the *Urgrund* and taught the paradoxical doctrine of the immanence of the transcendent in finite being. In light of this ontological vision, Tillich could maintain that everything which exists can do so only in virtue of its participation in being-itself, i.e., in God.

The "root-dialectic" in Schelling's philosophy is this paradoxical relationship of finite being to infinity; it is at the basis of all other dialectical relationships, such as that of subject and object and the interrelationship of ideas. In every act of thought, in all creative encounter, the subject comes into contact not only with the object but also with the Ground of Being who is at the same time the Ground of his own being. In light of these philosophical presuppositions, we can better follow the thought of Tillich, who wrote in 1926, that: *"Das itinerarium mentis ad rem ist nur möglich als itinerarium mentis ad Deum."*[31] Here we have at the same time the ontological and epistemological basis for Tillich's concept of "theonomy," and indeed for his whole theology of culture.[32]

The doctrine of the Fall This understanding of the dialectical relationship between the finite and the infinite, however, is still very much within the framework of Schelling's earlier negative philosophy. It is via man's *essence* that he is continually related to God. It is within man's essential being that his point of contact *(Anknüpfungspunkt)* with the divine, that his participation in the life and reality of the divine Being-itself, is discovered. Schelling never rejected the insights of his negative philosophy that was centered around the principle of identity *(Identitätsprinzip)*: all finite, relative, conditioned beings are qualities of the absolute, unconditioned reality and vice-versa. God is purely potential and undifferentiated identity or the principle of absolute indifference. In him subject and object, nature and consciousness, rational and irrational, finite and infinite all meet in unity.[33] But the empirical reality of the separation of subject and object, the conflict of rational and irrational, the estrangement of the finite from the infinite, all bespeak in the starkest way an essential aspect of the real, human situation that equally escapes Schelling's philosophy of identity as it does Hegel's rational dialectic. It was to do justice to this irrational and estranged aspect of real existence that Schelling in his later writings developed the doctrine of the Fall.[34] This doctrine constituted in his understanding the chief corrective or complement of the earlier negative philosophy and radically changed his own thought in the direction of more positive philosophy.

By "positive philosophy" Schelling understood a system of thought that would keep the thinking subject within his own historical, concrete, existential situation.[35] As we have seen, such empirical grounding must include first and foremost the radical and universal estrangement of the human situation.[36] Schelling's earlier understanding of the dialectical relationship between finite and infinite did not explain the reality of estranged existence. The transition from essence to existence is no longer dialectical but paradoxical. Only the irrational, the unpredictable, the image of a "leap" connoting decision and freedom, can explain the presence of finite, estranged reality.[37] Finite existence becomes intelligible only in light of a complete break, a gap, a removal, or in Schelling's mythico-philosophical language, a Fall *(Abfall)* from the Absolute. The finite universe in its totality is the self-revelation of the Absolute, its eternal self-objectification, according to the philosophy of identity; but with the corrective of positive philosophy it is seen that the uniqueness and individuality of finite existence cannot be explained by a necessary logical process. It can only be explained by an act of pure freedom, which to Schelling meant the possibility of opposition to the rational principle. The only real meaning of freedom is precisely the power to choose between good and evil, the selfish *Partikülarwille*[38] as opposed to the *Universalwille*: the creative and divine Life Urge *(Lebensdrang)*, which in man has achieved consciousness and struggles upward toward the conscious harmony and union with God. Although this arbitrary factor or pure willing *(Willkür)*[39] is continually overcome within the divine life, in man there is the real possibility of both freely separating himself from the Absolute or of freely choosing to return to divine unity:

> . . . there would be no life or joy of life in God, if the powers now subordinated did not have the continual possibility of arousing the contradiction against the unity, and were not also incessantly quieted and reconciled again by the feeling of that beneficent unity by which the powers are suppressed. . .
> . . . nature is not coercively but voluntarily subject to the eternal spirit. The sight and presence of that essential purity have no other effect on nature than to liberate it, so that it can yield to separation, or resist it and fall anew into the life of passion and desire.[40]

It becomes evident that for Schelling, as later for Tillich, the Fall is both necessary and free at the same time. It is necessary insofar as it is part of an inevitable process, with roots within the Divinity itself. It is free insofar as nothing short of freedom can explain the transition from essence to existence. As Tillich maintained in the Systematic, the Fall is characterized by both freedom and destiny—a polarity that constitutes one of the most basic elements which make up the ontological structure of being.[41] In light of this Schellingian ontology, then, Tillich maintained both the tragic universality and the personal human responsibility for the Fall.[42] In theological terms, there is a coincidence of the Creation and the Fall. They both occur simultaneously, so that there is not the one without the other, by way, however, of ontological fact or givenness, and not by reason of logical necessity. Tillich's theological perspective on sin and the Fall achieves structure in Schelling's philosophical doctrine of a transcendent Fall, rooted in the Godhead, and yet so free from dialectical necessity that he calls it a "leap" *(Sprung),* and describes its occurrence in terms of a "tearing loose" *(losreissen)* from the Absolute and true reality.[43]

The divine principle of self-defection   But what is to be understood by a "transcendent" Fall, and one which occurs within the divine Life itself? To attempt to answer this question we must bear in mind that Schelling's appeal to Platonic authority in his *Philosophie und Religion* was not just incidental. Schelling had seriously returned to Plato in his philosophical attempt to answer the problem of the intelligibility of finite existence.

Although still working within the framework of his "negative" philosophy, Schelling discovered in Plato's "divine ideas" the basis for the possibility of separate, unique, and individual existence. Such individual and finite existence he could envisage intelligibly only as the self-objectification of the Absolute. Still working within an idealist frame of reference, Schelling maintained that the Platonic divine ideas provided the link between the divine Absolute and the estrangement and irrationality of free process. The Platonic divine ideas were reflections of the Absolute; consequently, for them to exist as separate, individual things would actually constitute an alienation or estrangement from their true center or essence. In this sense they are not fully being, but rather a mixture of being and nonbeing (mē on), which was precisely Schelling's definition of finitude. In *Philosophie und Religion,* written during the early period of his idealist trend, Schelling stated the relationship between the "divine ideas" and the nonbeing characteristic of finitude: ". . . das Licht des göttlichen Wesens an dem Nichts sich gebrochen oder abgespiegelt habe, und hieraus die Sinnenwelt einstanden sei."[44]

But the divine ideas of Plato remained too essential, too abstract for the later Schelling as a fitting explanation for the transition from essence to existence. The something else that was needed was necessitated by the empirical reality of the irrationality, ambiguity, and raw givenness of finite historical existence. The older, more empirically minded Schelling continued to find this something else not only within ontology but also within the Godhead itself. This something else was an irrational moment of pure freedom within the divine Absolute itself. A logical jump from idea to existence was not possible, for ideas do not decide, and existence, like estrangement, is the effect of free decision. The answer had to be sought in that primordial character of being itself which determined the coming to be of finitude. Granted the Schellingian understanding of the relation of finite to infinite, it was inevitable that he should still find the answer within the divine Life itself.

Even while Schelling's approach became more empirically rooted and existential, he continued to understand God as the *Urgrund* and *das absolute Indifferenz*. What is new in the positive philosophy is that Schelling took the irrational or nonbeing into the divine *Urgrund* itself.[45] He posited a moment in God that is not God himself—a principle of opposition within the Absolute. He named this principle *das unvordenklich Sein,* immemorial or primordial being.[46] Schelling also referred to this moment in God as the "Dark Principle," the ultimate potency for freedom. He attempted to preserve at the same time, however, the holiness and impeccability of the Divine, by insisting simultaneously that this irrational Will *(Willkür)* is eternally overcome or conquered within the divinity. This is the meaning of the "transcendent" Fall, that it takes place outside of all time and space, as part of the eternal and divine process: "Dieser Abfall ist übrigens so ewig (ausser aller Zeit) als die Absolutheit selbst und als die Ideenwelt."[47]

But how valid is it to posit in God something that is other than God, even though it should be eternally conquered in the Godhead? Such a doctrine, no doubt, sounds strange to orthodox ears, but Schelling considered it to be better suited than traditional concepts to the biblical understanding of God—the living God of anger, passion, and compassion, who seems to "struggle," no matter how successfully, with the powers of evil and irrationality in the universe.[48]

Once again Schelling went to classical Greek philosophy to find insight and inspiration. This time the guidance came from Aristotle. With the help of the great philosopher's doctrine of "potency," Schelling was able to go beyond the purely rational and abstract notion of "divine ideas." He spoke of real potency *(Potenz)* not only in man but in God as well. To be in potency was to be "on the verge of being" and therefore to be already partially in separation and estranged existence. Potency in God meant finitude *in* God, and this Schelling did not hesitate to assert.

Striving persistently to find empirical grounding for his philosophy, Schelling did a great deal of psychologizing to support his intuitive insights. He began with man—finite freedom—and recognized that human personality is hardly something given; it is rather something to be acquired or won.[49] It was achieved only through continual struggle and conflict against selfish impulse and particular will *(Partikülarwille)*, which stood in the way of human self-integration. Schelling's concept of God as Ground of being and absolute Indifference, in which all contradictions and polarities are reconciled in absolute unity, led him to place the ultimate principle of opposition within the Godhead. This irrational moment in God explained for Schelling both the source of vitality in the Absolute and the self-exteriorization of the same ultimate reality in the form of the process of nature.

Potency in God is not idea or essence, but a real principle that is the cause of the self-manifestation of God *ad extra.* This principle in God is finite and therefore not God, but it accounts for the Fall and the separation of the material world *(die Sinnenwelt)* from its essential unity with the Absolute. Although the foundation of the Fall and estrangement, therefore, are in the divine *Urgrund,* their actualization requires an act of human freedom. Man's fallen state, therefore, involves both freedom and necessity—a doctrine that later became an important, though controversial earmark of Tillich's thought.[50] In the Fall, man freely separates himself from God, so that creation and estranged existence are identical. Separation or estrangement is, as it were, the price of creation; but the ultimate goal of creation: the transition from "nature in God" to God's "self-revelation in nature" justifies the heavy cost to be paid.[51] True to his understanding of the relation of the finite to the infinite, Schelling saw, therefore, a close analogy between the divine and the human conquest of personality. In a way that clearly anticipates contemporary philosophical trends he even spoke of God "making himself": "*Gott macht sich selbst.*"[52]

The first potency in the divine *Urgrund* has no reality aside from the actuality of a differentiated, conscious, and rational divine personality or will. This divine self-affirmation as subject, however, presupposes the first potency and overcomes the self-sufficiency and solitude of absolute indifference. The conscious Deity, moreover, is in potency (second potency) to reunite to the ground from which it has been separated. The reunion is actually achieved in the divine Spirit of love (third potency) that overcomes in eternal process the irrational and unconscious *Lebensdrang*, which is also the Ground of finite existence *ad extra*. Through these same divine potencies God manifests himself externally in finite existence and directs all creation toward reunion with its divine source. Ultimately, then, it is the ambiguous character of the first potency—the divine principle of self-defection—that makes the world process possible.[53]

It is important to bear in mind that in Schelling's theogony, God upsets the unity of the potencies within the Godhead and thereby releases the finitude of the first potency. This enables God to enter the world process, within which by the conquest of its irrationality, evil and alienation, he achieves his own "personalization." In order to understand Tillich's interpretation of humanism, it is imperative to set his doctrine within this Schellingian framework, from which Tillich never strayed. For Tillich, as for his philosophical master, the struggle of the Absolute Spirit within the world process takes place on the battleground of human consciousness, which stands at the summit of nature's development. The conflict of the divine with the irrational and destructive forces is fundamentally a struggle for humanity.[54]

In Schelling's ontology, then, it becomes apparent that we have the foundations of Tillich's doctrine of estrangement, of the irrational element in God, and of the immanent presence of the Divine creative Ground in all finite reality. These doctrines are essential to Tillich's whole theology of culture and further investigation will bear out the truth of David

Hopper's contention that "at the moments of his apparent deepest involvement in the questions of history Tillich was gripped by an even deeper systematic involvement in the questions of ontology."[55]

3

The Theology of Culture

On the Idea of a Theology of Culture

We now return to the actual historical context in which Tillich gradually began to develop his theological interpretation of culture. As indicated, Tillich had become the theoretician of the newly emerging religious socialist movement, and although he and his colleagues derived great inspiration and insight from Marx, they felt a very serious dissatisfaction with the socialist program and perspective as it was actually developing in Germany and Eastern Europe. Marxist socialism, with its atheistic and antireligious bias or direction, was in Tillich's terms, seriously lacking in *depth;* it only tended to broaden the gap between the sacred and the secular. It was too negative and simply failed to "recognize the extent to which it stood itself under the crisis."[1]

An awareness of this "depth" dimension in life and culture is Tillich's understanding of the authentically religious attitude,[2] for it is precisely at this level that man encounters the infinite and creative Ground, which is ever immanent (according to Schelling's ontology) throughout the world process and in all cultural acts. The innate weakness of Marxist socialism is that it has rejected *a priori* this depth dimension of reality, by reason of its protest against established, bourgeois religion. Marxist socialism had not distinguished between authentic and inauthentic religion, and had thereby lost a dimension of reality, the ultimate one in terms of meaning. Tillich recognized a number of clear symptoms of this spiritual dearth in the socialist movement at the time, among which he explicitly mentioned the following: the attempt to create a new epoch merely through technology and strategy; socialism's failure to extricate itself from the bourgeois presuppositions about science and its "objectifying" attitude; and the unconscious fostering of materialistic capitalist attitudes through an overemphasis on the goal of economic welfare and technical progress. But, most serious of all, in Tillich's view, was socialism's theory of education, which would make the intellect the tool of technical discipline and harness the will "for the purpose of an economic and political acquisition of power."[3]

Thus, despite Tillich's great enthusiasm for the socialist movement and its protest against the spirit of capitalism, he ran into direct confrontation with its view on education, insofar as this involved the dismissal of all religious values and spiritual concerns as forms of ideology. Until his emigration to America in 1933, Tillich had been engaged from 1919 as *Privatdozent* and then professor in several German universities. We have already seen that in 1919 he was serving as a *Privatdozent* in theology at the University of Berlin, and that here he had found the nucleus of the new religious socialist movement.[4] In this capacity Tillich felt the threat of Marxist socialism and its view of education in terms of its attitude toward the theological faculties in German universities.

These theological faculties, Tillich admitted, reflected the general isolation and irrelevance of the church to the general culture. For as the church was removed from the proletarian masses, so in like manner was the theological faculty isolated from the other disciplines in the university. Tillich was, therefore, very sympathetic to the socialist objections to the then current attitude and approach of these faculties and did not wonder that socialism would want to dispense with them altogether. Yet, he was equally convinced that without the religious dimension, the much longed for goal of socialism—a truly unified culture—could not be achieved.

Just as it was religion that Tillich saw as the major force of unity for a cultural situation in general (including, of course, the social, political, and economic realms), so also on the academic and intellectual level it was theology to which he ascribed this same kind of unifying role. Tillich's epistemology, it should be noted, was based on the conviction that to the *logos* or intelligible structure of the mind, there corresponded a similar *logos* structure of reality. This vision of mind and reality clearly affected his understanding of the academic disciplines and their relation to the living culture.[5] Accordingly, he expected that the function and role of religion in cultural life should be reflected in the relationship of theology to the other academic disciplines. His sympathy with the Marxist protest led him to criticize the theological faculties wherever they failed to fulfill their unifying function. This occurred, he maintained, primarily in two different cases: (1) when theology viewed itself as some sort of scientific knowledge of God and the world, competing with the other sciences, and (2) when it authoritatively fostered and imposed the claims of a particular religious denomination.[6] In either case the net result was to set theology apart as a completely separate science and discipline, heedless of its task of providing unity of meaning among the sciences, comparable to that of the religious dimension in the cultural situation. In doing so, theology only served to increase the gap separating the secular culture from the religious realm.

Here we have, then, the concrete context within which Tillich addressed himself in 1919 to the question of a theology of culture: a struggle to save the theological faculties in the German university system. Clearly, Tillich's position on the issue placed him once again in a situation "on the boundary," insofar as he opposed both the actual orientation of the theological faculties, on the one hand, and the socialist endeavor to remove them completely from the university, on the other. His stance could be identified neither with the main line of socialism nor with that of the established church. In an address entitled, *Über die Idee einer Theologie der Kultur*[7] given in 1919 at the University of Berlin, Tillich took up the challenge and developed his theory on the role of theology in the university. At the same time, he necessarily laid the groundwork, as his title clearly indicates, of a whole theology of culture.

Although this polemic over the theological faculties provided the immediate background to Tillich's lecture, it must not be forgotten that the address was delivered at a university conference convoked under the auspices of the newly found religious socialist group. An essential aspect of the program was an effort to overcome the sharp cultural tensions that characterized the central and Eastern European situation in the years immediately following World War I. Tillich was struggling to provide the theoretical framework to support a new understanding of the reciprocal relationship of religion and culture and a deep-rooted reconciliation of these so markedly divorced spheres of society. It is evident, then, that the specific question of the theological faculties provided the concrete situation in which Tillich tackled the far broader cultural problem of the relationship of religion to culture.

In this address, as has previously been implied, we have both the origins and the foundations of Tillich's theology of culture. This understanding of the importance of this early address by Tillich is shared by Jean-Paul Gabus, author of a very important study on Tillich's theology of culture: "Cette conférence est veritablement la conférence-programme du projet tillichien."[8] The major ideas of this address are now examined with additional help where necessary from later clarifications of some of these basic elements made by Tillich himself, especially in a series of works published in German during the 1920s. In this way, the study will be more in harmony with the actual historical sequence in the development of Tillich's thought.

The place of theology among the academic disciplines
Theology, according to this early Tillichian study, is "the concrete-normative science of religion."[9] It must be carefully distinguished from the philosophy of religion, which is a descriptive science, dealing with the universal forms of all

reality. Theology, on the contrary, as the definition implies, is concerned with the concrete, the unique, the absolute, the exclusive. Philosophy of religion, by reason of its philosophical attitude, must necessarily deal with the generalized conceptual structures. It is precisely these generalizing structures, however, that are resisted by the concreteness of the religious claim. Herein lies the intrinsic problem of the philosophy of religion.[10] Nevertheless, Tillich was convinced (and this remains a major insight for his theology of culture) that there is a point where the concreteness and uniqueness of revelation and the generalized concepts of philosophy of religion meet. To find this point of contact was the decisive task of the philosophy of religion.[11]

Envisaging, therefore, a synthesis rather than an opposition between philosophy of religion and the concrete claims of revelation, Tillich was by the same token able to reconcile and correlate theology—the science of revelation—with philosophy of religion:

> . . . philosophy of religion and theology are two elements of a single normative cultural science of religion. They belong inseparably together and are in continual interaction with each other and with the third element, the cultural history of religion.[12]

Tillich placed the science of religion in general among the cultural sciences *(Geisteswissenschaften)*, whose principal interest is with "meaning," for concern over meaning is what essentialy characterizes *Geist*. Like all the other cultural sciences, religion has three elements: the philosophical, which articulates the particular sphere of meaning to which the discipline belongs; the cultural historical, which systematically organizes and arranges the material or data of the empirical sciences in question; and the systematic or normative, which constructs a normative system on the basis of the philosophical categories and the cultural history. Theology is related to the philosophy of religion in the same way as normative aesthetics is related to the philosophy of art or a normative theory of law is related to the philosophy of law.[13] It is within this frame of reference that Tillich defines theology as the concrete normative science of religion. Insofar as it attempts to relate the philosophical universal to the concrete stance of directedness to unconditional meaning (or what he later called "ultimate concern"), Tillich at this period of his development referred to theology as a "theonomous metaphysics."[14] While Tillich later departed from this understanding of theology on the *theoretical* level, his theology of culture developed along lines, which, *in practice,* remained faithful to this early understanding of the role of theology among the academic disciplines.

The relationship of religion to culture   If theology is the intellectual systematization and methodological explanation of religion, as Tillich maintained, then its relationship to the academic disciplines must reflect the nature of religion and its connection with secular culture. In the 1919 address Tillich set the groundwork for his later, well-known treatments of this subject.[15] Religion, the young theologian insisted, is not simply one particular cultural domain besides others, such as it was for Kant, Hegel, and even Schleiermacher, who assigned religion to a particular psychic function. It is rather a dimension or quality of finite reality that is present and active in all spiritual acts and cultural creations. It is based upon the experience of an unconditioned and absolute reality (Schelling's *das Unbedingte*),[16] which is the correlative aspect of a no less radical and absolute experience of nonbeing and lack of meaning in all finite experience.

It is precisely this unconditioned element in human experience that gives it its religious quality. It is as a quality (again following Schelling) and not another being that Tillich would have us understand the religious dimension. It is the kind of relationship to this unconditioned element that constitutes the basis of distinction between religion and culture. Whereas religion is intentionally directed toward the unconditional or ultimate meaning-reality, culture is so substantially, but not intentionally. Culture, as an act of the human spirit, is necessarily rooted in the unconditioned meaning or ground of all meaning. By intention, however, it is directed toward conditioned forms, which, on the other hand, can achieve meaning fulfillment only by remaining transparent to the religious import or transcendent source of meaning which they contain. This transparency to the religious dimension— understood as the source of ultimate meaningfulness—must be brought to bear on all cultural activities if man is to attain a culture that itself has unity and meaning. The very separation of these spheres, which so characterizes the modern secular world, is the clearest manifestation of man's spiritual estrangement in our times. Religion and culture must not be separated: "Religion is the substance of culture, culture is the form of religion."[17] Theology, of course, must reflect this mutual interpenetration of religion and culture by bringing into relief and adequately expressing the "concrete religious experiences embedded in all great cultural phenomena."[18]

Form-import and the typology of culture Our consideration of Tillich's understanding of the relationship between religion and culture as well as his notion of the role of theology makes clear his concept of the task of a theology of culture. Although philosophy of culture concentrates on the form or autonomous aspect of a culture, theology of culture is concerned primarily with its spiritual substance or import.

It must always be kept in mind that for Tillich substance and form are aspects of "meaning." Otherwise, his interpretations of cultural phenomena based on these polarities will not be correctly understood. It must also be understood that for Tillich meaning *(Sinn)* is primarily the question of the "meaningfulness" of life. Although Tillich seemed to be well aware of the variety of concepts connected with the term *meaning,* his own principal concern was consistently that of ultimate meaningfulness. The most radical ontological question, "Why something rather than nothing at all?" is essentially and primarily to be answered in terms of "meaning."[19]

In his "Philosophy of Religion" (1925), Tillich distinguished three kinds of cultural meaning:

1. "the awareness of the universal interconnections of meaning"
2. "awareness of the ultimate meaningfulness of the inter-connection of meaning"
3. "an awareness of a demand to fulfill, to be obedient to, the ultimate unconditional meaning-reality"[20]

A culture that is aware of both the universal interconnections of meaning (no. 1) as well as the ultimate meaningfulness of the interconnections (no. 2) can still lose the sense of ultimate meaningfulness by lack of attention to concern for "obedience to the ultimate unconditioned meaning-reality" (no. 3). This for Tillich is the situation of secular culture. In this respect, Tillich is something of a prophet anticipating with great clarity of vision the wide consensus of so many modern interpreters of culture (see Chap. 1) who single out the cardinal contemporary cultural problem as a vivid sense of "loss of meaning."[21]

Drawing upon the model of expressionistic art, Tillich presented a picture of cultural typology in terms of the relationship of form, import, and content. By *content*, Tillich meant the objective existence that is raised up to the intellectual cultural sphere by *form*. Form, in turn, is the direct concern of the different autonomous, cultural activities—theoretical, practical, scientific, aesthetic, juridical, social, and so on. Each academic discipline, as the intellectual reflection of these varied areas of culture, possesses its own forms, which follow their own autonomous rules. It is for this reason that Tillich connects form with autonomy or secular orientation. *Import*, on the other hand, represents ultimate meaning-reality—the spiritual substantiality that gives form its significance. It is in import that *theonomy*—"transparency of cultural forms to their religious depth"—is grounded. Theonomy, which is the authentic religious attitude, as well as autonomous culture have to do with meaning. They differ as to the levels of meaning:

> The more the form, the greater the autonomy; the more the substance or import, the greater the theonomy. But one cannot

exist without the other; a form that forms nothing is just as incomprehensible as substance without form.[22]

With the help of this imagery, Tillich set up a whole typology of culture. The dominance of the formal element constitutes a profane or secular culture, whereas the preponderance of emphasis on import (*Gehalt*) is the essential sign of a religious culture. Finally, insofar as the preponderance of import at the expense or destruction of form creates the authoritarian distortion of religion called heteronomy, it is the delicate balance of form and import that indicates a classical or theonomous culture. In 1929, Tillich was still working within the *cadre* of this typology, when he wrote: "the highest stage of culture is attained where human existence, in complete and autonomous form is comprehended in its finitude and in its quest after the Infinite."[23]

There can be no doubt that even from Tillich's earliest endeavors to relate religion to culture, and theology to the other disciplines, the notion of theonomy serves as his foundation concept and ground principle. It is, in his own words, "under the banner of theonomy" that he envisaged both the struggle of religious socialism and the defense of the theology faculties in the university.

The task of a theology of culture   A theonomous awareness is achieved in the cultural disciplines when the predominant import shatters, without destroying, the autonomous forms, breaking through them, revealing their inadequacy, while pointing at the same time to the ultimate meaning-reality they contain. The task of a theology of culture is "to follow up this process in all the spheres and creations of culture," by indicating and bringing into relief the "concrete religious experiences embedded" therein. In the "Theologie der Kultur," Tillich uses the examples of art, philosophy, ethics, politics, and economics to show how theology must analyze, classify, and systematize the religious import of these disciplines. In the 1925 work, *The Philosophy of Religion*, Tillich continued to develop this theme by probing the religious and unconditional element to be discovered in what he terms the various "realms of meaning," under which heading he includes reason, law, community, aesthetics, and so on. When these areas lose awareness and directedness to the unconditional import of meaning, he contended, they will inevitably become meaningless—the necessary outcome of every purely secular culture.[24] From this it follows that one of the major tasks of theology, especially in a secularized situation, is to work toward successful meaning-fulfillment in all cultural functions.

To many a secular writer this kind of language arouses suspicions, lest Tillich was simply suggesting a more subtle kind of religious interference into secular, autonomous realms. Tillich insisted, however, that he was equally fearful of any kind of return to religious heteronomy. In the 1919 address he set up certain criteria for the theologian of culture to ensure that he will avoid this ever present religious temptation. It is especially in the constructive or systematic aspect of his work that the theologian will be tempted to trespass beyond the frontiers of his own legitimate task and create a situation of cultural heteronomy. The theologian, Tillich reminded the reader, must never fail to respect the complete autonomy and independence of the various disciplines, even while he brings the normative criticism of religious import to bear on all realms of meaning. The following guidelines are proposed to avoid the danger of religious infringement:

1 "The theologian of culture is not directly creative with regard to culture."[25] He must not attempt to create a system of law, of ethics, rules for science, political systems, or principles of aesthetics.
2 He is to adapt rather a critical (affirmative and negative) attitude toward autonomous productions from the perspective of his own concrete theological stance.
3 Furthermore, "he can indicate in a very general way the direction in which he visualizes the realizations of a truly religious system of culture, but he cannot produce the system himself."[26]

From the first enthusiastic, somewhat romantic vision that inspired Tillich's early efforts toward a theonomous culture—which envisaged the actualization of the religious principle in all spheres of spiritual and cultural life,[27] one might presume that Tillich is recommending a stage of culture in which Christianity becomes areligious and secularized, in prophetic anticipation of the more contemporary movement of "religionless Christianity." Nothing, however, could be further from Tillich's thought, for any utopian ambitions, which might seek to creep into his more romantic hopes, were strongly counterbalanced by a persistent and ever-vivid awareness of the universal estrangement of finite existence. Whatever affinities to contemporary humanism are found in Tillich's thought, and whatever difficulties some Christian theologians may have in recognizing the Christian character of his system, the impact of the Christian doctrine of original sin on his thought should serve as a warning to those critics who would too easily classify Tillich as a secular humanist disguised in the outer garments of Christian symbols.[28]

After his wartime experience, Tillich was more convinced than ever of the fundamental estrangement of the human condition. In view of this conviction, even in the enthusiasm of his involvement in the religious socialist movement, Tillich could not let himself interpret his theonomous vision as anything but an ideal—never to be achieved in more than a fragmentary way within history. For in the state of estrangement, the various cultural spheres tend to remain within the limitations of their own finite and conditioned forms. All the more so in light of the rational and reflective emphasis of our contemporary secular culture is the difficulty of transparency to the sacred and ultimate dimension of meaning greatly increased. For only the insight of faith reveals to man the religious depth present in all his cultural creations. Hence, the need in fact of special, particular religious structures, such as myth, liturgical cult, dogma, and church. In actual, estranged (fallen) human existence, there is need of a special religious sphere in order to bring attention and awareness to the sacred or depth dimension, and thereby prevent a universal profanation of culture.[29]

Apart from the religious structures just mentioned, there is need on the intellectual level of a special science of religion, and, in particular, of its concrete, normative aspect, which is theology. Such a concrete, normative theology is found only within the particularity of a specific religious community, possessing its own peculiar tradition and norms, "no longer derived from culture but with an independent history going back much farther than most other cultural creations."[30] Tillich is strongly urging the necessity of a church theology. But how is this to be related to the more general theology of culture concerning the nature and role of which the major portion of his address is occupied?

Theology of culture and church theology This is the principal issue with which Tillich concluded his first attempts to elucidate a theology of culture. This might also well serve as a reminder to some of his later critics that despite the strong ontological and metaphysical interests, the major thrust of Tillich's work from its very inception was theological. Tillich was not apologetic about his theological stance: existential estrangement of religion from culture demands a discipline that can indicate the fundamental unity and meaningfulness of cultural creation. Without the concreteness of a particular religious stance, however, such a project cannot begin to succeed. The religious dimension is the sphere of unconditional and ultimate meaning-reality. To retain its quality of ultimacy it must not cease to transcend the relativity of all finite forms. Yet even in his early work, Tillich knew that religious substance required embodiment in forms, that "like everything spiritual, religion is supported by a community."[31] Authentic religion demands the *paradoxical* concretization of universal and unconditional reality in particular revelational symbols of a historical community and tradition.[32] Not only theology of culture but also church theology, reflecting the religious experience and unique stance of a particular sacred community is essential to the task of creating a theonomous culture.

There are innate dangers to both theology of culture and church theology. The former tends to become a fashionable interpreter and prophet of the ongoing cultural development; the latter tends to forget the relativity of its own point of view. The only answer to both these dangers is the mutual complementation and balancing off of both types of theology. Tillich even suggested, though with obvious hesitation, that the best practical solution might be to have both tasks performed by one and the same theologian.[33] His insistence on the need of church theology, somewhat unexpected at this point of the address, seems to satisfy the author as an adequate safeguard against a faddist and fashionable theology of culture. And, after all, do not the restrictions and restraints demanded by loyalty to a historical religious tradition provide one of the best possible protections against "selling out," so to speak, to popular cultural tendencies? Tillich's concern, on the other hand, about the continuous danger of religion to absolutize its particular stance with authoritarian claims, urged him to be more specific about the kind of attitude that must be maintained by the church theologian if there is to exist the possibility of a constructive relation between church and secular culture, between theology and the secular disciplines.

Tillich distinguished three types of attitudes toward secular culture that church theology has historically assumed at different periods and in different social and political situations. The first is the typically Catholic attitude in which theology of culture is absorbed into church theology. Tillich rejects this approach as essentially authoritarian and heteronomous. Second is the old Protestant attitude, which, although, unlike Catholicism, preserves the relativity of church, cultus, and ethics, nevertheless sets divine and supernatural revelation as an absolute form of knowledge over against other forms of relative knowledge, deriving from the various sciences and academic disciplines. Neither of these two attitudes permits a genuine theology of culture. The third—which is his own view—would see the importance of maintaining the absoluteness of the "religious principle" while insisting at the same time on the significance and autonomy of the finite, relative forms within which the religious principle is to be discovered if it is going to have any meaning. Only this latter approach assures a positive relationship between theology of culture and church theology.[34]

For the early Tillich, then, of the period immediately following World War I, there were really two distinct theologies with two equally distinct, though thoroughly interrelated tasks. Tillich had to pass through several important stages of development in his philosophical and theological reflection before he could achieve his famous method of correlation, which would transcend his doctrine of two theologies. One might justifiably conclude (although the text of his 1919 address is far from unambiguous) that Tillich was recommending that the theological faculties fulfill two distinct roles: the more analytic function of a theology of culture and the more normative one of church theology. Whether Tillich envisaged these two distinct roles, as separate functions on the practical level, in the form of different sets of lectures, seminars, programs, and so on, or simply saw them as two distinct tasks necessary to every theological enterprise, cannot be ascertained from the address itself. Tillich simply did not direct his attention on this occasion to the practical details of such a plan, but rather restricted himself to enunciating the principles and guidelines for assuring the proper functioning of the theological faculties in the university.[35]

So far, we have considered the sense in which the theology of Paul Tillich can be considered a thoroughly humanistic theology, intrinsically geared toward a deeper understanding of man and a humanization of contemporary culture. From the point of view of this last element, in particular, we have seen that his theological endeavor from its inception was essentially directed to our current secular culture and the questions that arise therefrom. We have considered the historical context and situation within which the young Tillich began his theological work, and this study has made it unmistakably clear that Tillich's theological project was planned from the outset as a theology of culture. We now proceed to consider the developments that gradually emerged from this original blueprint of a theology of culture.

From a Twofold Theology to the Method of Correlation

To students of Tillich more familiar with his more mature writings of the American period (1933–1965), the concept of "two theologies," discussed in the previous section, will seem unfamiliar, even foreign. Yet, this was his standpoint, however uneasy, clearly evidenced in the "Theologie der Kultur," and never completely supplanted until the later formulation of the method of correlation. This latter achievement, in turn, would only be possible after Tillich had evolved a plausible philosophical interpretation of history, on the one hand, and a firm christological foundation, on the other. Prior to this, as was clearly seen from a consideration of his early works, the pressures of the immediate cultural and political situation had limited Tillich's concerns to questions of the nature and the role of theology among the academic disciplines, and the theological foundations for an authentic humanistically oriented culture.

The philosophical interpretation of history and the foundations of Christology Tillich followed up his 1919 address with a number of perceptive articles, the primary purpose of which was to clarify and work out in detail the principles of his master plan for a theology of culture. The following, in particular, should be mentioned: "Die Überwindung des Religionsbegriff in der Religionsphilosophie" (1922), Das *System der Wissenschaften nach ihren Methoden und Gegenständen* (1923) and "Religionsphilosophie" (1925).[36] Important as each of these early follow-up works is for a correct understanding of Tillich's intellectual development, they are still very much written within the frame of reference of a theology of culture distinct from a church theology. There are, however, strong indications already in these early works, especially in *Das System,* Tillich's masterful systematic classification of the sciences, that he was attempting to combine the two apparently distinct functions into one unified theological approach. Tillich identifies these functions as (1) the *confessional task* of discriminating and transmitting the "spirit of the original documents of revelation" and (2) the *cultural task* of "radiating theonomy into autonomous forms."[37] There remains a tension between these two tasks that Tillich does not yet succeed in resolving. Yet, he is clearly on the way toward integrating the two by establishing the intellectual basis for theology as a "theonomous" cultural science—which is a very accurate description of his whole systematic theology.

Furthermore, once having securely established the place of theology among the cultural sciences, Tillich proceeds, both in *Das System* and in the "Religionsphilosophie," to develop what he calls the "metalogical method" as the most fitting approach to the theological study of culture as well as to the philosophy of religion. By way of philosophical intuition *(Schau)*, metalogic can get beyond the formalism of logic and the particularity of empiricism, so as to express the "dynamic elements of meaning" . . . by leading . . . "beyond philosophical considerations to cultural history, and then to the establishment of norms."[38] Metalogic is aimed at the discovery of meaning within the dynamic "living stream of meaning realities, a stream that also includes the holy or religiously qualified realities."[39] Although the term *metalogic* proved to be short lived and ephemeral in Tillich's thought, it does represent a clearly "theonomous" approach to the cultural sciences, and, in addition, by reason of its serious concern for the dynamic process of the life of the spirit, opens the way for Tillich to a religious interpretation of history.

Despite all the insistence we find in these early works of Tillich's on the concrete normative aspect of theology, they are very far from revealing the exact nature of this particular confessional stance, and especially of its relationship to the theonomous science of religion. Granted that Tillich is writing as a Christian theologian, it is quite remarkable that there should be such a glaring absence of a clearly christological perspective. In the "Theologie der Kultur," for example, there is not even mention of a christological theme. Yet this is the central, confessional stance of the Christian communities. Accordingly, Tillich's references to the necessity of the concrete, normative function remain as yet abstract and blood-less. This is quite in sharp contrast to his theology of culture, which, firmly grounded in a consistent and profound ontology and philosophy of culture, already appears vital, exciting, and creative. A study of Tillich's early works reveals that it was only after he had achieved a much greater historical consciousness that he was able to establish a firm foundation for a convincing Christology, which, in turn, served to concretize the confessional, normative stance.

One of the most significant steps Tillich made in this direction is evidenced in a 1924 article, entitled "Kirche und Kultur." By this time, Tillich had begun to shed a great deal of the philosophical idealism and romanticism that had been evident in his "Theologie der Kultur,"[40] so that whereas he presents revelation as the answer to the cultural split between the sacred and the secular, by way of creating new theonomous forms, Tillich does not identify this conquest or victory with the Kingdom of God. For the victory of theonomy is only a partial and temporary one, and is only a directedness toward the Kingdom of God.[41] Theonomy is itself not the work of man but a divine act, for which human efforts are only a preparation or openness.

A still more decisive development in Tillich's thought occurred in a series of articles written between 1924 and 1929, in which Tillich complemented his earlier "vertical" understanding of the breakthrough of eternal import into the finite order with a "horizontal" emphasis that places the manifestation of the unconditional within the historical process itself. The influence of Marx's historical thinking has made its full impact on Tillich's theological analysis. With this concern for historical destiny Tillich combined a sense of freedom, decision, and risk within the historical process. In the context of our historic situation we must decide in light of the *eschaton*—the call of an ultimate reality standing at the end of time. Tillich was speaking the language of Barthian Crisis theology and of the philosophers of existence, especially of Kierkegaard. Together with Marx, these thinkers helped divest Tillich of the last traces of Hegelian idealism. As a net result, during this period Tillich's thought was able to grapple fully with the question of the meaning of human existence within history.[42]

In order to do justice to the uniqueness and concreteness of historical reality, Tillich developed the concept of *kairos*[43]—"a breakthrough of ultimate reality into the historical process." *Kairos* was an unrepeatable event of world-historical nature and had to be met with freedom, decision, and involvement. Tillich could now maintain that it is only through this kind of risk-filled participation in the historic situation that knowledge of unconditional and ultimate reality is possible. Within this context of historical thinking, Tillich proposed the philosophical perspective he termed "belief-ful realism" *(gläubiger Realismus)*—the application of the theonomous attitude to the philosophical interpretation of history. Through this intuitive method *(schauende Methode)*, Tillich was attempting to reconcile the tension between faith and realism, historical awareness and self-transcendence, philosophy of history and theology, for he was convinced that this method would reveal the identity of the ultimate reality with the ultimate meaning of history.[44] Only at this point could Tillich find a fitting and solid structure in his theology of culture for a concrete theological norm.

Tillich now believed he could confidently affirm the christological dogma without having recourse to what he termed supernaturalistic and heteronomous thought. Christology is no longer simply a speculation on the two natures, human and divine, in Christ. To reduce it to this would be to fail to fulfill the function of theology as Tillich saw it. He now saw Christology as an interpretation of history from the point of view of a community that has engaged itself in the historical process through decision and commitment. For this community, supported by its ancient tradition, Christ becomes the meaning of history, being at once its center and its ultimate goal. At the same time it is in Christ that the unconditional and ultimate reality has manifested itself in a concrete, decisive, and nonambiguous way: the *eschaton* has broken through into our time.[45]

The inclusive christological norm and the method of correlation As Christ, the center of history, became unambiguously the concrete norm for Tillich's theology of culture, his theology became more firmly rooted in the confessional stance of the Christian communities, and thereby enabled him to do away with his former uneasy distinction between church theology and theology of culture. Without in any way surrendering the important goals he had connected with the latter, Tillich could now do full justice to the concrete, confessional aspect he had maintained was an essential ingredient of theology as a cultural science. He accomplished this by a paradoxical reconciliation of the universal and the particular, determined to avoid the temptation to heteronomy that so easily accompanies the concrete stance of faith. Christ, as the center of history, could be seen against the background of a universal *Grundoffenbarung.* Despite the original influence of Barth's Christology on his own thought, Tillich set his own thought in direct opposition to the basic Barthian spirit and methodological assumptions, which, in Tillich's view, created a radical opposition between divine and human reality, between Christian revelation and autonomous culture. Barth's theology, in other words, represented for Tillich a "christological exclusivism," which was bound to prevent any serious dialogue with secular culture. Although fully endorsing Barth's Christocentrism, Tillich affirmed with equal insistence the universal and all-inclusive nature of the Christ-event. The Christ-event is received by a universal revelation and the theological norm is used in a theonomous perspective.[46]

This double concern of Tillich's christological theory is evidenced even in an early very important article, "Rechtfertigung und Zweifel," published in 1924. Here we find careful and explicit development of the notion of *Grundoffenbarung*—the most fundamental and universal revelation that attests to the divine presence in everything that exists. This concept is already implicit in Tillich's earlier theology of culture, by way of direct inheritance from Schelling's ontological principle of the paradoxical immanence of the infinite in the finite as well as from the basic Lutheran theological doctrine: *finitum capax infiniti*.[47] For Tillich, to put it in another way, there is a direct correlation between the revelation of Jesus as the Christ, and the most profound human experience of the presence of ultimate reality within the depths of man's being and historical existence. Just as Saint Paul explained to the Athenian philosophers that the same hidden God whom they worshipped in mystery as the unknown God had revealed himself in Jesus of Nazareth (Acts 17:22–31), so also did Tillich's theology of culture relate the Christian revelation to the *Deus abconditus* or unconditional element that was present in all autonomous cultural forms. As Tillich's theological system developed, a clearer description of this relationship was also evolved. The ultimate reality and infinite presence that man experiences in the religious and anxious awareness of his own finitude, and in the courage to assert his being in spite of the threat of nonbeing and meaninglessness, which constitutes his estranged condition, has manifested his healing presence in a unique, decisive, and historical manner in Jesus as the Christ. The universal tragic condition of human estrangement is overcome in the new God-man relationship established in Jesus as the Christ:

> . . . the biblical picture of Jesus as the Christ confirms his character as the bearer of the New Being or as the one in whom the conflict between the essential unity of God and man and man's existential estrangement is overcome. Point by point, not only in the Gospel records but also in the Epistles, this picture of Jesus as the Christ contradicts the marks of estrangement which have been elaborated in the analysis of man's existential predicament.[48]

This universal and inclusive christological norm enables Tillich to preserve intact one of his principal theological aims: to interpret the import of the Christian message to those many of his contemporaries who were searching for ultimate meaning within a strictly secular context. By seeing his Christology over against a universal *Grundoffenbarung* Tillich is able to maintain his basic insight into the relationship of religion and culture; namely, there is no culture so secular, autonomous, or profane that it is not rooted in the infinite and divine reality. This means that even modern technological and secularized society with its sense of spiritual void can be revelatory of the divine, and that accordingly, contemporary secular man, despite his loss of transcendence and his doubt about God, can be justified and find God within the very cultural situation that seems to have no place for him. Tillich is telling us, in brief, in a favorite phrase of his that: "The Holy embraces itself and the secular."[49] Luther's *simul justus et peccator* becomes *simul justus et dubitans*.

Gabus, in his introduction to the French translation of Tillich's 1958 collection, *Theology of Culture,* shows a very penetrating insight into the special character and significance of Tillich's Christology. The following passage merits being quoted in full:

> Without any doubt, Christianity represents a paradox, namely, the affirmation that in the person and message of Christ, the universal Truth becomes concrete and particular truth. In Jesus Christ, and in him alone, the absolutely universal and the absolutely concrete coincide . . . Christianity cannot reduce this paradox without denying its own originality, its very *raison d'être.* But this is the only Christian paradox. Unlike Kierkegaard and Karl Barth, and all the more so Protestant fundamentalism, Tillich refused to multiply the paradoxes of the Christian faith. He would never oppose those pairs that contemporary Protestant theology delights in placing in contrast: Athens and Jerusalem, culture and faith, reason and revelation, philosophy and theology. To the extent that the Christological event is inclusive and universal, Tillich was convinced that he could show that there was in fact a necessary correlation between these apparently antithetical pairs.[50]

Tillich explicitly saw his work in continuity with the "logos" theology of the early Greek fathers.[51] The inner dynamic of *Deus absconditus—Deus revelatus; Grundoffenbarung*—Christian revelation; the universal logos and the concrete logos constitutes the very core of Tillich's future doctrine of correlation, as Gabus clearly implies in the quoted passage. With the achievement of this method, the need for two theologies—one of church and the other of culture—was definitely overcome, and the resulting synthesis was essentially directed toward continuing the dialogue with secular culture that was outlined in Tillich's 1919 address. The old problem of the relationship of philosophy to theology takes on a much more radical and decisive role in Tillich's system. It is no longer a peripheral question, but becomes the question of the very essence and aim of theology. For in Tillich's view, theology can only begin with the philosophical questions, with ontology, with the *Grundoffenbarung* within human existence.[52]

It would be beyond the scope of this investigation to attempt to establish the exact beginnings of an explicit method of correlation in Tillich's developing system, especially since this has been done elsewhere.[53] What is significant here is that the achievement of this method by Tillich enabled him to unify and synthesize the most fundamental tensions that remained unresolved as long as he viewed his theology as a "theonome Metaphysik," as was the case in his early writings. The conflicts represented by the opposition of church theology and theology of culture were absorbed into the tension of kerygmatic and apologetic theology, which was in turn resolved by the method of correlation. This latter was aimed at doing full justice to both message and situation with a methodology that was adequate to the task.[54] The second significant factor is that the method of correlation, which supplanted the "two theologies" approach of 1919, was possible for Tillich only after he had established a concrete, historical, christological stance.

Theonomy and the Method of Correlation

The first thing to be said when considering the relationship of theonomy to Tillich's method of correlation is that in looking back over his earlier works Tillich recognized many of his more mature concepts as already being contained implicitly in the earlier formulations. Tillich explicitly mentioned the notion of theology as "theonome Metaphysik" defended in *Das System* (1923), as expressing in germinal, though insufficient fashion, what he would later call the method of correlation.[55] A few general remarks about the nature of this method are sufficient for our purposes, as it has already been the object of many scholarly studies.[56]

Correlation is essentially Tillich's view of the relationship of cultural situation to Christian message in terms of theological approach. For the theologian the correlation is centered primarily around the dialectic between philosophy and theology. The theologian looks to philosophy for an analysis of the cultural situation and of the discovery of the questions of ultimacy that are inherent within it. By reason of his faith commitment, however, the theologian realizes that the answers to these questions that arise out of the very structures of estranged human existence are outside of the potential of the human mind and the resources of human power:

> These answers are contained in the revelatory events on which Christianity is based and are taken by systematic theology from the sources. . . They are "spoken" *to* human existence from beyond it. Otherwise they would not be answers, for the question is human existence itself.[57]

Another important aspect of Tillich's method of correlation that must be borne in mind if one is to avoid misrepresenting this complex dialectical method is that the correlation is not simply one of philosophical question and theological answer. This has been widely recognized by a number of current studies on the subject.[58] The philosophical question and theological answer are more correctly seen as "interrelated" and "interdependent." The impact of the divine answer is already present in the concrete theological stance or theological circle that constitutes the theologian's existential commitment. Yet it is the same theologian who is philosophically analyzing the human situation. Thus, for example, the Chris-

tian faith of the theologian will influence, though not determine, his philosophical conclusion that the question of God is
implied in human finitude. On the other hand, the
philosophical analysis will so influence the theological answer
such that, for example, if God is going to be treated in the
Systematic theology at all, He "must be called the infinite
power of being which resists the threat of nonbeing."[59]
Accordingly, the philosophical understanding of the human
situation will also deeply affect the peculiar character and
formulation of the theological answer.

The relationship between correlation and Tillich's earlier
works, especially the "Theologie der Kultur," is such that it
represents a carefully elaborated method of theology based on
the fundamental insight already found in the earlier works.
Once Tillich's concept of *theonomy* ("the presence of the
divine Ground in all human cultural creations") could be
translated to the horizontal level of the breakthrough of the
infinite reality into the historical process, Tillich could find a
fitting place in his philosophical vision for the christological
norm. Jesus as the Christ was the depth of culture, the bearer
of the New Being. Only now was correlation between Christian *kerygma* and human cultural situation possible. *The
method of correlation, therefore, is an extension of the
theonomous vision that is central to Tillich's thought from the
outset.*

In his Introduction to Volume 1 of the *Systematic,* Tillich
indicates his awareness of the dangers that are inherent in
both a kerygmatic as well as an apologetic approach to
theology.[60] It was precisely through the method of correlation that he maintained that the extremes of either approach
could be offset and the values of each could be both preserved
and reconciled. Tillich's early work represented, in these
terms, a more exclusively apologetic theology, with very
explicit concern for discovering the religious element in secular, cultural forms. Although even his early writings were
ultimately directed toward relating the same religious depth
present within secular autonomy to the specific, concrete
stance of the Christian message, the latter was not very clearly

integrated into his method until he had developed a viable historically based Christology, and finally, the notion of correlation itself. By the same token, whereas Tillich's more mature works proved more successful in incorporating more fully the concrete norm contained in the Christian symbols, they never failed to lose sight of the original Tillichian concern of 1919, namely, that of maintaining a vital dialogue with contemporary secular man. Tillich made this point very clearly in his preface of his collection of essays published in 1959, under the title *Theology of Culture:*

> In spite of the fact that during most of my adult life I have been a teacher of Systematic Theology, the problem of religion and culture has always been in the center of my interest. Most of my writings—including the two volumes of *Systematic Theology*—try to define the way in which Christianity is related to secular culture.[61]

We have now seen the intellectual stages whereby Tillich was able to move from the concept of a twofold theology to a unified method of correlation in which he reconciles the tasks of the formerly distinct theologies, correlating the philosophical interpretation of culture with the religious symbols of Christian revelation. At the same time, it became evident that throughout these changes in methodology and approach, Tillich's theology always remained essentially a theology of culture. We can now proceed to a more detailed and thorough analysis of Tillich's concept of theonomy, for it is the focal and central concept of his entire theology of culture.

4
Theonomy: The Keystone of Tillich's Theological Construct

Even a cursory glance at the index of Tillich's collected works gives the reader a significant clue, even quantitatively, to the importance of the term *theonomy* within the skillful architectonic structure of the entire opus.[1] The term is both frequent and persistent from his first article to the last volume of the *Systematic*. Theonomy, furthermore, is defined in many places in the course of Tillich's writings, and significantly, not always in the same terms. This is not the result of a lack of consistency, but rather of the variety of contexts in which he finds it helpful to apply this focal concept. We have here but another indication of the manner in which this crucial idea permeates Tillich's entire theological inquiry.

Theonomy and the Dialectic of Culture

Tillich's most succinct, yet most general, statement on the concept is found in an article written for *Religion in Geschichte und Gegenwart* in 1931, entitled simply "Theonomie."[2] At the very outset of the article Tillich establishes an important aspect of his understanding of theonomy, one that he insisted upon throughout his long career, no matter how hard, at times, his opponents tried to move him from this position. Theonomy, according to Tillich, is not opposed to autonomy—to the inviolability of human freedom or the dignity and independence of human intelligence. Theonomy does not signify religious authority—a divine law imposed from without. Theonomy is to be contrasted, rather, with what Tillich terms "heteronomy," by which he meant precisely "the destruction of autonomous human forms of thinking and acting by a law which is foreign and external to the spirit."[3] The kind of secularity that dominates in Britain and the United States is usually uncomfortable dealing with the category of religion, when it is understood, as Tillich did, in this "theonomous" fashion. For theonomy does not permit clear-cut distinctions and classifications of religious and secular, of revelation and reason, as if these involved extremes of polarization.[4]

Not only was theonomy not to be opposed to autonomy but, in Tillich's view, theonomy was indeed a higher (or better, "deeper") autonomy—in fact, the only really authentic autonomy. "Theonomy is autonomous reason united to its own depth."[5] Tillich never failed to make it very clear in his interpretation of culture that he was in no way opposed to human autonomy or to the humanistic spirit which it implies. He was opposed only to what he termed "shallow" or "self-complacent" autonomy,[6] insofar as such autonomy lacks completeness—it lacks direction toward ultimate meaning. It is not authentic autonomy. By this Tillich did not mean merely to assert that lack of theonomous depth would create a situation of somewhat inadequate or deficient autonomy. He meant rather that it would lead inevitably, as if by an intrinsic and necessary law, to new forms of heteronomy. The reason for this, Tillich maintained, is that the human spirit, in either its individual or collective form, cannot continue very long without the meaning provided by an ultimate concern. But ultimate concern is not experienced in individual finite meanings but only in the depth or ground of all meaning; in the sense of a total meaningfulness of all life and reality. The difficulty with a *self-sufficient* or *purely secular* autonomy is that it has lost this dimension of depth, and must eventually fill the resulting void by attributing ultimacy to something finite and limited—the very essence of idolatry. "But an autonomy which is left to itself leads to emptiness, but since a vacuum cannot endure even in matters of the spirit, it seeks fulfillment in the form of demonically destructive powers."[7]

The twentieth-century brand of demonic, false absolutes that creep into our culture wherever genuine ultimacy is lost was the subject matter of Tillich's Bampton Lectures, given at Columbia University in 1963. It is clear that the same fundamental dialectic of culture, centered around the ideal of theonomy and its deviations (autonomy and heteronomy), remains the guiding principle of Tillich's thought and analysis even in the last years of his life. The demonic distortions or idolatries that arise in our secularized, technological culture to replace the loss of genuine transcendence and the dimension of depth are called fittingly "quasi-religions," for they make a claim to man's total commitment, attempting to offer new answers to the ultimate meaning of life.

> In secular quasi-religions the ultimate concern is directed to-wards objects like nation, science, a particular form or stage of society, or a highest ideal of humanity, which are then considered divine.[8]

Although such secular forms of quasi-religion are never rejected *in toto* by Tillich, precisely because of the religious intention implicit within them,[9] they are, nevertheless, seen as inadequate substitutes for religious depth, necessarily leading to destruction or existential frustration. Nothing short of the Infinite itself can satisfy and fulfill man's quest for ultimacy in meaning and in being. Autonomy, Tillich maintains, is indeed a very important dialectical stage in the growth of humanity. It is a wholesome, prophetic protest against heteronomy—against the inhumanity that so frequently accompanies the specifically religious sphere. [10] When secular autonomy neglects what Tillich calls the Odyssey aspect of the human drama, the cultural situation is menaced by the inwardly necessitated catastrophe of purely autonomous thought. [11]

If we reflect on the various attitudes that Christian theologians have taken to the secular, as discussed in Chapter 1, it is clear that Tillich is correctly classified among those who take secular culture very seriously and yet remain cautious and circumspect about their approbation of secularity. [12] Given Tillich's understanding of the cultural dialectic, to speak of "secular Christianity" would be to affirm as permanent and ideal what must by its very nature be a transitory dialectical stage. For Tillich autonomy must always strive for a new theonomous cultural unity.

Theonomy: An Attitude
of Christian Humanism

The most accurate and helpful way to understand Tillich's concept of theonomy is in terms of an *attitude* toward secular culture. Profane or secular culture, for Tillich was substantially religious. Tillich considered his famous dictum, "Religion is the substance of culture and culture the form of religion" to be "the most precise statement of theonomy." [13] The peculiarity of finite created forms is that they can either hide or reveal the absolute meaning and ultimate dimension which supports and judges them. The profane and the holy are not really distinguished except by reason of the intention that the individual or the culture brings to them. A theonomous attitude is one that is intentionally directed to absolute and ultimate meaning, without destroying the single finite forms of meaning and their relationships.

Just as we were able to speak in Chapter 1 of a secular *mood* or secular *spirit* as a fundamental attitude toward life, [14] so also can we speak of theonomy as an all-pervasive attitude that guides and affects Tillich's entire intellectual effort. Theonomy takes on content only when it is applied to specific cultural areas, such as human science, morality, philosophy, art, politics, and historical interpretation. This is also another reason for the diverse definitions of theonomy presented by Tillich in different sections of his work.

The most distinguishing and essential characteristics of this attitude are reflections to a very great extent of the author's own personality and character. We recall how in his youth Tillich was already faced with the threat of a split-consciousness, especially as he encountered the classical humanism of the German *gymnasium*. [15] This same kind of dichotomy between Christian and humanist ideal continued to challenge him during his university days, and, indeed, it can well be maintained throughout his entire career. Consistently, even from those early years Tillich opted for synthesis rather than polarization, for mediation rather than condemnation. Tillich became a humanist in his school days and remained so until his death. What was peculiar to his attitude, however, was that, unlike so many of his contemporaries, Tillich found his humanism complementary to the Christian creed rather than opposed to it.

We already noted that Tillich would never tolerate any Christian interpretation of God and religion that would extol the divine majesty at the expense of human dignity. It is precisely this attitude that so characterized Tillich's whole personality that is conceptualized and systematized in his concept of theonomy. "The idea of theonomy," he writes in Volume 3 of the *Systematic,* "is not antihumanistic, but it turns the humanistic indefiniteness about the 'where-to' into a direction which transcends every particular human aim." [16] Like his theological teacher, Martin Kähler, before him, Tillich became a theologian of "mediation" [17] between the humanistic and the specifically Christian viewpoints. Theonomy became the conceptual criterion by which he judged the contemporary cultural scene, both religious and secular. At its most fundamental level, *theonomy is the intellectual symbol for a religious humanism.*

Our current cultural situation, as Tillich saw it, with its great emphasis on technology and empirical method, leads inevitably to the dehumanization of society, and Tillich's intention was nothing less than "to work for the reconstitution and rehabilitation of the human, including spiritual and material concerns, in the context of modern life."[18] Culture is for Tillich the self-creative function of life in the dimension of spirit; in its practical goal it is aimed at "humanity," by which he means the personal and social self-fulfillment of the individual man.[19] But the self-creative function of life is not enough; there must also be a self-transcendence of life under the dimension of spirit, which Tillich identifies with the religious function. Here again, "humanity," or the self-fulfillment of human potentialities, is not to be sacrificed, though this is exactly what occurs in every heteronomy, or demonic distortion of religion.[20] Ideally, therefore, the self-transcending or religious function should help man attain the essential humanity from which he is estranged, rather than oppose it. Finally, even in his interpretation of so specifically Christian a symbol as the Kingdom of God, Tillich sees the humanistic ideal as essentially present. It is the very ambiguity of the religious dimension itself that raises the question of the Kingdom of God, and this Tillich identifies with the ideal of a fulfilled humanity:

> . . . The Kingdom of God gives eternal meaning to the individual person. The transhistorical aim toward which history runs is not the extinction but the fulfillment of humanity in every human individual.[21]

This basic and overriding concern for the dignity and fulfillment of humanity totally integrated, at the same time, into a religious and Christian vision of reality is the essence of Tillich's humanism and the fundamental practical meaning of "theonomy." It is evident that we are dealing with an attitude that is far broader than any particular methodology, system, or concept. For this reason it is justifiable to assert that the most accurate term to express the spirit and *Weltanschauung* that pervade Tillich's entire theological enterprise is what James L. Adams calls "the theonomous attitude."[22]

Theonomy and the Artistic Model

Like several other important Tillichian notions,[23] the concept of theonomy is derived ultimately from a concrete, existential experience. To put it in another way, the concept of theonomy is autobiographical in origin. Tillich derived his vision of theonomy from the very powerful impression that his first serious encounter with the study of art made upon his whole personality and understanding. The major influence of expressionistic art on Tillich's dialectical notions of form, content, and import, from which the notion of theonomy is derived, has already been noted. From Tillich's autobiographical sketches it is a relatively simple matter to pinpoint the situation from which this critical aesthetic experience derived. During a furlough from the battlefront in World War I the young chaplain visited the Kaiser Friedrich Museum in Berlin, pursuing the interest in art he had already developed through studying prints of the masters, as a diversion and relief from the horrors and ugliness of war. At the museum he came upon a Botticelli portrait of the Madonna, which moved him so deeply that he experienced it as a sort of divine revelation. According to Tillich's own testimony, some of the most fundamental of his philosophical and theological categories were derived from reflection on this experience; he mentions specifically those of "form," "substance," and "breakthrough."[24] Tillich was very much aware of the great affinity between the religious and the aesthetic experience. His philosophy of religion concerned itself chiefly with the theoretical foundations of this boundary experience. In view of this general outlook that brought Tillich to the question of the relationship between religion and culture, it is no longer surprising that his all-important religious symbol of "theonomy" is derived from the artistic model.

We are drawing attention at this point to the aesthetic imagery that lay at the roots of Tillich's theological construction primarily because it helps us to understand the concept of theonomy as such, the subject of our present consideration. In addition, this aesthetic imagery of Tillich's also provides a helpful background and insight for understanding several other important aspects of Tillich's thought in general, especially his use and understanding of religious and theological language. Gabus shares this view of the great significance and impact of the artistic model on the whole structure or fabric of Tillich's theological approach:

> All his philosophy of religion and culture, as well as his idea of divine revelation are based on this experience. He understands that an artistic or religious symbol has the function of opening up a new dimension of being as well as a corresponding dimension of the soul. [25]

Lest we should feel that Gabus might be overstressing the importance of the influence of the artistic vision on Tillich's conceptual apparatus, we need only consider some of Tillich's own observations on the subject:

> . . . Painting is a mute revealer and yet to the interpreting spirit it often speaks more clearly than the word that conveys a concept . . . [26]
> . . . Though I have not produced anything in the field of the creative arts, my love for the arts has been of great importance to my theological and philosophical work. [27]

The symbolic character of Tillich's theological concepts and the problems that arise therefrom are discussed in greater detail later in this chapter, and a critique of Tillich's symbolism insofar as it affects his interpretation of culture is presented in the final chapter. In both instances, the question of the influence of the artistic model on his conceptual framework and formulation will be of prime importance. For the present, we confine our considerations to the specific categories of "form," "content," and "import," that Tillich derived from the study of expressionistic art. [28] Some have maintained that Tillich's cultural typology and dialectic are essentially a carryover of nineteenth-century idealist construction, which he imposes artificially on the human, cultural situation. If this objection were true, this would certainly cast great doubt on the validity and usefulness of the concept of theonomy. In light of the foregoing analysis, however, it appears that there is little foundation for this assertion. The process was, in fact, quite the reverse: Tillich's conceptual categories for the interpretation of culture were rather the product of his aesthetic experience, the reflective expression of a powerful personal and cultural experience. It was the experience of the religious character of art, in other words, that colored his conceptual categories, rather than the reverse. If one must relate Tillich to nineteenth-century philosophy, and there is good reason to do so, it would be far more accurate to call him a romanticist rather than an idealist.

We now consider Tillich's study of expressionistic art and the effect it had on his thought. It was in the works of men such as Schmidt-Rottluff, Nolde, Kirchner, and Heckel as well as in the paintings of such masters as Cézanne and Van Gogh that Tillich first encountered the beginnings of expressionism. In this new art form Tillich saw a revolt against the earlier nineteenth-century naturalism and impressionism— the artistic reflections of the capitalist and technological temper.[29] In the works of these men the object or content seemed to lose importance. In his well-known series of reflections on art called *Museum Without Walls*, André Malraux maintains that what really matters in this revolutionary art is the inner pattern or schema, the subjective rather than the objective, "which may *or may not* take the shape of objects. . . Gone are the copper pots and pans and all the other objects brought to gleaming life by the reflection of light."[30] In impressionism, men and things were all seen alike on the surface as objects are in a complacent capitalist culture. The light of impressionism illumined the surface alone, for this was an age in which man sought meaning in finite forms, in what Tillich terms the spirit of "self-sufficient finitude."[31] In expressionism, as Tillich saw it, Eternity broke through, proclaiming No to the absolutizing of time and finite things.

But the role of expressionism was negative and had to be complemented by a more positive art form, a "new realism" in which "things were envisaged in their cosmic meaning and in their depths."[32] Expressionism and the new realism, as represented by the works of George Grosz and Otto Dix, broke through the *surface* of objects, not only to shake the complacency of human autonomy but also to reveal the *depth*, the "inner infinity of things," which give meaning to empirical, finite reality, while at the same time depriving it of absolute independence.[33] It was through art that Tillich experienced so poignantly the "Yes and No of being and meaning"—the infinite and inexhaustible ground and abyss that breaks through from the depth of finite reality, shattering but not destroying its autonomous forms (*durchbrechend nicht zerbrechend*).[34] From this experience of expressionistic art he was able to formulate the categories of form, content, and import that provided the pattern of interrelationships with which he could distinguish the various cultural styles. Likewise, from the new realism in art Tillich derived his methodological concept of "belief-ful realism."

Within this conceptual framework, theonomy was the ideal relationship that could maintain between form, content, and import. It was the essential relationship and the ground and basis of all others. Autonomy and heteronomy are rooted in theonomy[35] just as form and content in expressionism are rooted in import (*Inhalt*). In the new realism, after the purifying effect of the expressionist protest, a new emphasis could once again be given to content, but this time with a new, deeper meaning manifesting itself from within the depths of the shattered forms—forms that could no longer postulate their own absoluteness.[36] From this experience of ecstatic awareness of ultimate meaning breaking through the surface from the uttermost depth of reality, Tillich came to envision the cultural ideal of theonomous unity. This vision is reflected conceptually in the *Systematic*, for instance, when he writes: "Theonomy does not mean the acceptance of a divine law imposed on reason by a highest authority; it means autonomous reason united with its own depth."[37]

Wherever this unity is broken, there is an excess in one direction or another. Here lies for Tillich the essence of the drama of human cultural growth. Instructed by his own hard-learned lesson connected with the failure of religious socialism, Tillich frequently reminds his readers that there is no perfect theonomy under the conditions of existence. Guided by the artistic model, he saw autonomy as an over-emphasis on form; heteronomy as the external imposition of a special content and theonomy, as the balanced concern for import or ultimate meaning that never destroys the form or content. In his 1919 address on theology of culture, Tillich offered this dictum: "The more the form, the greater the autonomy; the more the substance or import, the greater the theonomy."[38] The history of human culture was that of the continual fluctuation between the predominance of one of these three types. Tillich ends his article on theonomy in *Religion in Geschichte und Gegenwart* with the statement that the challenge of theonomy is that of struggling through the problems of autonomy toward a culture and society that is filled with transcendent import.[39] This is the analysis of a philosopher-artist.

Theonomy and *"Belief-ful Realism"*

Tillich's theonomy was thus much more than a particular concept. Although it did express a cultural relationship involving the dialectical categories drawn from art, it could extend well beyond both interpretation of art and typology of culture. The artistic and aesthetic image was the basic one for Tillich—or at least he believed it to be so.[40]

There is no doubt that Tillich's theonomous vision is ultimately founded upon his ontological understanding of the relation of finite to infinite, of conditioned to unconditioned being in every sphere of cultural experience. Another important expression of this attitude appeared in an early concept—that of "belief-ful realism," the origin of which he traced once again to an aesthetic experience—that of the new realism in art.[41] The notion of "belief-ful realism" (Tillich later changed the term to "self-transcending realism"), like that of metalogic was one of the more ephemeral concepts in Tillich's intellectual growth. It was developed in answer to the pressing problem of the interpretation of history that challenged the young theologian as he actively engaged in

politics following the cultural upheaval in Germany after
World War I.[42] In his collection of articles dealing with this
question, gathered under the heading *The Interpretation of
History*, Tillich's main theme was that the burning theological
question of the day was the relationship of the Christian
message to the whole of history. His own theology of history
centers around this concept of "belief-ful realism" *(gläubiger
Realismus)*, which is fundamentally an application of the
theonomous attitude to the problem of the meaning of history.

From his study of modern art, Tillich viewed expressionism as a protest against the nineteenth-century "faith in
the self-sufficiency of the human and finite world."[43] This
protest against the emptiness of modern, secular, industrial
society was taken up by a number of cultural movements, and
especially, by existentialism in literature, the arts, and
philosophy. It all pointed to the cultural void and spiritual
dearth that resulted from living on the "surface of things,"
from surrendering to the "objectifying" tendency of technology. Expressionism, as part of this protest, brought out the
negative judgment of theonomy. For the theonomous attitude
is rooted in the Ground of being *(Sinngrund)*, which is for
Tillich not only the ultimate source of meaning but also the
ultimate criterion of judgment—the Abyss *(Abgrund)*,
threatening all finite reality with the awareness of its own
meaninglessness. In the new realism in art Tillich saw the
other complementary side of his theonomy that reaffirms the
importance of finite form in all its uniqueness, but in such a
way as to indicate its essential reference to the ultimate
meaning-reality.[44] What the new realism effected aestheti-
cally, Tillich hoped to do philosophically through his concept
of "belief-ful realism," by which he hoped to reveal the
ultimate meaning beneath the surface of our current political
and social movements.

It was especially within the context of meeting the challenge of the interpretation of history, a challenge presented
both from the side of Marxism and from "crisis
theology"—that Tillich employed the idea of a "belief-ful

realism." We have seen that the development of Tillich's Christology had been preceded by the addition of a horizontal historical dimension to his thought. The addition of this historical dimension to the concept of theonomy creates the image of eternal import entering into the historical process itself, as opposed to the mere vertical breakthrough into finite forms. This aspect of theonomy, which is belief-ful realism, takes time and the present with extreme seriousness, seeing in faith and decision its ultimate relationship to eternal meaning.[45]

Belief-ful realism is actually Tillich's theological reflection on an interpretation of history, connected with writers such as Troeltsch, Rickert, and Dilthey, and which Tillich called "historical realism."[46] Tillich's involvement in the political and social situation in postwar Germany so shaped his own thought that he found the emphasis of this school on the principle of "contemporaneity," the importance of the here and now, as very congenial to his outlook and to his own efforts at working out a theology of history. This focus on the present was a safeguard against both the romanticism and the Utopianism that Tillich was trying to combat through the religious socialist movement. This is what he considered to be the "realist" aspect of historical realism.

The "historical" side of this view of history could be seen in its sharp opposition to what Tillich called paradoxically any "non-historical" interpretation of history, among which he classified "mystical realism" and "technological realism," insofar as:

> They do not look at concrete existence, its "here and now," in order to discover the power of things. They abstract from it— technological realism for the sake of means and ends, mystical realism for the sake of essence and intuition.[47]

In other words, these interpretations attempt either to go beyond finite things to look for the "really real" in the eternal essences that transcend time and empirical reality, e.g., as in the mystical realism of the Middle Ages; or, they identify the "really real" with the calculability or utility of things, as is a predominant mood of contemporary secularity. Tillich maintained that technological realism had achieved almost total victory in our own social and intellectual situation; this will remain a determining aspect of his theological interpretation of the present. Historical realism insists upon the importance of the present in a way that is closely analogous to the emphasis of the new realism on maintaining the reality and independence of the finite, concrete form. In both cases ultimate meaning was to be discovered within the very concreteness and uniqueness either of the finite forms or of the historical present.

Even by temperament and inclination Tillich was keenly aware of the limitations of technological realism. He also referred to the latter in the broader perspective of "self-limiting realism,"[48] insofar as it refused to look for self-transcendence within empirical existence. If technological realism accepted religion at all, it could do so only as a separate realm—and this was totally opposed to Tillich's theonomous vision of reality. His struggle against what he calls "mystical realism," on the other hand, represents an inner conflict with a powerful, natural tendency within his own intellectual and emotional structure. For there is a striking contemplative aspect to Tillich's thought—a meditative, passive, receiving attitude that is open to the mysterious presence of the divine in everything that is. By way primarily of Schelling and Boehme, Tillich had imbibed very early in his thinking a deep draught of Neoplatonism.[49] The "God-above-God" of his *Courage to Be,* for instance, is clearly reminiscent of the Neoplatonic search for the ultimate power of being in that which is beyond being—in the "good," the "pure actuality" or the "One." Tillich was strongly drawn to the quiet contemplation of this Eternal, Unchanging One, as well as to silent meditation of Its hidden presence in nature, in man and in cultural creativity. Upon reading some of the philosophical sections of his work, as well as many of his sermons and his theological interpretations of art, the reader is quickly made aware of the power of this contemplative attraction. Tillich obviously delights in pure speculative, philosophical reflection, and it took the moving experiences of the trenches of World War I and the social revolution in the postwar period to shake him free from the snares of this subtle temptation. He writes in his memoirs of this change of mind: "It soon became clear, though, that a one-sided devotion to contemplation was based on the same escape from reality as my flight into literary fantasy."[50]

German scholarship, in general, Tillich admitted, tended to be quite abstract and theoretical. Amidst the cultural upheaval and political revolution that followed World War I in Germany, Tillich and others were finally healed of this one-sided tendency, so that politics, the social order, class struggle, and the cultural movements of the present became an integral part of their philosophical reflection.[51] Tillich, in other words, became a historical realist, in the sense just described. The cultural situation of the time—contemporaneity—took on a new vital and essential importance. Tillich did not, on the other hand, abandon his ontological search for ultimate truth—for the permanent and unchanging element in reality. He remained a mystic in this sense, but transcended mystical realism by maintaining a solid grounding in the social and historical context.

By combining the insights of mystic faith and historical realism, Tillich sought, within an active involvement in social struggle and political change, to grasp the "depth of reality in which its divine foundation and meaning become visible."[52] What was required was a realism that was at the same time "belief-ful" or "self-transcending,"[53] as well as contemporaneous and concrete. Belief-ful realism unites in tension two sharply conflicting attitudes: realism and faith—attitudes that are often judged in our secular culture to be mutually exclusive. As difficult as he recognized it to be, Tillich maintained that culture must attempt to remain and embrace the radical tension of these two polarities in order that it might give due attention to the seriousness of the historical process and situation, while at the same time remaining open to the eternal meaning which it contains. Such is the perspective of "belief-ful realism"—"the religious depth of historical realism."[54]

But how does one relate the eternal or religious viewpoint to the world of time? Tillich's answer to this crucial question centered around the notion of *kairos*, which has already been discussed in Chapter 3. In his cultural analysis "belief-ful realism" represented *kairos* thinking in contrast to *logos* thinking. *Logos* thought is characterized by the search for the eternal, timeless presence of unconditional reality within the universe and the human mind. Idealism, with its emphasis on the absolute and its reduction of finite reality to a gradual, conscious unfolding of this same Absolute, is the major extreme of Western *logos* thinking. All mysticism likewise shares this unconcern for the significance of the present moment. *Kairos* thinking, on the other hand, is historical thinking, which includes passion and involvement and takes place within an active participation in the historical situation of the present. "Belief-ful realism" must, however, also include the element of *logos*, for it was to remain open to those special moments in the temporal process when the eternal breaks into historical time, creating a crisis in the depth of human existence. Kairos thinking is "belief-ful" for it is attentive to ultimate meaning and truth; it is realistic insofar as it is dynamic and contemporaneous:

> . . . belief-ful realism . . . does not idealize or spiritualize its objects. It is the skeptical, unromantic, unsentimental attitude which accepts the objects in their stark givenness.[55]

The *kairos* moment is "belief-ful" also because it can be recognized only through faith. It is a kind of knowing that involves decision; it implies belief, hope, and daring. "There is no concrete interpretation of history without faith."[56] This faith, which emerges from amidst full involvement in the concrete historical situation, is not irrational; it does not "by-pass a full consciousness of experimentally verified knowledge."[57] The *logos* element remains even though it is transcended, for whereas the recognition of the presence of

Ultimate Reality within historical time depends upon the ecstatic state of being grasped by Infinite Being, it must still be expressed in a way that has its own inner coherence and rationality. This is why Tillich never opposes reason to faith, for faith is reason carried beyond its normal state: it is *reason in ecstasy*.[58] But the meaning of history is only present to faith.

For Tillich the event of Jesus as the Christ was the decisive *Kairos*, or breakthrough of the eternal into time and history. Despite his strong philosophical orientation, Tillich was by no means uninformed on the question of biblical eschatology. Although Christ is the end of history (realized eschatology), Tillich recognized that for Christian faith the ultimate goal *(telos)*, the Kingdom of God, is yet to come (future eschatology). In the meantime, history continues, and this is not only sacred history which has divine significance, for there is only one history, just as there is only one reality. History is both sacred and profane, and the meaning of this ongoing historical process from the Christ-event to the *eschaton* is the burning theological question.[59]

The answer to this question Tillich saw in terms of *kairoi*, decisive historical moments in which the divine Presence is manifest, and which derive their power from the great *Kairos*, which is the Christ-event. These are moments that demand not only acknowledgment but also decision and active response, here and now. The recognition of the *kairos* within secular history, despite its fragmentary and ephemeral appearance, assures the man of faith that the final victory is already won and lies hidden as Kingdom of God within the very ambiguity of the historical process. To be thus aware and responsive to the *kairos* moment within the reality of the historical situation of the present is to express a "belief-ful realism." It means to take secular history seriously; it means to think with contemporaneity about the ultimate meaning of existence. It is an attitude that enables the theologian to have a theology of history, and not just a doctrine of sacred history. It constitutes a call for a new theonomy within a social order that is more in tune with its own spiritual depth. "Belief-ful realism" is thus another expression of Tillich's central concept of theonomy, when applied to the historical dimension. For Tillich's meaning of a coming theonomy is this: "to be belief-ful in and through the autonomous form of knowledge and action."[60]

Theonomous Reason and Theonomous Culture

Tillich did not originate the term *theonomy*. It derived immediately from a typology of authority found in the works of Richard Rothe and Ernst Troeltsch. Tillich was very much aware of the powerful impact that the work of Troeltsch, in particular, had upon his own thought.[61] More remotely, the term came from Kant, who employed the expressions "autonomy" and "heteronomy" in relation to the question of man's inner moral conflict.[62] In the *Systematic*, Tillich first used "theonomy" and its dialectic counterparts as aspects of the dynamic tension and ambiguity within human reason. The use of these terms in this context gives a rather different emphasis to their meaning, yet it is by no means totally inconsistent with the usage of his theological predecessors, including even Kant. The use of "theonomy" as an aspect of reason also corresponds to the chronological introduction of this term into Tillich's early work, for even in the 1919 address on theology of culture, theonomy was treated as an aspect of human reason that should manifest itself in the various academic disciplines.[63] But even here in his initial usage of the term, Tillich obviously extended the concept well beyond the realm of what we usually understand as human reason. For already he was speaking of a "theonomous culture," the concretization of this attitude of mind in the practical order. In his 1922 article, "The Conquest of the Concept of Religion in the Philosophy of Religion," Tillich applied these same categories to the classification of historical periods, and by 1925, in "The Philosophy of Religion," the notion of a theonomous culture is beyond all question a major theme.

The transition from a category of reason to a category of

culture is relatively easy to understand, insofar as it is the individual who possesses reason, and it is a group of individuals who creates culture. A culture that is guided by individuals whose power of reason moves in a certain direction will also move as a whole in that same direction. Furthermore, Tillich understood rationality in a very broad sense—that which he named "ontological reason"—"the structure of the mind which enables the mind to grasp and transform reality."[64] It was an important aspect of Tillich's epistemology that to the rational structure of the mind there corresponds an intelligible structure of the world. But "world" for Tillich is an existential term—correlative to the ego-self, who creates a world. In his anthropological analysis, it is precisely man's ability to look upon encountered reality as a world, which lies at the root of man's having a culture.[65] It becomes evident, granted this broad concept of rationality, that theonomy as a category of reason so understood, will automatically become a category of culture. For Tillich, it became the normative category of culture and the symbol of an authentically religious situation.[66]

5
Theonomy and the Meaning of Contemporary Culture

To understand Tillich's application of this normative criterion of theonomy to the interpretation of the contemporary cultural situation requires a further consideration of his notion of "ontological reason," for it is the loss of ontological reason with its concomitant deprivation of the dimension of depth that Tillich considered to be the most significant characteristic of the modern cultural and spiritual situation. In this chapter, we consider Tillich's notion of ontological reason and his religio-philosophical symbol of depth.

Ontological Reason versus Technological Reason

According to Tillich's understanding of the history of philosophy, the ontological concept of reason has been the dominant view in the classical philosophical tradition. For Tillich it was also the most adequate, complete, and all-inclusive interpretation of human rationality. Ontological reason does not only think *about* the world and the things that man encounters therein—it participates in them. It includes the cognitive, aesthetic, theoretical, and practical realms of knowledge. It is both objective and subjective. It is the *logos* of classical reason present in both mind and reality, as exemplified in the *eros* of Plato, the *apatheia* of the Stoics, the *appetitus* of finite things in Aquinas, and the "intellectual love" of Spinoza. Only ontological reason has the potential of openness to the depth of reason. Thus, theology, according to Tillich, should concern itself directly and essentially only with ontological reason, for this alone embraces the religious dimension of reality.[1]

To ontological reason Tillich opposed technological or technical reason, whose aim is to remain detached and distinct from the reality it encounters and objectifies. It is not difficult to understand the analogy with the previously discussed technological realism.[2] Clearly, technological realism is Tillich's expression for technical reason, when applied to the question of the interpretation of history. Because of its concern for the way things can be used and for their function, technical reason tends to reduce things "to something less than their true reality."[3] The technical concept of reason dominates in our period and tends to remove "reasoning" from *reason* in the broad, ontological sense in which Tillich understood it. Tillich conceded that technical reason had achieved in our time a total victory in the intellectual realm, just as he had recognized the complete hegemony of technological realism in the historical realm. This victory guaranteed and assured the primacy of the trinity of natural science, technology, and capitalist economy. Insofar as Tillich saw the fate of each of these phenomena as totally tied in with each other, he also referred in more general terms to the "triumph of the spirit of capitalist society,"[4] or more philosophically, to "the spirit of self-sufficient finitude."[5] The dehumanizing and alienating effect of this spirit and the powerful existential protest against it constitute the principal cultural struggle of our times.

"The lost dimension"   In a 1958 article, entitled "The Lost Dimension in Religion,"[6] Tillich claimed that our present-day culture, both within and without the churches, had lost the dimension of depth in its experience of reality. If Tillich was right in asserting that only ontological reason is open to the depth of reason, it would follow logically that the triumph

of technological reason would entail the loss of depth. But what is this "depth" of which Tillich spoke so often? It is another metaphor to express the image of the divine import breaking through from the inner reality and meaning of all intelligible structures. More fundamentally we are confronting once again the ontology of the later Schelling, with its assertion of the paradoxical presence of the transcendent and infinite Ground within all finite being. Reason experiences this depth as "something that is not reason but which precedes reason and is manifest through it."[7] Culture experiences this same depth as substance and meaning: religion is the substance of culture. Secular culture has separated the structural and formal element from the substance and has thereby lost the dimension of depth. Ultimately, then, the loss of substance and the concomitant dehumanizing effects can be traced to the one-sided hegemony of technological reason. Accordingly, Tillich bleakly describes the contemporary secularization of consciousness as:

> . . . The concentration of man's activities upon the methodological investigation and technical transformation of this world, including himself, and the consequent loss of the dimension of depth in his encounter with reality. Reality has lost its inner transcendence, or in another metaphor, its transparency to the eternal.[8]

Cultural crisis and the alternatives   Loss of substance or loss of depth for Tillich is the same as loss of meaning. Yet the very function of the human spirit is to seek and create meaning.[9] Particular, finite, conditional meaning, however, is not enough for the human spirit; a sense of ultimate meaningfulness is also required. Secular culture has lost this sense and is plagued with emptiness and meaninglessness. Philosophical and theological literature over the last two decades, as well as the studies of sociology, have been replete with this message. Tillich's own very popular work, *The Courage to Be,* deals in great detail with the nature of this very serious problem.[10]

Faced with this predicament, and yet finding the message of

the traditional creeds difficult to the point of unintelligibility, contemporary man has two alternatives from which to choose. The first is to restrict his human self-affirmation to the limited sector of reality that his highly advanced technological reason can handle and handle well. Much of contemporary philosophy, in Tillich's view, has accepted this alternative.[11] This way has the advantage of avoiding anxiety, of escaping, at least for a time, the deeply disturbing question of the meaning of human existence. As stated in Chapter 1, secularism is the affirmation in principle of the characteristic mood of contemporary secular culture. With particular reference to this issue, secularism represents a denial of the depth of reason, a limited affirmation of the self and of reality. In Tillich's terms, therefore, this certainly would be a poor, even neurotic choice, for it would constitute an escape from the anxiety demanded by authentic human existence, in short, a failure of courage in contemporary culture.[12] A culture built on this ideal of a diminished but safe and anxiety-free humanity can, from Tillich's perspective, end up only with a loss of humanity.

The second alternative is to courageously accept the ambiguities and anxieties resulting from a fully asserted humanity. For this reason Tillich is not opposed to human autonomy, but for him a full humanity is necessarily religious, which also means to be anxious. Man is an anxious animal. Once man ontologizes, or asks the question of his own being, he is necessarily filled with anxiety—not with a neurotic and unhealthy anxiety, but with what Tillich terms "existential anxiety."[13] Anxiety goes with man's finitude, which is his essential nature. It is anxious man, shaken from the very foundations of his being and asserting himself despite the threats of meaninglessness and emptiness that arise from his existential estrangement, who is the creator of meaningful culture and purposeful society. Contemporary existentialist protest has courageously opposed the absurdity, ambiguity, dehumanization, and loss of meaning that are so prevalent in a technologically oriented culture. But this negative recognition of a spiritual vacuum is not enough. A *new* sense of ultimate concern, a *new* awareness of depth, and a *new* search for ultimate meaning must accompany this protest. In this way, the cultural vacuum will become a "sacred void," awaiting a new *kairos* ("breakthrough of eternal meaning"), and thereby find a new theonomy within the very spiritual emptiness of contemporary autonomous culture. Jean-Paul Gabus, in his detailed commentary on Tillich's theology of culture, provides us with an excellent summary of the new quest for theonomy that Tillich envisioned within the context of our present secularized and technological culture:

> Technology has therefore been profoundly alienating for man. But this alienation is not necessarily fatal. Under the impact of the spiritual, divine presence, the technological processes can themselves become theonomous and open to ultimate meaning. . . . They can become humanized and recover a true sense of meaning for man; they can serve as a means toward an end which transcends them, and help man to realize himself as a person.[14]

The Critique of Secular Humanism

An analysis of Tillich's critique of secular humanism has been deferred until now, for a correct understanding of this critique presupposes an awareness of the principles of his theology of culture and his interpretation of contemporary culture that have been described in the preceding pages. Although much of Tillich's understanding of secular humanism should already be self-evident as a result of the foregoing analysis, a summary of Tillich's specific appraisal of this widespread, contemporary cultural mood will be of value here.

For Tillich, a secular culture is identical with an autonomous one, in the sense previously described, and *humanism* is the highest contemporary expression of the secular spirit.[15] Tillich considered the emphasis of humanism on human goals and the search for meaning within human existence as a justifiable and necessary protest against the authoritarian and heteronomous interference in the name of religion with the "autonomous processes of civilization."[16]

On the other hand, Tillich also maintained that although in our present cultural situation, this humanistic spirit had successfully destroyed what he termed the "demonic" distortion in religion, it had in the process lost contact with its own spiritual depth and left the way open thereby for a new heteronomy from the side of secular "quasi-religions." Contemporary humanism, as Tillich saw it, approves in principle the viewing of reality from this single *surface* dimension of the measurable, the calculable, and the useful. It is in this context that Tillich referred to humanism as "shallow."[17] That is, humanism, according to Tillich, sees its autonomous protest in the name of humanity as a permanent ideal rather than as a necessary dialectical stage. Having lost the dimension of depth, humanism sees God as superfluous and would make man in his stead the center of the universe. Tillich identified this aspect of secular humanism with "the spirit of industrial society."[18]

Humanism, when imbued with this spirit, makes creativity an exclusively human quality. It disregards man's fundamental estrangement or what traditional biblical religion calls man's fallen state: "Man has shortcomings, but there is no sin and certainly no universal sinfulness."[19] Accordingly, it is expected that man's goals can be achieved and his problems overcome through good educational processes. Man's actual state is regarded as his essential one and the possibility of unlimited, continued, and progressive fulfillment of his potentialities is seen as a realistic goal. On the communal level, the advance of science and technology are seen as the principal answer to the reunion of mankind.

> As the universe replaces God, as man in the center of the universe replaces the Christ, so the expectation of peace and justice in history replaces the expectation of the Kingdom of God. The dimension of depth in the divine and the demonic has disappeared.[20]

What began, therefore, as a legitimate protest in the name of humanity, has for Tillich, made a *volte face* only to divinize man, while overlooking the ambiguities and the tragic element of the human situation. This was the spirit of "self-sufficient finitude" that evoked the existential protest in art, literature, and philosophy, and concerning which Tillich was able to predict, as early as 1925, that it would prove to be inadequate under the impact of severe social-ethical shocks.[21]

On the philosophical level, Tillich interpreted secular humanism as a form of idealism. Although he wholeheartedly approved of the zealous concern of secular humanism for humanity and its dedicated protection of human autonomy, Tillich maintained with equal conviction that humanism did not understand the nature of its own prophetic impulse. It failed to recognize the unconditional element in its own commitment and enthusiasm, and made of this enthusiasm for human fulfillment an end in itself—an ultimate concern. The emergence and the appeal of secular humanism in our time corresponds with the victory of "technological realism."[22] There is much in this attitude and approach that is revelatory of a real religious depth and power (which only serves to confirm, for Tillich, his thesis that religion is the substance of culture). The detached and ascetic attitude of the scientific ideal of knowledge reflects "an attitude that corresponds to the immovable, eternal element in all knowledge."[23] The "controlling knowledge," which characterizes technological realism, and which sees the theoretical calculability and practical utility as that which is "the really real"[24] of things, carries with it an undeniable enthusiasm in the feeling of freedom and unlimited power over nature. This same enthusiasm inspires a total commitment to honesty—an unconditional imperative that drives the radical secularist to an unremitting quest for the truth and an ardent dedication to the achievement of human progress. Enthusiasm of this type, according to Tillich, has a definitely "ecstatic" quality and, therefore, can easily be given a "quasi-religious" aura. Hence, no matter how far a cultural attitude is profanized by a denial of self-transcendence, it cannot escape the sacred and unconditional Ground from which it draws its power and inspiration. Religion remains in its essential form of "ultimate concern."[25]

This confusion, however, of the enthusiasm of secular humanism with the unconditional Source of its power denies the holiness of life, and in its anxiety to preserve human dignity and autonomy it profanizes culture, for culture, like life itself, must transcend itself. Without self-transcendence, the profane receives the glory of holiness;[26] that which is conditioned and finite becomes the object of ultimate concern, and thus a new heteronomy and a new demonic situation is established. The honesty and dedication of the humanist is religious, but not theonomous, for on the level of culture, theonomy, for Tillich, means precisely "the self-transcendence of culture."[27]

> Autonomy is not "irreligious," although it is not a vehicle of religion. It is indirectly religious through the form; it is not directly religious. The humility of the scientific empiricist is religious, but it does not appear as such; it is not theonomous. The heroism of Stoic self-control is religious, but is not theonomous. The mystery of Leonardo's Mona Lisa is religious, but it does not show that it is.[28]

In a theonomous cultural attitude, all cultural forms are seen in their relation to the unconditional. In secular humanism they appear only in their finite relationship; despite his various religious qualities, the humanist does not see his own autonomous creations in their theonomous depth. Yet the seriousness of the humanist's concern makes the humanistic ideal into something ultimate, and as such, creates of it a new "quasi-religion"[29] that offers to contemporary culture a new answer to man's eternal quest for a sense of destiny and meaning. In the past, this answer had always been provided in the Western world by biblical religion. The difficulty with this new answer, as Tillich saw it, was that it overlooked the tragic element in human existence and disregarded the ambiguities and sinfulness of the human situation. Accordingly, it presents to modern man an unrealizable ideal: "the actualization of all human potentialities."[30] Granted the universal estrangement of the human condition—the basic finitude of human nature—many significant human potentialities will of necessity remain unrealized. Secular humanism has no answer to this dilemma other than its enthusiasm and optimistic idealism.

This is the sense in which Tillich referred to humanism as an "idealism," that is, he claimed that it confused the ideal with the real, by idealizing the real rather than transcending it, which could only be done through faith or "belief-ful realism."[31] Secularism, as Tillich saw it, was a form of technological realism, which rejected self-transcendence for fear of trespassing the limits of the empirically given. In philosophy, positivism, pragmatism, and empiricism were all manifestations of technological realism. The humanism that grew out of modern secularism was not realism but idealism. It also denied "self-transcendence," but in its own way—by relativizing the gap between the finite and the infinite and blurring the lines that separate the conditional from the unconditional. Secularism is a realism that is not self-transcendent, and humanism, if it can be called "self-transcendent," would be a self-transcendence which is not realistic.[32] The idealistic nature of secular humanism, Tillich maintained, lies in its confusing man's existential situation with his essential being.

> The conflict between what man essentially is and what he actually is, his estrangement, or in traditional terms, his fallen state, is disregarded. Death and guilt disappear. . . . Man's actual state is hence mistakenly regarded as his essential state, and he is pictured in a position of progressive fulfillment of his potentiality.[33]

But this confusion, Tillich thought, could lead only to existential frustration, insofar as it involves a radical commitment to that which remains less than ultimate—a noble but finite ideal, which can neither be achieved nor hope to fulfill the expectations of those who have so committed themselves. Humanism, in short, has made of human fulfillment and personality development an ultimate concern, which is to reject self-transcendence, and create thereby an "idolatrous faith." By "idolatrous faith" Tillich understood the attempt to make ultimate that which is not in fact ultimate, that which is conditioned and finite. When secularism remains in the state of protest against religious heteronomy, it easily becomes idolatrous, for which it must pay a heavy price. Humanity in the state of estrangement does not make a fitting object of ultimate concern, and Tillich reminds his readers in his *Dynamics of Faith*, that although the content or object of ultimate concern does not matter as regards the formal definition of faith, it does matter infinitely for the faith of the believer:

> In true faith the ultimate concern is a concern about the truly ultimate; while in idolatrous faith preliminary, finite realities are elevated to the rank of ultimacy. The inescapable consequence of idolatrous faith is "existential disappointment," a disappointment which penetrates into the very existence of man! This is the dynamics of idolatrous faith: that it is faith, and as such, the centered act of a personality; that the centering point is something which is more or less on the periphery; and that, therefore, the act of faith leads to a loss of the center and to a disruption of the personality. The ecstatic character of even an idolatrous faith can hide this consequence only for a certain time. But finally it breaks into the open.[34]

It is clear that Tillich attributed a specifically "religious" quality to secular humanism. He frequently insisted that the humanist is already on the way to theonomy.[35] But despite all many self-complacent Christian believers. As an idealist, the humanist is already on the way to theonomy.[35] But despite all these positive features that he saw in humanism, Tillich was anxious to save contemporary secularists from the inevitable failure and emptiness that follows from an idolatrous ultimate concern. We can now better understand the assertion that Tillich addressed the bulk of his theological effort to strictly secular men: scientists, artists, philosophers, sociologists, and psychologists, who although embracing a very noble humanistic ideal and life-style, are fundamentally estranged from traditional creedal religion.[36] Even the specifically Christian aspects of Tillich's work are geared to people, who though remaining within the church, are secular in their thinking and require a reinterpretation of biblical symbols, along more modern ways of understanding. We fail to understand Tillich's appraisal of secular humanism if we forget the genuine sympathy and attraction he felt for the humanist outlook, and especially for its sharp critique of so much that tries to pass under the name of religion. Tillich did not hesitate to maintain that the Spiritual Presence itself is often more readily discernible among humanists than in the churches in the present cultural situation. Religion has no monopoly on the divine, nor humanism on the demonic distortion thereof.[37]

Through his theological interpretations of culture, Tillich was continually inviting serious-minded humanists to look into the depths of their own humanity and ideals to discern therein the ultimate Source of their own self-transcendence. For despite all his sympathy with the humanist protest, he was equally convinced that "only a self-transcending humanism can answer the question of the meaning of culture."[38]

In order to understand the kind of "self-transcendence" that Tillich had in mind, we must also recall that he was working very much within the Platonic and Augustinian tradition of religious philosophy.[39] It is from this perspective that Tillich saw contemporary culture as one that urges man to live on the surface of things: to confuse the ordinary visible, empirical realities with that which is really or ultimately real. Although this is an innate tendency of man in the state of estrangement, as history will testify, Tillich felt that our contemporary technological culture with all its emphasis on calculation and controlling knowledge, as well as upon industrial organization and institutional growth, had an unusually powerful thrust on encouraging the human tendency to get totally caught up in preliminary and finite concerns. Like Plato, Tillich was also thoroughly convinced that the true meaning of reality was not to be discovered on the *surface*, but in the *depth* of things, and for Tillich, at least, (and very likely for Plato, as well) this discovery of the really real occurred only in the ecstatic experience of faith. In support of his own notion of transcendent depth, Tillich cites Plato's concept of *parousia* in the *Gorgias,* to the effect that "things have being by the presence *(parousia)* of the good in them; the true being of things is their good, appearing in them, but at the same time concealed by them."[40]

It was to this dimension of depth—at once immanent and transcendent—in which ultimate reality breaks through from its concealment within the concreteness of the finite forms and empirical situations that Tillich appealed as the corrective to secular humanism's one-sided protest against religious heteronomy. Accordingly, he saw this theonomous vision, or what he also termed "self-transcending realism," not as a negation, but as a fulfillment of humanism. In theonomy "the idea of humanism is transcended without being denied."[41] Humanism itself leads to the question of culture transcending itself.[42] Through the theonomous ideal, contemporary man can preserve and foster humanism, while transcending it at the same time, if he will only recapture that "lost dimension" of depth, with all its sacred and healing power.

The faith that Tillich proposed as the way to recover the depth dimension is neither an irrational mysticism nor an obediential passivity to divinely inspired commands from another realm. He understood faith as rather a "real, thoroughly human, but ecstatic experience based on full awareness of the significance of the 'here and now' ":

> The ultimate power of being, the ground of reality appears in a special moment, in a concrete situation, revealing the infinite depth and the eternal significance of the present. . . The power of a thing is, at the same time affirmed and negated when it becomes transparent for the ground of its power, the ultimately real. It is as a thunderstorm at night, when the lightning throws a blinding clarity over all things, leaving them in complete darkness the next moment. When reality is seen in this way with the eye of self-transcending realism, it has become something new. Its ground has become visible in an "ecstatic" experience, called "faith."[43]

There is little doubt that the whole tone and texture of

Tillich's approach seems somewhat poetic, if not fanciful, to modern secular and empirical thought, enmeshed as it is in scientific method and technological concerns. Before dismissing Tillich's challenge as irrelevant and vacuous, however, there are two reasons that should give the secular man serious cause to stop and reflect:

1. It was precisely Tillich's claim that it is the cultural loss of an important human dimension that makes notions such as depth and ultimate reality appear foreign and meaningless to contemporary man.

2. If Tillich should, by chance, prove to be correct, there could be much to lose in failing to heed him, for his strongest challenge is that secular man—without faith—is lacking the principal ingredient for constructing a truly human society.

But it is one thing to take seriously a theory on the meaning of culture, and it is quite another to determine how that theory may be effectively evaluated. Tillich was well aware of the problems of verification (or falsification) connected with his thought. He insisted, for one thing, that empirical methods of verification—although most appropriate to scientific statements—were not applicable to the ontological reflection which dominates in theological discourse. By the same token, however, he also maintained that theological and ontological statements are not purely subjective—they must stand up under rational and objective scrutiny, or, to use his own terms, they must "serve the Logos."[44]

Granted that the language of Tillich's interpretation of culture is highly poetic and symbolic, he did not see this as a limitation or liability. Indeed, Tillich insisted that symbolism is the natural language of theology and philosophy, insofar as they deal, each in their own way, with the outer boundaries of human experience, i.e., with questions of ultimate reality which are not expressible in direct or literal language. In short, responsibility to the logos, or respect for rational criteria, will take a different form within the religious or metaphysical context than within a strictly empirical or scientific one. Recognition of this distinction has won wide acceptance today in the major philosophical schools, especially under the influence of the later Wittgenstein with his stress on "language games."

In response to critics who challenged him to establish the truth conditions or rules of verification for assessing his own thought, Tillich assumed two principal lines of strategy:

1. Statements that express the truth experienced in the depth of reason are not of the type to be verified *experimentally*. On the other hand, they can be tested *experientially*, i.e., within the life process itself. Tillich readily admits that such verification is less precise and less objective (no doubt, we might also add, more resistant to falsification). As Tillich puts it: "The test, therefore, will always be indefinite and preliminary and never do away with the necessity of risk."[45] Whether or not we find this an agreeable situation, most of our truth judgments in life fall into this category.

2. The truth of ontological and religious assertions can be determined—always with cognitive risk—by what Tillich called "an intelligent recognition."[46] On this second point, Tillich's position has a remarkably contemporary ring, clearly suggestive of the most recent discussions in philosophy of science. Whereas at first glance the notion of intelligent recognition might seem unduly subjective and defiant of the accepted norms of public verification, a comparison of Tillich's approach with recent developments in the debate over the nature of scientific theory puts him clearly in line with a growing and respectable school of scientific epistemology. Thomas Kuhn, Michael Polanyi, N. R. Hanson, and Ian Barbour,[47] to mention but a few leading proponents, have each stressed the impossibility of designating rules for major paradigm shifts in science. In contrast to earlier positivist views, their new epistemology downplays the role of observation, proofs, conditions of verification, and the use of formal rules in the process of making scientific judgments. Without denying the empirical foundations of science or discrediting the ultimate impact of cumulative evidence, these authors have convincingly drawn attention to the more subjective aspects of scientific discovery and the importance of personal judgment in the assessment of scientific theories.

Although Tillich never developed in detail his notion of "intelligent recognition," this concept could certainly be defended along the lines of current scientific epistemology, insofar as it serves as an analogue for religious and metaphysical knowledge. Obviously, if scientific judgments, with their traditionally strong claims for empirical footing and experimental verification, are inherently dependent on insight, conversion, and personal judgment, we can hardly be justified in making stricter empirical demands for the verification of theological and ontological assessments. If these current views on science are correct, we can avoid the extreme of reducing theological assertions to matters of personal preference, while substituting the criterion of "good reasons" for the positivist demands of empirical evidence.[48]

It is obviously beyond the scope of this study to attempt a full-scale critique of Tillich's theology of culture. Nevertheless, any intellectually responsible assessment of Tillich's critique of secular humanism requires a thorough analysis and evaluation of his principal grounds for rejecting the humanist outlook.

We have already established that despite Tillich's positive appraisal of secular humanism as a protest in defense of human dignity and intellectual autonomy, he seriously objected that it had lost its sensitivity to a principal area of human meaning and growth, which he described as "the dimension of depth." But how much objective reality is actually designated by this Romantic metaphor of "depth"? Is it possible that we are dealing primarily with a clever metaphorical device, or is there really an essential structure of human culture, generally neglected or bypassed by secular humanists, and which is fittingly designated by the symbol of depth?

Our contention is that the Tillichian notion of depth, despite its mythopoeic appearance, is far from an empty symbol, but actually points to an important feature of human awareness and cultural structure. As a world outlook, secular humanism is seriously inclined to neglect this very real and very vital human dimension. In line with our understanding of verification as it has been described, we hope to offer "good reasons" to support these claims and to leave to the reader the judgment of intelligent recognition.

6

The Depth Dimension of Culture

The "Spiritual Vacuum" and the King's Chapel Lectures

In view of our discussion that concluded the preceding chapter, we can assume that metaphors, such as "depth," serve a legitimate cognitive function. By the same token, however, we recognize the necessity of indicating the experiential referent of such metaphors, in order to clarify the cognitive content and to make certain that we are not dealing with an empty or "irreducible metaphor."[1] Tillich, as we have seen, identified as the distinguishing feature of our contemporary cultural situation the complete victory of technical reason and purely secular thought. Although the battle had been fought in the name of human dignity and autonomy, the victory was a Pyrrhic one, for the autonomy that was gained was *shallow* and the secular culture that it produced had lost the dimension of depth.

In evidence of his indictment Tillich pointed to the "spiritual vacuum" that is also a prominent feature of the cultural situation of today. This "inner void" (to use another of Tillich's favorite figures) is the direct effect of the loss of depth, and, structurally speaking, represents the symptomatic and experiential side of this loss. At first glance, the logic of this procedure seems somewhat questionable, for does it not leave us with the frustrating situation in which our understanding and evaluation of "depth" becomes dependent upon that of an equally evasive and indefinite metaphor—"spiritual vacuum?"

Fortunately, in this case, Tillich provided a careful and unusually detailed description of what he meant by the "spiritual vacuum" in a series of lectures that he gave at King's Chapel, Boston in 1958. In the course of six addresses, Tillich tried to diagnose the pulse beat of modern Western society. He explored a wide variety of cultural expressions, ranging from literature and the arts, philosophy and science, religion and theology. From this broad and diversified scene Tillich proceeded to trace, step by step, a general pattern that would make sense and give unity to the whole cultural situation. Unfortunately, the picture that emerged is not an encouraging one: it is the frightening image of modern man mercilessly, inevitably driven toward making himself into an object or thing among the many objects of his own creation. On a somewhat more optimistic note Tillich's portrait of modern man also reveals him as struggling, even furiously, against his own depersonalization,[2] but even this struggle appears to be filled with futility and despair.

A few examples of Tillich's analysis in the course of these lectures might best serve to illustrate how he went about constructing a blueprint from these varied materials, and, more importantly, will clarify and give more concrete substance to Tillich's notion of a "spiritual vacuum."

The loss of unity   While reflecting on the various stages and schools in the history of art in this century, Tillich made the following observations about the Cubist movement:

> The organic forms of the human body and human face were resolved into cubes and geometrical figures. The artists of this period still wanted to give us the image of man, but the image of his body and face was reduced to the fundamental mathematical and geometrical elements of physical nature. The especially human had disappeared or was only indirectly indicated.[3]

He was convinced, nevertheless, that cubism, like sur-
realism and abstractionism, were honest forms of art insofar
as modern technological society does tend to swallow up the
individual human person as an object among objects. This
tragic loss of individuality in contemporary society produces
a new and stifled cultural type: the "mass man." Mass society
and mass man is a theme that runs throughout the lectures,
and without any doubt, is for Tillich an essential feature of
the loss of depth. Fortunately, he also took great care to
clarify what he meant by these expressions:

> "Mass man" is the man who moves not out of the center of
> himself, but who moves as a particle of a mass . . . In our period
> in history a quiet but definitely effective power is at work which
> makes us into a particle of a mass.[4]
> A "mass society" is a unity of human individuals kept together
> by laws of social dynamics whose cohesion has such a character
> that the human differences are irrelevant to the movement.[5]

The faceless man of modern art is identical with the mass
man who appears in literature and the social sciences. In both
cases the *individual* is lost—lost in the very world of things he
has created. This creation of a mass society with its concomitant loss of individuality is the result of the victory of controlling knowledge in our time. Controlling knowledge tends to
transform elements of nature and culture into existential
objects. To live as an object among objects is to live without
depth. Those who feel this continuous threat to our humanity
that issues from the very core of technical, industrialized
society are more likely to discern what Tillich meant by loss
of depth and to share his sense of a "spiritual vacuum."

The loss of meaning   But this is only one side of the portrait
of modern culture that Tillich painted in these lectures. The
anxiety and despair raised by this specter of man losing his
own personhood and individuality has also raised a powerful
protest. The greatness of our contemporary period is that
man will not be deprived of his humanity; he will not accept
becoming an object. Contemporary literature is replete with

this spirit of stubborn and tenacious resistance, though it often appears more despairing than hopeful. The desperateness of the struggle, Tillich claimed, was nowhere presented more vividly and powerfully than in the American theater:

> The American playwrights Arthur Miller, Tennessee Williams and Eugene O'Neill are not tragedians. They simply show the desperate situation of man. Because in order to be tragic, there must be a principle which is broken through . . . Here is the pure negativity of man who has lost an ultimate principle of meaning, of man who has become a thing, and who fights desperately to remain a man.[6]

The theater, like the novel, according to Tillich's analysis, frequently captures with great insight the loss of meaning and general spiritual poverty so frequently found in society today. The plea is urgent enough, but it is rarely accompanied by an answer or even the suggestion of a new direction. Despite the ongoing protest in the arts and literature, the plight of man in contemporary culture seems hopeless and his future meaningless. To live in such a state is to live in a "spiritual vacuum."

The loss of subject   An analogous interpretation of the current human predicament Tillich derives from his reflections on the present trends in both science and philosophy. Through modern physics more than through any other discipline we have become aware of the striking degree to which we as "knowers" actually construct or create objects. That even our apparently objective observations of nature are all "theory laden" has become a byword in philosophy of science. We construct models, we build paradigms, and we put together patterns that make sense of our observations. In short, *objects* are not just there in nature; whereas objects must certainly conform to actual structures that are given in nature, the object, as such, is, to a great extent, a construct of our own intellect and imagination.

If we can construct objects out of immediately encountered reality, it is certainly possible that we can also turn human beings into objects. It is Tillich's serious contention that the great success of scientific method in our century has inclined us to apply its concepts and principles to all issues of concern, even to that of our own self-understanding. More and more in our day man is studied through exclusively scientific procedures; the unity of man is lost. He is thought of as a combination of atoms, chemical processes, biological changes, and the like. In short, "man has lost himself in the world of objects he has created."[7]

The loss of language   In philosophy, as in science, the tendency is also to exclude personal attachment and involvement. The emotional and psychological elements are barred from the arena of reflection, and, as a result, man is reduced to a knowing or logical subject. In such fashion, argued Tillich, the whole of human language is reduced to mathematical calculus and man is made into something that begins to resemble a mechanical brain. Just as the human face disappears in modern art, so does authentic human language begin to vanish in modern philosophy:

> Human language is reduced to science, but human language has not only meaning—logical meaning: it also has power, expressing something of the person who speaks, of the encounter of the culture with the world. When this power is lost man is deprived of his language.[8]

Clearly, Tillich had in mind the more positivistic trends in contemporary philosophy, and we might have wished him to distinguish this outlook from other contemporary movements in philosophy and even from the more recent developments in linguistic and analytic philosophy. Certainly, if one thinks of the philosophical contributions of a Gilbert Ryle, John Austin, or P. F. Strawson, to mention but a few leaders of the new philosophy, one could hardly accuse them of depriving man of his language. Much less could one justify *in globo* certain dramatic accusations made by Tillich, such as the following: "I believe that present day analytic philosophy is intimately related to the understanding of man as a thing, first as creating things, then as becoming a thing himself."[9]

Nevertheless, positivism is not completely absent from contemporary philosophy, and even though it has practically lost any intellectual respectability among academic philosophers, there is good reason to believe that the positivist spirit permeates a great deal of contemporary popular culture. To the extent that these assertions are true, we have another area indicated by Tillich where a loss of depth undercuts human potential and fulfillment, i.e., the undermining of significant dimensions or levels of human language. Certainly, many sensitive social commentators of the late 1960s and early 1970s expressed great concern about the loss of symbolic, mythological, and poetic language under the impact of technocracy.[10] With Tillich's critique of contemporary philosophy, we have added an additional piece to the puzzling picture of a "lost dimension."

In summary, the structure of Tillich's argument in these lectures is as follows: the loss of individuality and purpose as revealed in art and literature is paralleled by the loss of self and language in science and philosophy.[11] The unified and ultimate meaning of this loss to humanity in various sectors of culture is discovered in Tillich's analysis of current movements in religion and theology, for "the religious question is in the depths of all questions."[12] The religious question is precisely a question of depth; the loss of self, purpose, and so on as described, are all aspects of man having lost his dimension of depth. On the positive side, it is right within these very depths of his own being that man can discover his essential nature and can begin to acquire self-understanding "in terms of the Ground of Being Itself."[13] In the long run our own sense of meaning and our preservation of our own personal uniqueness will depend upon our centeredness in an ultimate reality:

> The finite center cannot maintain its centeredness over against the continual temptation to be transformed into a thing. Without resting in an ultimate center, without an ultimate center of meaning and being, no finite center can resist against the destruc-

tive power which comes from that which the self himself has created, namely, the world of things, in theory and practice.[14]

A culture that is open to the transcendent and ultimate center will discover a new sense of purpose as well as the source of courage to affirm itself, despite its finitude and contingence. Tillich believed that such a reconciliation of modern man with his own true being was really possible, for a complete picture of the human situation today reveals not only a "spiritual vacuum"—our estrangement from our essential goodness—but also a process of healing "in which the original forces which are given to men in creation are reestablished."[15] In order to receive this healing, modern culture must foster ontological as well as technical knowledge and must get beyond the limitations of immediately encountered reality by developing a sensitivity to ecstatic, revelatory experience.[16]

Psychology and the Dimension of Depth

It would be a gross exaggeration to claim that Tillich's King's Chapel Lectures are free of his typical ontological abstractness. Nevertheless, they are unusual for the degree to which they attempt to illustrate and concretize his notion of depth. The lectures are basically successful in clarifying for the audience what Tillich intended by loss of depth and the subsequent spiritual vacuum that pervades today's culture. But once having clarified the meaning of Tillich's critique we must attempt to judge the validity of his charge. Since throughout the lectures, as well as in his work in general, Tillich makes frequent appeal to the discoveries of depth psychology in support of his interpretations, we might do well to start our evaluation from this perspective. We should find much help here in that a number of innovative and creative schools of psychology have begun to explore with great seriousness and openmindedness the human significance of religious or depth experience. We will also then be ready to compare the ideals of secular humanism with the psychological demands for a genuine openness to depth.

The so-called "third psychology," which would include the existentialist, humanistic, and phenomenological movements in psychology, was, at the time of Tillich's major theological interpretations of culture, already pursuing similar concerns and issues as those involved in the concept of depth. It should not be surprising, therefore, that outstanding humanistic psychologists and psychoanalysts, such as Erich Fromm, Victor Frankl, Rollo May, and Abraham Maslow have responded with enthusiasm to aspects of Tillich's interpretation of culture. Psychology, to be sure, has only a limited interest in cognitive content of an interpretation, preferring to focus attention instead on emotional reference, unconscious origins, symbolic power, and the like. Apart from any other value, the rich use of symbolism and the powerful dramatic quality of Tillich's work would alone account for its strong appeal to the psychologist. Whatever might be the full explanation, there are many parallels in outlook between Tillich's theology and the new emphases in psychology. In a striking number of instances we can even find terminology as well as basic insights in psychology that are derived directly from Tillich's thought.[17]

Depth and ecstatic experience: the work of Abraham Maslow An outstanding example of this direct dependence and open reliance in psychology on Tillichian terms and concepts is found in the writings of the late American psychologist Abraham Maslow. Maslow's works are studded with a variety of expressions that have a very familiar ring to students of Tillich's thought. "The dimension of depth," "awareness of Being," "ultimate concern," and "ecstatic experience," to cite only a few, are all used frequently by Maslow and in a way that is quite central to the core of his doctrine.[18]

Maslow, who was a professed secular humanist,[19] shared not only many of Tillich's positive values and insights but was generally in close agreement with Tillich's negative criticism of our culture. Maslow, for example, showed an even greater impatience than his theological ally with what he considered the offhand dismissal of the problem of transcendence by so many contemporary British and American philosophers.

Maslow was convinced that in neglecting experiences of transcendence, especially as they occur in the so-called "peak experience," these philosophers would cut off modern man from the experience of being-itself, which lifts him to "greater than normal heights of awareness,"[20] from which the meaning of life can be more truly and fully perceived or intuited:

> Most official, orthodox philosophers today are the equivalent of legalists who reject the problems and the data of transcendence as "meaningless." That is, they are positivists, atomists, analysts, concerned with means rather than with ends. They sharpen tools rather than discovering [sic] truths.[21]

Maslow, like Tillich, is overly harsh in his criticism of contemporary philosophy, failing to make very refined distinctions about the various trends in the different leading philosophical schools. Nevertheless, Maslow's overall impression is that current philosophy is inimical or at best insensitive to an area of human experience which, according to his psychological research, is the most vital for achieving a sense of meaning and direction. What is even more significant is that Maslow recognized with Tillich the sharp dividing line in our culture between those who relate to life on the *surface* level and those who search into its depth. This difference had so fascinated Maslow that a great part of his long years of research was devoted to the study of those human "peak-experiences," which claim revelatory insight into the authentic meaning of reality, and which occur in the deepest recesses of the personality.[22] The subject matter and concerns of Maslow's work by themselves justify a more thorough study of his findings, for they immediately raise the possibility of throwing some "scientific" light on the issue.

The real question for Maslow was whether a secular humanist culture necessarily led to a blindness to that aspect of human experience which traditionally had been called the "ineffable" or the "mysterious," and which Tillich described as the "dimension of depth."

Maslow's work employed all the questionnaires, observations, and clinical studies that are characteristic of the empirical-minded researcher in psychology. But it went far beyond the interests of the average clinical psychologist; Maslow had no less a project in mind than a psychological, humanistic interpretation of our culture.[23]

Maslow shared Tillich's view as to where the real spiritual division of mankind is to be discovered. This division is no longer based on categories of denomination or religious affiliation. It is rather a question of surface or depth—and Maslow saw the "peak," or ecstatic, experience as the key to increasing our openness and awareness to depth. For this reason, he and his disciples devoted years of determined and careful study to the nature, frequency, and implications of peak experiences.

When viewed from this unique perspective, even the most basic of the older religious distinctions, such as theist and atheist, believer and nonbeliever, begin to lose significance. On the surface of things, no doubt, a Buddhist in his ritual still looks like his fellow Buddhist; an atheist in his rejection of worship appears similar to his fellow atheist; and a Christian and Jew in their customs seem close to their fellow Christians and Jews. Once we scratch the surface, however, Maslow assures us, we will discover that men are really divided religiously along very different lines:

> What we wind up with is a new situation in the history of the problem in which a "serious" Buddhist, let us say, one who is concerned with "ultimate concerns" and with Tillich's "dimension of depth," is more co-religionist to a "serious" agnostic than he is to a conventional, superficial, other directed Buddhist for whom religion is only habit or custom, i.e., "behavior."[24]

In a way that is clearly reminiscent of Tillich's early observation concerning atheism, namely, that "he who seriously denies God, affirms him,"[25] Maslow sees contemporary man then as really divided into two camps, as far as his authentic inner attitude is concerned: one, the serious-minded and the other, the "moment-bound."[26] By the "moment-bound" Maslow means those who no longer ask the fundamental questions, whether or not they are estranged from the church organizations. These he calls "true" or "full-fledged" secularists. The serious-minded, by way of contrast, are "ultimately concerned" with the meaning of existence. There is no doubt that for Maslow it is the moment-bound who are less authentically human; they are only concerned with means, with practical issues; they never look into the depths to ask the big question about existence itself.

The predominant and fundamental meaning of the term "religious" in Maslow's humanistic psychology is precisely this openness to the depth and fullness of being. A really mature person is by definition "self-actualizing," that is to say, growth-motivated, self-expressive, capable of perceiving beings, personal or otherwise, in all their uniqueness. The self-actualizing person is one in whom:

> the powers of the person come together in a particularly efficient and intensely enjoyable way, and in which he is more integrated and less split, more open for experience, more idiosyncratic, more perfectly expressive or spontaneous, or fully functioning . . . more truly himself, more perfectly actualizing his potentialities, closer to the core of his Being.[27]

In brief, a "self-actualizing person," Maslow's term for the highest level of psychological development, is characterized by "openness" to experience and to "Being," a view that, he claims, is supported by empirical research. This person who "ontologizes" rather than analyzes and measures; whose activities are "end-activities" rather than "means activities," is for both Tillich and Maslow, the truly religious man.[28] Another point of convergence of equal importance in Maslow's and Tillich's analyses of authentic human development is Maslow's conviction that the self-actualizing personality is ultimately rooted in relatively frequent and intense ecstatic experience. For Tillich this is the very nature of the experience of faith—reason in ecstasy; it is part of man's "essentialization." For Maslow, it is the mark of a personality that has achieved the greatest maturity, individuation, and fulfillment. Maslow calls such personal illuminating episodes "peak experiences," "core religious," or "transcendent experience."

Again, for both Tillich and Maslow, it is the person who is so open to the ecstatic disclosure of Being—to the awe-inspiring and threatening ontological question—who is the truly religious person.

The question of Being, for Tillich, is not just one question among many; it is *the* question raised by human existence itself. For man is a mixture of being and nonbeing. This is the very essence of human finitude and drives man to the search for the "really real," for ultimate reality—for that which does not partake of nonbeing. Man experiences nonbeing in the form of anxiety,[29] which, in turn, provides the occasion (ontic shock) of revealing that which is beyond finitude—Being itself. This focal doctrine of anxiety in Tillich's anthropology is dependent upon his ontological doctrine of the relationship of the finite to the infinite: "the anxiety of finitude . . . is eternally taken into the blessedness of the divine infinity . . . blessedness comprises itself and the anxiety of which it is the conquest."[30]

Despite the elaborate architectural intricacy and the ingenious conceptual construction of Tillich's massive system, it is important to remember that it is ultimately based on the individual ecstatic experience of the power of Being itself—the very source of man's power and courage to overcome the anxiety that is the necessary consequence of his own finitude.

Maslow attributes a special type of knowledge—B-cognition (Being-cognition) to the self-actualizing person—who is also the person open to "peak-experience." Unlike psychological studies of the past, Maslow's research is directed toward emotionally healthy people.[31] This fact makes his identification of the "peaker" with the self-actualizing personality even more significant. But the B-cognizer is not simply one who is open to periodic ecstatic experience; he generally perceives the world around him with the clarity and richness that the average human being can have only in "his highest moments" (peak experiences), if at all. The B-cognizer, moreover, is more *open* to the possibility of such experiences, receives them more frequently, and is more deeply affected by them in his personal life. He is more *open* to the world around him insofar as his perception is detached from purely pragmatic concerns. He does not cipher out from the object only those qualities that are relevant to human moods and purposes, and as a result, he is able "to see more truly the nature of the object in itself" . . . "to perceive the world as if it were independent not only of the perceiver but even of human beings in general."[32] Maslow compares B-cognition to the awareness of the mature lover, who, he claims, sees more in the beloved than could possibly be seen by one who does not look with the same regard of care and concern.

Another aspect, which according to Maslow's research is most characteristic of B-cognition, especially in the peak experience, is that it is "much more passive and receptive, much more humble, than normal perception is. It is much more ready to listen and much more able to hear."[33] This last point is of special importance for an evaluation of Tillich's interpretation of secular humanism, for, in his view, it is only "receiving knowledge" that is open to the dimension of depth—the dimension that has been lost to the secular consciousness. "Receiving knowledge," filled with *eros* and longing for union with the object of its perception is essentially the same as Maslow's "B-cognition." Like B-cognition it penetrates "into the depth, into the essential nature of a thing or an event,"[34] and thus gets beyond the surface of sense impressions and changing appearances. In short, Maslow's studies support not only the validity of "receiving knowledge" but also strongly suggest that there is a real dimension of "depth" to which it corresponds, and which can only too easily be lost amidst the activities and concerns of a control-oriented, technological culture.

Maslow was also in accord with Tillich's analysis of culture in that he recognized, with obvious regret, the victory of "technical reason" in our day. Maslow, contrasting this type of knowledge with his B-cognition, used the term "D-cognition" (Deficiency cognition) to indicate that kind of knowledge that is based on the needs and aims of the knower. In D-cognition, as in Tillich's controlling knowledge, the agent looks upon things to see how they can be used as means in relation to his own ends. This is the ordinary, everyday knowledge of a practical type that is absolutely indispensable in order to survive or prosper in the world of means and ends, cause and effect. Because of the great development and precision, the success and reliability of this type of knowledge in our culture, D-cognition enjoys tremendous esteem. In a highly advanced technological and scientific culture the physicist, for example, seems much more important than the metaphysician or the poet.

Maslow did not attempt to demean this sort of practical and logical cognition any more than Tillich despised what he termed "technical reason." But Maslow did look very unfavorably, from the point of view of personalistic psychology, upon the individual attitude that would restrict itself to D-cognition as the only proper avenue of dealing with reality. For this attitude was inimical to peak experience; it cut man off from possible openness to the dimension of depth. D-cognition is too one-sidedly human-centered, self-centered, active, and aggressive to leave man open to the revelatory power of nature and reality. It sees the world "only from the vantage point of the interests of the perceiver,"[35] as containing means and instruments for resolving various human needs. D-cognition is too egocentric for self-transcendence; it needs the balance of B-cognition in order to be self-transcending, unmotivated, and not-needing. Essentially, the same understanding of man is behind Maslow's claim that only B-cognition is open to the transcendent or peak experience, and Tillich's persistent emphasis on the openness of ontological reason to the "depth of reason."[36] Tillich's concern about the dominance of technical reason and its harmful effects upon the openness of the mind to self-transcendence in revelatory experience is never merely a question of individual psychological balance or growth. Theonomous reason is a cultural as well as an individual category. Maslow, too, shares this cultural concern, lest attitudes that inhibit the possibility of transcendent experience should create a culture which is less than human.

Still another aspect of Maslow's psychological research into the nature of the peak experience lends support to Tillich's interpretation of culture in terms of openness to depth. Maslow shared Tillich's understanding of the close relationship between the ecstatic experience in art and the ecstasy of the religious or mystical type. We recall how Tillich had drawn the model of his religious interpretation of culture primarily from the aesthetic experience of expressionistic and new realist art.[37] Indeed, theonomy is the symbol of the presence and breakthrough of the divine within all cultural forms of creation. What religious and artistic symbols have most in common for both writers is their "function of opening up new dimensions of being as well as a corresponding dimension of the soul."[38] This twofold aspect of the opening up process is important, for it shows that both Tillich and Maslow understood the awareness resulting from such experience as something more than a description of one's psychological state. Symbolic language, a common language of ecstatic experience, has an ontological as well as a psychological reference, for which Maslow uses the term "ontopsychological."[39]

In light of Maslow's understanding of the importance of the peak or ecstatic experience for human growth, it is not surprising that he strongly proposed an educational approach that would create sensitivity to B-cognition. The practical application of this educational psychology put great importance on the role of the arts and aesthetic experience. In the following passage from an article appearing in the *Humanist* we get a clear indication of Maslow's educational perspective, as well as of the close connection he saw between the aesthetic and the religious experience:

> . . . the arts are so close to our psychological and biological core, so close to this identity . . . we must let them become basic experiences in our education. They could very well serve as a model: the glimpse into the infinite that they provide might well serve as the means by which we might rescue the rest of the school curriculum from the value free, value neutral, goal lacking meaninglessness into which it has fallen.[40]

Tillich could hardly have wished for a clearer expression of the theonomous attitude in education than this proposal of Maslow. Maslow had the ability to express in a more concrete and specific form some of the rather broad abstractions or symbols of Tillich's theology of culture. As was observed in Chapter 5, Tillich objected to the expectation of humanism that all man's goals could be fulfilled through good educational processes. Tillich was quite correct in recognizing the intimate connection between humanism and education, and this correlation is a very important part of humanist self-understanding.[41]

Tillich's objection to this expectation consisted in his conviction that humanism had no clear notion as to the direction in which education must lead. The humanist goal of the actualization and fulfillment of all human potentialities is simply not realistic, "since decisive human potentialities will always remain unrealized."[42] Furthermore, Tillich maintained, if the goal could be fulfilled to any degree at all, it would only be for elite groups and individuals, for "the human condition always excludes—whether under aristocratic or democratic systems—the vast majority of human beings from the higher grades of cultural form and educational depth."[43] Tillich's solution to the dilemma was that education must be "into the mystery of being."[44] Such an expression might stand for something very profound, and indeed within the context of Tillich's major ontological presuppositions one can have a fairly good *general* idea of what he was getting at in these terms. On the other hand, the expression is general enough to permit several possible practical interpretations under the same rubric "mystery of being." Maslow's suggestion for the improvement of education, could be said to represent a practical, authentic concretization of Tillich's abstractly expressed ideal. It spells out, in other words, what could be meant by education into the "mystery of being."

Finally, Maslow saw the peak-experience as the clue to the real significance of religious revelations and illuminations. The peak or ecstatic experience is substantially what religious experience, and ultimately religion itself, is all about. Mar-

ghanita Laski, to whom Maslow acknowledged his deep
indebtedness, maintains the same position in her unique
study, *Ecstasy: A Study of Some Secular and Religious Experiences*.[45] Laski's whole approach in general, which considers
the experiences of the religious mystics, the visionary flights
of literary artists and poets, and the popular accounts of
transcendent feelings all under the general rubric of ecstasy,
reveals more than any specific statement her basic understanding of the question. Nevertheless, her sharp distinction
between the religious experience itself, and the *overbelief,* or
subjective interpretation of the experience, clearly demonstrates that for Laski the essential element is the religious
experience of transcendence rather than its theological or
symbolic explanation.

> Overbelief made its first dictionary appearance in the 1933
> supplement to the *Oxford English Dictionary* where it is defined
> as: "Belief in more than is warranted by the evidence or in what
> cannot be verified." The first use cited was in 1900, but the
> best-known example of its use is William James's in *Varieties of
> Religious Experience* first published in 1902. Here James uses
> *overbelief* as I shall principally use it, to name the subjective gloss
> or interpretation placed by people on their experiences, and
> although, he believed, as he put it, that "the most interesting and
> valuable things about a man are usually his over-beliefs," he still
> thought it proper, in trying to discover the nature of religious
> experience, to disregard the overbeliefs and confine himself to
> what was common and generic.[46]

Both Maslow and Laski lament the fact that the dominant
empirical and scientific attitude of our culture does not encourage us to investigate ecstatic or religious experience,
which provides man with a unique source for achieving a
sense of purpose and meaningfulness of existence.[47] Although
Maslow was a self-declared Secular Humanist, and, in consistency with our definition, rejected the traditional answers
of the creeds as inadequate, he nevertheless strongly objected
to that kind of secular spirit that would throw out the
religious questions together with the answers it had rejected.

For these religious questions, maintained Maslow, must be dealt with in order to achieve a truly human situation, both on the individual and the cultural level. The affinity to Tillich's view on this issue is quite striking, and both Tillich and Maslow see a certain positivistic and empirical attitude in our culture as the greatest obstacle to openness in this direction.

Secular Humanist ideals and the permeability of a culture
Thus far we have discussed secular humanism as a general outlook and attitude rather than as a particular movement. Given the interests of this study, this emphasis was appropriate, for Tillich's own reflections on secular humanism rarely, if ever, refer to a specific movement, but deal rather with the broad, usually unthematized cultural perspective described in Chapter 1. On the other hand, there is no doubt that Tillich was well aware of the existence of a Secular Humanist movement.[48] For the sake of efficient methodology our examples are drawn primarily from writers who have explicitly expressed adherence to this movement. This procedure will provide an objective norm for the selection of representatives of the secular humanist outlook.

Both Tillich and Maslow attributed much of the present loss of depth in our time to an excessive positivistic spirit in modern culture. To the extent that positivism and shallow empiricism can be shown to dominate the contemporary Humanist outlook, its influence in modern culture will clearly be detrimental to the fostering of depth awareness.

Despite the provisional character of Maslow's and Laski's studies, they provide us with sufficient evidence to indicate beyond a reasonable doubt that many men find in ecstatic or peak experience a greater awareness of the world around them, a clearer sense of their total meaning and direction in the scheme of things, and a source of courage, joy, and motivation which deeply affects their human conduct. Accordingly, any willful or systematic neglect of so important an area of human experience certainly would reveal a shallowness and a closed mind.

Tillich was also aware that not all Secular Humanist writers shared this hostility or closedness to the religious or depth dimension. Certainly Dewey, Randall, and Huxley, for example, would not fit under this heading of shallow-minded or closed-minded Humanism.[49] Despite these important exceptions, Humanism, as a movement, too frequently fell victim to its own empirical spirit, and closed itself off from a serious study of these highly significant experiences. The degree of Humanism's failure in this respect can be gathered from a study of divergent reactions among Humanist writers to the ecstatic or peak experience and other claims of transcendence. Before we review these reactions, a brief recapitulation of our analysis of Maslow's work as it bears on Tillich's interpretation of culture is in order.

Tillich claimed that humanism, which he considered to be the highest expression of the secular autonomous spirit, was thoroughly justified in its reaction against religious heteronomy. On the other hand, he also maintained that in its praiseworthy and zealous defense of human dignity and independence of human intelligence, humanism had profanized culture and lost its sensitivity to the self-transcending aspects of culture.[50] In light of Maslow's (and Laski's) empirical studies, the notion of ecstatic experience, the concept of "receiving knowledge," and the awareness of depth all take on a greater degree of credibility and concreteness, and appear far less poetic and fanciful. From Maslow's perspective, the self-actualizing and fully developed personality enjoys a special quality of openness, which he also describes as "permeability." Permeability means very much the same as receptiveness to the impact and penetration of all aspects of reality and Being upon one's awareness and consciousness.[51]

Just as in the case of Tillich's "theonomy," Maslow's permeability is also a quality desirable for a culture or movement as well as for an individual. The clearest indication of the permeability of culture, for Maslow, is its openness and sensitivity to the ecstatic or peak experience. In order to determine the accuracy of Tillich's judgment on the lack of openness of secular humanism to the religious or depth dimension, we must ask ourselves whether or not the principal ideals of Secular Humanism, as a movement,[52] are inherently opposed to this attitude of permeability. Since this question can best be answered by considering both negative and positive Humanist reactions to the ecstatic or peak experience of reality (or, if one prefers, to the perception of depth), we now turn our attention to several representative examples.

Negative Humanist reactions to the call for transcendence and depth awareness   In the provocative and carefully argued thesis of the late Columbia philosopher and Humanist spokesman, Charles Frankel, we have a classic example of the humanist polemic against the religious appeal to moral absolutes, eternal verities, and ultimate spiritual realities.[53] Frankel launches his most vehement attack against those religious apologists who invoke the perilousness of the world situation and the growing sense of anxiety in our time as proof of the urgent need of a religious transformation of culture and a return to the absolutes of faith.

Frankel's principal objection to this kind of argument is that it is really based on a thinly disguised "loss of nerve,"[54] which effectively diverts our intelligence and energy from the real issues of political and social existence. Accordingly, those religious leaders and cultural commentators who insist on treating us to a "language of ultimates" and prescribing for society a heavy dose of transcendent ideals are *au fond* "prophets of doom,"[55] whose inspiration will eventually lead us to the frustration of imaginary hopes and unattainable goals.

Frankel's work, although undeniably controversial in style and intent, is by no means close-minded and insensitive to the opposition. He shows a genuine and sympathetic understanding of the negative critique that has recently been brought to bear against the humanist view of culture, and which is clearly reflected in the writings of both Maslow and Tillich. Frankel willingly admits, for example, that liberal and democratic humanism has been seriously shaken in its optimistic prognosis for the future of human civilization. The Secular Humanist has been forced to recognize that much more is wrong with human nature than one can hope to eradicate by education and social reconstruction alone. Political power and military force, for example, play a far greater role in forging the directions of society than the humanist was ever willing to admit. World War II, in particular, shattered the liberal humanist faith in the inevitable progress of human culture through science and technology. The thin lining of civilization proved to be too weak to contain the break-through of barbarism, and technological growth was usually accompanied by even greater ills than the good it produced.[56]

Nevertheless, Frankel insists that the message of the "prophets of doom" is both misleading and unproductive. We gain nothing by emphasizing the ambiguity of human intelligence, the radical evil in man, and the subsequent need for a resurgence of religious absolutes. Indeed, we can only lose when we surrender our confidence in human nature, for only through self-confidence will we be able to meet the challenge of the real, concrete problems that face modern culture:

> The great problem, in short is to reconstruct the liberal tradi-tion to make it applicable to an age of technical specialization, bureaucratized power and mass movements . . .
> But however difficult these problems with which liberalism is confronted may be, it is clear that they are institutional, not psychological—political not moral. They cannot be dealt with by reaffirming our faith in absolute moral principles, or by reducing our faith in human potentialities, or by admitting that rationality is a will-o-the-wisp, or by waiting for spiritual transfiguration.[57]

The basic conflict between Frankel's view and Tillich's interpretation of culture is apparent. Furthermore, Frankel's dismissal of any appeal to transcendent values or spiritual transformation as "loss of nerve" clearly runs counter to Maslow's stress on the importance of B-cognition and peak-experience for overall personality development. As has been observed, Maslow has contended that the B-cognizer, in his openness to revelatory experience, tends to develop a character that is more "responsible, active . . . , more self-determined, more a free agent . . . most able to transcend the ego or the self and to become selfless . . . more loving and more accepting."[58] If Maslow's analysis is correct, it certainly seems far more suited than Frankel's interpretation to explain the frequency with which praiseworthy social and political programs end in defeat by reason of a lack of inner freedom, responsibility, or human sensitivity on the part of voters and citizens.

Another example of a negative attitude among Humanist writers toward a religious or transcendent view of culture is found in the works of the philosopher Sidney Hook.[59] Hook, who is also a frequent contributor to Humanist publications and a signee of Humanist Manifesto II, shares Frankel's diffidence in the biblical conviction that improvement in the social order demands an inner transformation or conversion of the individual. Hook bases his argument primarily on the claim that whereas the Christian social gospel has had two thousand years in which to order the world on a moral basis, it has, in fact, failed quite miserably in its appointed task.[60] On these grounds Hook is unambiguously opposed to any attempt on the part of religionists to substitute "consolatory ideals" and pious exhortations about the hope of blessedness in a future life for responsible social planning and effective political action. Such Humanist fears about the misdirection of supernaturalistic and religious concerns clearly have some justification in light of the overall performance of the churches in recent centuries. Too frequently the churches have been inclined to offer spiritual solace and comfort in issues such as racial injustice, the proliferation of wars, and population explosion, where practical and concrete solutions would have been much more to the point. Indeed, this false supernaturalism has certainly provoked a great deal of protest from within the very ranks of the churches themselves, especially during the last two decades.

On the other hand, to speak of the poor record of the "churches" is a somewhat questionable method of debate, for the term *church* is clearly a blanket one, including under its very general heading a wide variety of religious groups, which express highly divergent attitudes toward social responsibility. But even if, for argument's sake, the overall performance of these many communities and groups, Jewish as well as Christian, is assumed to be so poor as to justify a total dismissal of their voice in matters of social and cultural concern, we can still question with Maslow whether this justifies throwing out all interest in the valid religious questions with which the churches have traditionally been concerned.[61] Substantially, Maslow is raising the same objection expressed by Tillich in more abstract form when Tillich claimed that in purely secular culture, the humanistic, autonomous spirit has overreacted against heteronomous interference of authoritarian religion by rejecting its own religious depth in the process. This rejection, in Tillich's view, resulted in a loss of self-transcendence in life, a neglect of the ultimate meaning-dimension, and the general profanization of culture.

Humanism, as a movement, in both Britain and America, has enjoyed the prestige of a membership that is striking for its large representation of scholarly, brilliant, and highly talented elements of our society. This fact has been used both as a claim for its credibility on the part of its supporters and as the basis for the accusation of elitism on the part of its opponents. Maslow, who knew Humanism from within, maintained that in view of its rich intellectual resources the Humanist movement has exerted little influence on our culture at large. Maslow's explanation for this phenomenon was precisely the fact that Humanism had neglected this whole area of ultimate value and transcendent emotion, which men simply "refuse to be done out of."[62]

In a similar vein, the European Humanist and philosopher Gerhard Szezesny lamented this same weakness of humanism and secular culture, which, in his view, had set the stage for a revival of Christianity, at least in its institutional form. For Christianity, he claimed, has remained, in a way, "richer and deeper," insofar as "it knows more about man's inclination to turn to the mysteries, to form some notion of what lies beyond the rationally knowable."[63] In his exciting and controversial work, *The Future of Unbelief,* Szezesny strongly objects to the Christian domination of Western culture on the grounds that it represents the uneasy survival of a primitive theology, which is fundamentally at odds with the loftiest ideals and greatest achievements of Western civilization. Although Szezesny's work is undoubtedly an appeal for greater rationality and renewed confidence in human intelligence in our culture, he nevertheless recognizes the significance of ecstatic experience, and obviously does not find it inconsistent with this rationality and intelligence. And although man does not gain any additional factual knowledge (controlling knowledge) in such experience, he can nevertheless achieve therefrom greater spontaneous insight into the mystery of being and life.

> . . . in times of transition an overpowering sense of security and liberation may suddenly arise, just when it has long been thought forever lost. When this occurs the basic connectedness of a world that had seemingly disintegrated into millions of phenomena and processes stands revealed in a new experience of space and time and a new encounter with being. At these rare moments of spontaneous insight the mystery is lighted up, that very mystery which the religious believe they alone possess and alone can communicate, but in the face of which, in truth, they fail.[64]

For Szezesny, then, it is quite clear that a cultural situation like the present, in which transcendent or ecstatic experience is seen by theologians and Humanists alike as the exclusive and proper interest of the religions and the churches, is unfortunate indeed. With Maslow and Tillich, Szezesny is appealing for a greater openness within secular culture to what Tillich calls "the dimension of depth."

If neglect of the religious dimension and the closely related ecstatic experience should prove detrimental to the creation of a truly human cultural situation—as the analyses of Maslow, Tillich, and Szezesny indicate—then there is certainly something seriously defective in that strand of Humanism which is "full-fledged" secularistic.[65] To show the defects inherent in this outlook, however, is not to offer an adequate answer to Frankel's and Hook's objection that the appeal to religious renewal and awareness of the depth dimension are both impractical and misleading.

Hook also raises an even more fundamental difficulty about talk of ultimacy, which is particularly relevant to the Tillichian notion of the Unconditional and of ultimate concern. For ". . . is there any war," asks Hook, "so fanatical and bestial as a religious war in which the conditional values of social and personal interests take on the awful authority of unconditioned claims?"[66] The same basic objection is brought forward by Leonard Wheat, particularly against the notion of "ultimate concern," which he also considers to be a "fiction." Wheat, much influenced by the thought of Walter Kaufmann on this issue, takes a view that is very representative of Humanism's "down-to-earth" approach: the truly "humane person is apt to have several deep concerns which balance one another,"[67] rather than to be guided by one overarching drive. Wheat maintains that to actually live out Tillich's doctrine of ultimate concern is tantamount to moving in the direction of fanaticism.[68]

Humanist objections and Tillichian responses   Before we consider Hook's charge of the impracticality and diversionary nature of "language of ultimates," we do well to explore in greater detail the objection of implicit fanaticism mutually raised by Wheat and Kaufmann, as well as by Hook. Wheat cites the illustration of the bacteriologist whose ultimate concern is finding a cure for tetanus. Should a family crisis occur that would make such demands of his time and energy as to jeopardize the scientific project, the bacteriologist would logically have to neglect his family needs and obligations. It is evident from Wheat's example that he obviously forgets that Tillich's notion of ultimate concern is balanced by an equally serious warning against idolatrous ultimates. To commit oneself to an ultimate that is anything less than the Unconditioned, Infinite Reality is to condemn oneself to existential frustration. Tillich's theology, although it is directed especially to secular man and maintains a sensitivity to the religious element that is implicit in secular ideologies and outlooks, is nevertheless an apologetic for the Christian faith. By his own admission the notion of "ultimate concern" is the philosophical analogue to the great commandment: "The Lord, our God, the Lord is one; and you shall love the Lord your God with all your heart, and with all your soul and with all your mind, and with all your strength."[69] To choose the example of dedication to the cure of tetanus is to miss the real meaning of Tillich's ultimate concern.

Hook's argument, on the other hand, is much more subtle than that of Wheat's, and cannot be dismissed so easily as the latter's. One aspect of Hook's argument, as we have seen, is historical, for he claims that the historical record clearly demonstrates that inner conversion and emphasis on spiritual transformation, so essential to the gospel outlook, have had precious little effect on human society. Christian historians have been able to argue that despite the many failures within Christian civilization, Christianity has nevertheless brought about a great many reforms and improvements in human society. H. J. Blackham and Corliss Lamont, both leading Humanist spokesmen, readily concede this balancing factor in their classic summaries of the Secular Humanist outlook.[70] Tillich's reaction to the kind of objection raised by Hook is, on the other hand, primarily one of agreement. In Tillich's dialectical interpretation of culture, the greatest distortion and ambiguity of humanity will *necessarily* appear in religion and the religious realm: "In every act of the self-transcendence of life profanization is present or, in other words, . . . life transcends itself ambiguously."[71] Although ambiguity and distortion are present in all dimensions of life, such distortion in the religious dimension becomes "demonic" insofar as finite reality is accorded unconditional dignity and significance.

Tillich's criticism of religion is for this reason sharper than his objections to a purely secular or "shallow" humanism.[72] Like Maslow, Tillich called both groups to radical reform and renewal through the establishment of a transparency and openness to Being-itself—to the sacred depths present within all finite reality. The opposition found in both Hook and Frankel to a theological perspective of culture that could attempt to simply call man back to old conceptions and formulations of religious absolutes is quite justifiable. Such a procedure would certainly constitute a going backwards—a retrogression to what Bertrand Russell called "beliefs and passions appropriate to a bygone age."[73] But Tillich's humanistic theology did not call for such a reactionary return. What he offered is really a third way—an intermediate alternative. Modern man must discover a *"new* sense of ultimate concern, a *new* awareness of depth and a *new* search for ultimate meaning,"[74] within the very structures that constitute our secular, autonomous society. Tillich did not call for opposition to secular and scientific progress or an undermining of our political, democratic, and social achievements in the Western world for the sake of concerns that are primarily spiritual, mystical, psychological, and moral. The ideal of theonomous culture is one in which culture "in complete and autonomous form is comprehended in its finitude and in its quest after the Infinite."[75] Tillich, in brief, while remaining loyal and responsible (at least in his own view) to the biblical and Christian tradition, did not envisage the future of Christianity in terms of adherence to old belief systems: Christian symbols had to be radically reinterpreted in view of man's present cultural situation.

A brief comparison of Tillich's theonomous vision with Julian Huxley's evolutionary humanism further illustrates how removed Tillich's thought was from any kind of intellectual or cultural retrogression in the name of religious absolutes. Huxley and Tillich both maintained that the future development of human culture depended upon a broadening of the concepts of both religion and science and the subsequent harmonization of these two powerful human forces. Consider the following statement from Huxley's *Religion Without Revelation*:

> The concept of evolutionary humanism has helped us to see how, in principle, at least, science and religion can be reconciled. It has shown me outlets for ideas and sentiments which I think

can legitimately be called religious, but which otherwise would have remained frustrated or untapped. And it has indicated how vital a contribution science can make to religious progress.[76]

Huxley belongs to that group of Humanists, who though secular in their rejection of supernatural religion and their firm trust in scientific method, are nevertheless religious in the sense of Tillich's or Maslow's openness or permeability to the sacredness of reality. Scientific culture in general and the social sciences in particular have, in Huxley's view, neglected the "transcendent forces"[77] that constitute so important an element in human self-understanding. Accordingly, he like Maslow and Tillich, stressed the importance of overcoming the dichotomy of the sacred and profane, the religious and the secular. A truly scientific humanism will not, Huxley maintained, neglect man's religious impulse. The religious dimension is needed to help arrive at a new sense of destiny as man moves into a radically new situation. At the same time, from the other end of the polarity, "scientific study is needed to give religion a fuller understanding of destiny."[78]

From the point of view of Tillich's theonomy there is nowhere in his writings where the same optimistic hope for a unified culture, in which religion and science are reconciled, is so clearly and enthusiastically expressed, as in his original blueprint for a theology of culture traced out in his 1919 address: In this admittedly romantic and idealistic vision of man's future possibilities, Tillich describes the "theonomous society" as:

> the universal human community, built up out of spiritual communities and bearing with it all cultural functions and their religious substance, with the great creative philosophers for its teachers, artists for its priests, the seers of a new ethic of the person and the community for its prophets, men who will lead it to new community goals for its bishops, leaders and recreators of the economic process for its deacons and almoners.[79]

When we add to this earlier picture the subsequent developments in Tillich's overall vision, especially his awareness of the possibilities of religious depth right within the scientific and technological processes,[80] we see how strikingly similar is the notion of theonomy to Huxley's forward-looking, humanistic ideal. Finally, if Maslow is correct, then, the religious questions and the concern for depth and ultimacy are not only scientifically respectable but are absolutely essential to any realistic and humanistic cultural development.[81] Hook's position, by way of contrast, implies an unjustifiably sharp dichotomization of science and religion, of religion and culture. Hook's position is not open to a broader and more comprehensive view of science and of modern culture, which will include in its ambit those most cherished values and experiences that men have always called "religious." Accordingly, if Hook's objection has any validity, it is only against a certain type of "supernaturalistic" religion, for an appeal to ultimates and a concern for man's religious yearnings need not be connected with either indifference to practical concerns nor with attitudes productive of fanatical behavior. We have seen ample evidence that Tillich's interpretation of culture is essentially free from both such religious distortions.

We must take sides, therefore, with those Humanist writers, such as Maslow, Huxley, and Laski,[82] who contend that the reaction of secular autonomous humanism to traditional creedal religion is too often excessive, rejecting legitimate and important aspects of human experience along with the creeds themselves. Unfortunately this excessive response is not limited to a few exceptional authors, such as Hook, Frankel, or Kaufmann. Even the very conciliatory and moderate British Humanist leader H. J. Blackham informs us that Humanism "does not retain the religious categories—the numinous, the sacred, the holy, the worshipful, the eternal, the absolute. . . . Humanism is a rejection of these categories."[83] Corliss Lamont, his American counterpart, though showing a degree of appreciation for Maslow's research on peak experience, on the whole, dismisses any specifically religious experience as a totally unreliable source of truth, and warns the reader that it is frequently the result of epilepsy, hysteria, or some other morbid condition.[84] Edwin Wilson, the former director of the American Humanist Association, sees the value of humanistic psychology, such as that found in Maslow, to consist essentially in a way of offering the churches a way to save face by claiming that the religious experience discussed by these psychologists is what they were talking about in the first place.[85] Roy Wood Sellars, the American Naturalist philosopher and active Humanist, specifically criticized Tillich's use of terms such as "Being-Itself," "the Unconditional," and "the Ground of Being," as techniques for "by-passing the world around us," and assured us that he preferred "a matter-of-fact confrontation with material things."[86] Both Hook and Sellars dismiss Tillich's talk about "Being-Itself" as a kind of "mytho-poeic construction."[87]

It would be distorting the facts, on the other hand, to depict all Secular Humanists as supporting this positivistic appraisal of reality. Maslow and Laski both considered themselves Secular Humanists, and yet they obviously shared Tillich's serious concern for the depth dimension in human culture. Likewise, dedication to preserving the sacredness of life and nature had obviously attained the fervor of a religious commitment in the work of the Humanist and biologist, Julian Huxley.[88] Several well-known American philosophers, all of whom were actively involved in the Humanist movement, have also shown a remarkable, if not puzzling, concern for the experience of transcendence. A brief look at their understanding of the meaning and significance of the religious dimension of culture provides a more balanced picture of the Humanist outlook and a more accurate basis for judging Tillich's critique of a purely secular and humanistic cultural situation.

Positive Humanist reactions to religious experience and the depth dimension of culture Tillich acknowledged that many Humanists manifest a greater awareness of the religious dimension than people within the churches.[89] There is little doubt that the concern of Humanists in this direction frequently far surpasses that of a large portion of regular church membership.

We should not forget, however, that these writers are

"Secular" Humanists in the sense that we have defined this term; i.e., man, not God; scientific knowledge, not divine revelation constitute the centrality of their concerns. The religious domain may be of interest—even of vital interest—to them insofar as it represents a significant aspect of human experience or has filled an important function in directing human affairs. Humanists of this orientation (there is a dispute as to whether they should call themselves "religious humanists") are thoroughly convinced that a "full-blooded" humanism cannot afford to neglect any vital area of human existence. In support of this view, Humanists of this propensity are wont to quote the Latin poet Terence: "nil humanum mihi alienum puto."[90] They recognize, in other words, that biblical religion has come to express some of the noblest human aspirations and the most generous human feelings. Although they do not fail to point out the harm that religious distortion and fanaticism has effected at various times in history, they also tend to emphasize the ennobling and enriching benefits that religion has brought to Western civilization:

> It [Christian belief], in this case, has focused men's ambitions and aspirations, clarified them, and led men on to new insights. It has given them courage and power and consolation, in communion with their fellows and with the saints who lived of old. It has provided another world for the mind of man to dwell in, a realm of ideals from whose contemplation men return with renewed vigor. The enriching of this realm of insight and imagination to express more and more of human interest, feeling, passion, action and thought has been the greatest human achievement of Christendom.[91]

One of the leading, earlier proponents of this religious stream of the Humanist movement was the philosopher John Dewey. In his concern to assist modern man to find his way through the maze of rapid cultural change, Dewey stressed the importance of the "religious attitude" as an organizing faculty to provide man with a sense of direction. Although Dewey strenuously opposed supernatural religion and warned his readers, in a way similar to Frankel's, of religion's power to divert energy from ideal values and from actual conditions,[92] he nevertheless thought it imperative to rescue the religious attitude from its distortion in the religions.

The Columbia philosopher John H. Randall, Jr., picked up Dewey's project, but with a unique emphasis that was his own. Randall saw great significance in the *functional* power of the religious symbol. William James, the pragmatist, considered it an issue of major philisophical concern to examine the varieties of religious experience. Curtis Reese, Religious Humanist, preacher, and writer, emphasized the reconciling effects of religious consciousness.[93] F. J. E. Woodbridge wrote with sensitivity and zeal about the religious "perspective" and its importance for human happiness. His fellow Naturalist Irwin Edman stressed the human need of "cosmic piety." Joseph L. Blau, a contemporary disciple of Dewey's, emphasized the power of belief in God for shaping human destinies.[94] On the British scene, we have already noted Julian Huxley's enthusiastic defense of what he described as "the quality of holiness in things"—a quality that produces peace, reconciliation, and rapture.[95]

Perhaps one of the clearest expressions of this genuine Humanist esteem of the religious dimension of life is found in Randall's description of his philosophical development. At a certain point in his career, after going through more negative and critical stages in his attitude toward religion, Randall reached a position where he began to doubt "whether any philosophizing can be other than truncated,"[96] which fails to address itself seriously to the religious questions. A philosophy that was consistently built on this premise could hardly fail to fulfill the essential requirements of what Tillich has called a "theonomous philosophy." It is no wonder that Randall became Tillich's principal dialogue partner in his ongoing discussion with Secular Humanism, and that at times it was difficult for an audience to see where both men differed other than in terminology.[97] We have yet to discover in this investigation whether any substantial differences separate Tillich's theonomous vision of culture and the religious humanism of writers such as Randall. For the present, we can say with certainty that Tillich's assertion that Humanism had lost sight of the religious dimension cannot be applied to these Religious Humanists, at least not in the same way as to their more purely Secular fellow Humanists.

It is not difficult to understand, in light of these sharp differences, that Humanists in the Randall camp are hesitant to have their position described as "secular" humanism. In a 1970 personal interview, for example, Randall was reluctant to identify with the label "Secular Humanist" and acceded only when it was made clear that the term "secular" was being used in the stricter sense of "noncreedal" or "nontheistic." He refused to support any notion of secularity that implied an "antireligious" attitude of any sort. To emphasize this latter point Randall also revealed that he had seriously hesitated to sign the First "Humanist Manifesto," fearing that it might entail a denial of the religious dimension.[98]

There is no doubt, then, that two sharply divergent attitudes toward religious experience can be found in the Humanist tradition; this cannot be overlooked in evaluating Tillich's critique of Secular Humanism. At least one major group of Secular Humanists reveal an unambiguous sensitivity and awareness of the religious or depth dimension that is present in all cultural forms. But is not this sensitivity and awareness of depth the very essence of Tillich's notion of theonomy? "Theonomous awareness," as Tillich described it, is only accessible to reason "in ecstasy." The greatest danger of secular culture, wrote Tillich in 1925, is that "religious ecstasy disappears and with it the ecstatic symbolic character of religious objects."[99] Despite the intricate intellectual structure of Tillich's theology, the key concept of theonomy is ultimately based on ecstatic religious experience.[100] Whereas one strand of Secular Humanism is open to such experience as revelatory of deeper structures of meaning, the other, larger segment of the movement dismisses it as illusory or even harmful.

It is evident, therefore, that Tillich's critique of Humanism as shallow or superficial in its loss of the religious dimension was directed more at the "matter-of-fact," positivistic, and "purely secular" variety of the movement. The striking similarity of his own views with that of humanistic psychology and of naturalistic philosophers such as Randall and Huxley permits no other interpretation. In the following chapter we take another and closer look at this religious branch of Secular Humanism to see whether it is ultimately distinguishable from Tillich's theonomous outlook. At this juncture a summary of our appraisal of Tillich's charge that a purely secular humanism loses sight of an authentic and essential aspect of reality would be useful, for until we have completed this evaluation we cannot dismiss the possibility that Secular Humanism might be right—refusing to confuse imagination with reality, emotive experience with authentic knowledge.

Thus far we have seen two arguments in particular that appear to support Tillich's claim. The first is *psychological* and depends primarily on the findings of Maslow and Laski. It is their strong contention that ecstasy is essential to human development and self-integration, and that in the peak-experience, healthy personalities receive a type of insight that helps them to grow, experience a sense of meaning and joy, and find motivation "to do something good for the world."[101] The second, though closely connected with the first, is *sociological*. We refer to the fact that a good number of the Humanist ranks belongs to the intellectual elite and to Maslow's and Szezesny's observation that secular humanism has nevertheless had little effect on our culture because of an overemphasis on conceptual intelligence and rationality with a corresponding neglect of transcendence. Neither of these two writers, it should be clear, are calling for an abdication of reason and intelligence, for in their view ecstatic awareness is not opposed to rationality. They are both in concurrence with Tillich's conviction that "the ecstatic experience of an ultimate concern does not destroy the structure of reason. Ecstasy is fulfilled, not denied, rationality."[102] Finally, even from the ranks of the Secular Humanists themselves there have been significant voices promoting a greater concern for ecstatic religious experience.

The Lost Dimension in
Historical Retrospect

Since the publication of Szezesny's work, almost two decades ago, radical and unexpected cultural change has served to corroborate both of these arguments. During this period there has been a rapid and powerful growth of a countercultural movement, which constituted a genuine rebellion against secularized society and its scientific world view. This rebellion took many forms, especially among students and the youth in Western countries: the hippie movement, the pop folk culture, psychedelia, occultism, oriental religion, yoga, zen, revolutionary humanism, existentialism, mysticism, and Jesus restoration are all manifestations of this new consciousness that resists the restrictions of the empirical and scientific model upon what counts for valid knowledge and experience. It was the growing momentum of this very "unsecular" attitude in the late 1960s that urged former evangelists of secularity, such as Harvey Cox and Peter Berger, to write books like *The Feast of Fools* and *A Rumor of Angels*—both representing a sharp about-face from their previous glorification of secularity as the will of God.[103]

More recently, Theodore Roszak, whom we mentioned earlier as one of the more outspoken representatives of the counterculture, called for a renewed sense of "nature sanctified". . . "alive with a transcendent presence" and an openness to "sudden ecstasy, an awareness of the heavens and earth swept by awesome presences, the mind on fire with rhapsodic declaration."[104] Critics have fittingly pointed to the excesses and the lack of clarity and precision that characterizes Roszak's work. Tillich would certainly have faulted Roszak's approach for its lack of rational criticism, but would, at the same time, have concurred with the latter's conclusion that "the energy of religious renewal . . . will generate the next politics, and perhaps the final radicalism of our society."[105] Whether one agrees with Roszak's solution or not, it is evident that the youthful generations for which he claims to speak will, to a large extent, refuse to accept technical proficiency in place of spiritual values, or social and political programs which are not accompanied by inner transformation. Accordingly, if Secular Humanism is going to offer a real alternative in the predictable future, it will have to restore the religious or ecstatic awareness to a respectable place in our culture; it will have to recapture the dimension of depth. Maslow not only shared this view himself but also saw that Tillich and he were fundamentally in the same camp on the issue:

> . . . it can be demonstrated that . . . the religious questions (which were thrown out along with the Churches) are valid questions, that these questions are almost the same as the deep, profound, and serious ultimate concerns of the sort that Tillich talks about and of the sort by which I would define humanistic psychology. . .[106]

Maslow also concluded from this argument, that if they become more aware of the religious dimension "these humanistic sects could become much more useful to mankind than they are now."[107] Maslow's conclusion undercuts the typical Humanist objection that concern for ultimate and religious absolutes serves as a diversion from the real practical issues that face mankind. It would indicate, to the contrary, that to satisfy man's social, political, and utilitarian needs is not enough. Furthermore, the historical argument that religion has in the past served to drain human energies that could have been spent far more productively understands the term *religion* in a way that is quite different from that of Tillich's and Maslow's "ultimate concerns." The Secular Humanist critique of religion is thus valid only if it is addressed to what Tillich called "heteronomous" religion.

In short, Tillich's interpretation of Secular Humanism as a cultural outlook and movement is essentially on target. It seems undeniable that a purely secular, strictly autonomous humanism contains principles that are logically prone to ignore, if not reject, the meaning-producing dimension that Tillich calls "depth."

The fact that a number of Secular Humanist representatives, especially in this country, recognize and struggle to overcome this serious weakness in our culture does not invalidate Tillich's thesis. To the contrary, it reinforces the accuracy of his interpretation, since it illustrates that the loss of depth in modern secularism can be recognized even by those who are outside of the "theological circle." At the same time, however, this religiously sensitive strain within the Humanist movement serves as a reminder that even the most brilliant intellectual construction—such as Tillich's theology of culture—must continually be challenged by demands for empirical fit. In this case, the dialectical interpretation of culture in terms of heteronomy, autonomy, and theonomy must not be allowed to swallow up real and important differences that are found within the Secular Humanist outlook. In a very general way, on the other hand, Tillich did recognize the religious potential within Humanism, which, as an idealism, he insisted, was already on the way to theonomy.[108]

Now that we have completed our analysis of Tillich's theology of culture and evaluated his critique of the secular humanist outlook, only one major question remains. Is Tillich's theonomous vision of culture really distinct from the world view of the Religious Humanists whom we have discussed? Are the similarities to be explained, as Tillich claimed, by the fact that Humanism is "on the way to theonomy"? or is it possible that Tillich's humanistic theology is more humanistic than theological? In the following and concluding chapter we discuss this issue in the dramatic form raised by Leonard Wheat: "Was Tillich really a theological imposter? Was he a Secular Humanist in disguise?"

7

Theologian or Humanist in Disguise?

The principal purpose of this chapter is to test whether Tillich's religious interpretation of culture is in the long run substantially different from the secular humanist point of view. We have thus far accepted the validity and the importance of insisting on the "depth" of human culture. Furthermore, we see no convincing grounds for interpreting Tillich's theology of culture as just a more subtle form of religious heteronomy. In short, we fully recognize the genuineness and authenticity of the humanistic element in Tillich's thought. We are now inquiring about the sincerity and legitimacy of Tillich's Christian faith and theology. Was Tillich really a Christian theologian at heart, or was he, as Leonard Wheat suggests, a thoroughgoing skeptic and fraud, whose principal achievement was that of deceiving the theological world into accepting him as one of their own, indeed, as one of their greatest representatives. As Wheat sees it, Tillich's real message was a sheer humanism—strictly secular and atheistic—which nostalgically (as well as strategically) clung to traditional religious symbols, such as God, Church, Holy Spirit, and Kingdom of God, while ascribing to them a completely new and strictly humanistic meaning. Once we break through the outer deception to the core meaning of Tillich's thought, we begin to understand that theonomy really stands for a fully integrated and harmonious human cultural situation and that the famous "God above God" is nothing other than humanity understood as ultimate concern.[1]

Although the more sensational and extravagant aspects of Wheat's theory can be dismissed offhand as journalistic exaggeration, one aspect of his thesis requires a serious response. Leaving aside the question of Tillich's inner motives and intentions—concerning which his three biographers do not always agree—the legitimate question raised by Wheat is whether the very structure of the theology of culture leads by an inner logical necessity to the espousal of a purely secular humanism. In other words, once we strip away the theological language and the religio-mystical trappings, do we have anything left that is substantially different from what has been said more forthrightly by a Dewey, Randall, Huxley, or other representatives of the "religious" wing of Secular Humanism? There are, it must be admitted, some very striking similarities between these apparently opposing points of view.

The Basic Agreements

Present-day Secular Humanists agree with Tillich's contention that the rapid social changes and serious human failures of our time have created in modern man a spiritual vacuum in terms of meaning and a sense of direction. The Humanist might find very different terms from Tillich's to express this very serious problem of our culture. The Humanist temper is also such that he would be unlikely to stress this kind of general cultural malaise and to put much more energy into addressing specific, isolated, and concrete problems—which, he would assume, will eventually reduce if not cure the malaise. Humanism is by definition optimistic, or at least melioristic: it shies away from existential or metaphysical analyses and prefers to identify concrete problems that are capable of rational methods of solution. Humanists consciously offer an alternative to modern man in the midst of his desperate search for meaning without encouraging him to lose time brooding over the ambiguities and limitations of the human condition. We do not find it difficult to muster sympathy for the positiveness of this approach, nor will we deny a certain impatience with Tillich's sometimes prolix diagnoses of human estrangement.

To be fair to Tillich, on the other hand, it must be recalled that human estrangement is the starting point and assumption of his entire philosophical theology. This estrangement constitutes, in fact, an important apologetic element against any purely secular view of man, which, like Humanism, either disregards or rejects the Christian doctrines of Original Sin and Divine Grace. Nonetheless, even the believing Christian might very well feel a great deal of sympathy toward the Humanist attitude of getting down to concrete tasks. Tillich felt very much this way after World War I, and proceeded to dedicate himself to the very practical issues of religious socialism.

One could also read carefully through the three volumes of the *Systematic* without coming across many of the specific issues of the kind the Humanist considers primary. We must not forget, however, that for Tillich man's current predicament in technological society is only one phase or manifestation of his basic existential state of estrangement. Accordingly, Tillich's work was not addressed exclusively to some specific sociopolitical problems of the moment, but rather to a discovery of the theoretical understanding and grounds for evaluating *whatever* religious or Christian decisions had to be made within the contemporary human situation.

What emerges, then, is that whereas both the Humanist writers and Tillich agree that modern man needs a new way of thinking about himself—a new self-understanding and sense of direction within the context of contemporary culture— each views the nature of the crisis in a radically different way. For the Humanist, the problem is created by a constellation of social, political, and economic changes, and is, therefore, to be met along the lines of these same categories. For Tillich, it arises ultimately from man's basic estrangement from the

Ground of his being, and must be approached in terms of overcoming this estrangement and by the creation of New Being through openness to the Spiritual Presence.

In addition to this fundamental agreement as to the seriousness of a meaning-crisis in our culture, Tillich's theology of culture shows noteworthy similarities to the characteristically Humanist outlook in two other specific and crucial areas. Both are of a sufficiently serious nature to merit special treatment.

The convergence of the religious and the secular spheres "There is no wall between the religious and the non-religious," wrote Tillich in the *Protestant Era.*[2] The meaning of this statement is immediately clear in light of the picture of Tillich's theology of culture, which was sketched in Chapter 3: religion is the substance of culture and culture is the form of religion. The theonomous situation is one in which autonomous cultural forms are asserted and preserved, while remaining transparent to their ultimate power of being and source of meaning. This theonomous interpretation of culture is rooted, furthermore, in Tillich's understanding of the ontological relationship of the finite to infinite Being,[3] as inherited primarily from Schelling's later philosophy. In Schelling's system, God is the creative Ground present in *all* finite reality. Hence, the secular as well as the religious domain is ultimately rooted in the same divine Ground. There is no part of finite reality that is not capable of becoming transparent to the religious dimension of reality. Tillich saw and understood the full implications of this metaphysical doctrine, for his interpretation of culture. This was already clear at the time of his 1924 article, "Rechtfertigung und Zweifel,"[4] in which he developed the notion of universal revelation *(Grundoffenbarung)*, as informing the whole of man's cultural experience. Tillich also possessed the courage and honesty to face the radical conclusion that logically followed from his philosophical position—namely, that the Divine Reality can be no less present to the doubter, the atheist, and the unbeliever than to the pious believer. There is only one reality and it is rooted in its entirety in the Divine Ground. Any separation of the secular from the sacred, culture from religion, is a distortion and the clearest sign of sin and estrangement.

Autonomy and heteronomy are tensions within theonomy, which can lead to a breaking asunder and thus to the catastrophe of the spirit, for the essential relationship of culture and religion is theonomy.[5]

Toward the end of his career Tillich referred to the convergence of culture and religion as "the principle of the consecration of the secular," which theologically he supported with the doctrine of the freedom of the Spirit.[6] Guided by these principles, Tillich felt a great confidence about reaching out to secular culture and its concerns. In other words, Tillich's theology of depth, which began with the assumption of the Divine Presence in everything that exists, enabled him to approach the secular sphere with the same "ultimate concern" with which he addressed himself to the specifically religious realm.

Secular Humanism, in its turn, is equally opposed to any division of the sacred and the secular. Except for those Humanists who may simply deny the reality of the sacred quality of existence and life, the "sacred" can be for Humanism, as well, an important aspect of human experience, an essential quality within man himself. *Humanist Manifesto I* is unambiguous on this issue: "The distinction between the sacred and the secular can no longer be maintained."[7] One can still find Humanists of the outdated polemical mold, still fighting the battles of the past century. For such writers the "sacred" is an empty concept; it is simply based on illusion and wishful thinking, or at best on fecundity of imagination. More often, contemporary Humanists find some sympathy with ideas about the sacred element of reality, provided it is understood as a human quality and does not interfere with man's autonomous activities and reasoning power. Such Humanists may even look tolerantly on the existence of "sacred" communities and the assertion of "religious" truths, so long as these former are amenable to the same criteria of human justice as secular institutions and the latter are subject to the same rules of empirical testing as nonreligious or secular propositions.[8]

It is with the "religious" Humanists that Tillich's thought on the relation of the sacred and the secular has most in common, for both he and they see the sacred as a real dimension or quality of reality and of human experience. With all Secular Humanists Tillich shared the vision of the unity of reality, and in this he was just as "antisupernaturalistic" as Dewey or Randall.

Unlike Dewey and Randall, however, Tillich's antisupernaturalism was not accompanied by a leveling of biblical revelation or of the reality of the divine Presence. Tillich was looking rather for a more intellectually acceptable framework for expressing traditional Christian faith—one to which he remained loyal to the end of his life. This last aspect of Tillich's thought seems strangely enough to be frequently overlooked by some of his critics, secular or religious, who are inclined to dismiss him offhand as a pantheist.[9] Jacob Taubes, for example, an otherwise astute critic of Tillich, stresses only one side of the theonomous perspective when he describes Tillich's theology as "Dionysiac"—"an Ecstatic naturalism" that interprets all supernatural symbols in immanent terms."[10] For although Tillich's God is certainly not a supernatural Being or a God "out there," it would be incorrect to leave the impression that Tillich has denied the divine transcendence. From the days of his Schelling theses, Tillich would always insist on *die absolute Spannung zwischen dem Bedingten und dem Unbedingten.*

> Being-itself infinitely transcends every finite being. There is no proportion or gradation between the finite and the infinite. There is an absolute break, an infinite "jump." On the other hand, everything finite participates in being-itself and in its infinity. Otherwise it would not have the power of being. It would be swallowed by nonbeing . . . All beings are infinitely transcended by their creative ground.[11]

Taubes realized, of course, that as a Christian theologian

Tillich wanted to retain the uniqueness of the Divine Reality and the radical distinction between the finite and the infinite. His point is that Tillich's theology of mediation is in continuity with the tradition of dialectical theology that goes back to Origen, and which never could be approved by the church. The basic reason for this inevitable rejection by the church is that a theology which involves the divine in human dialectic logically must lead to a theology of pure immanence—"The divine become immersed in the world, becomes an immanent principle."[12] Taubes sees this tradition of dialectical or logos theology as culminating in modern times in the Hegelian synthesis, and it is precisely in terms of Hegel's dialectic that he would have us interpret Tillich's theology.

Tillich has, indeed, derived much of his thought and categories from Hegel. Tillich also recognized with Taubes the continuation of the logos theology of Origen, as well as the notion of the coincidence of opposites (as found in Joachim of Flores and Nicholas of Cusa) in Hegel's dialectical philosophy. On the other hand, Tillich was also well aware that the logical and necessary reconciliation involved in Hegel's thought was bound to blur the distinction between the divine and human, the infinite and the finite, and accordingly referred to this element in Hegel's thought as *hybris,* ("the self-elevation toward the realm of the divine.")[13]

Despite the close structural and formal dependence on Hegelian dialectic, the roots of Tillich's thought are to be traced, not to Hegel, but rather to those who used Hegelian categories, such as "estrangement," to refute Hegel's attempt to reconcile in thought what was not reconciled in reality.[14] It is to Marx and Nietzsche, Kierkegaard and Schelling that we are to look for our clue to the meaning of Tillich's dialectic. In view of Tillich's academic background and the genesis of his intellectual growth, we are not surprised to discover strong traces of Hegelian concepts and categories, as well as terminology, in Tillich's formulations. But we must not conclude from this that Tillich used these concepts and categories in the same sense and in the same way as Hegel. In a reply to the philosopher Gordon D. Kaufman, Tillich reminds the reader of this important distinction concerning his dependence upon Hegel:

> The concepts of "estrangement" and "reconciliation" are important in all periods of Hegel's thinking: but I learned their realistic significance only through the attack on Hegel's belief in an already reconciled existence, as was done by his pupils, Karl Marx and Søren Kierkegaard, who used Hegel's own concepts against Hegel.[15]

The principal divergence of Tillich's thought from that of Hegel centers around the transition from essence to existence. For Tillich, following Schelling, it was the irrational, that is, an act of pure freedom,[16] as opposed to Hegel's necessary dialectical deduction from essence, that accounted for the reality of finite existence. In Hegel's system there was no real Fall: existence was viewed as a necessary, temporary process, and estrangement within the process was overcome by its own inner and necessary dynamic: "There is only distance between the actual and the ideal, which optimistically is ever decreasing."[17]

Daniel Day Williams has rightly pointed out in this regard that Tillich's most important debt to Boehme and Schelling is his assertion of "the reality of freedom in the life of God himself"—a freedom that brings about reconciliation through freely bestowed grace, rather than through objective reason.[18] The injection of this element of the irrational or pure freedom into the basic pattern of Hegelian dialectic leaves Tillich's system open-ended, as opposed to Hegel's. Furthermore, it guarantees the preservation of divine transcendence, at least in Tillich's terms. For although there is a clearly epistemological element in Tillich's notion of transcendence, i.e., man cannot know God unless God reveals himself to man, transcendence also has a more basic ontological significance. It means that the gap between the finite and the infinite is impassable: *transcendence is essentially related to the gratuity of the divine Grace or Spiritual Presence.* As a finite being I cannot come to God, unless He chooses to manifest his presence to me.

The human spirit is unable to compel the divine Spirit to enter the human spirit. . . The finite cannot force the infinite; man cannot compel God.[19]

The infinite is present in everything finite, in the stone as well as in the genius. Transcendence demanded by religious experience is the freedom-to-freedom relationship which is actual in every personal encounter.[20]

Tillich's principle of the convergence of the sacred and the secular, although sharing certain convictions with Religious Humanism, does not blur the distinction between the divine Spirit and the human spirit. Tillich's God does not become "an immanent principle," nor can his theology be adequately described as "dionysiac" or "ecstatic naturalism" without effecting a serious misunderstanding of his thought. Similarly, the evidence we have considered establishes that Tillich is not a "humanist in disguise." What he shares with humanism is a rejection of supranaturalism that would make God a "highest Being" and set the divine law over against autonomous reason. Theonomy is autonomous reason united to its own depth, but this depth has an abysmal character and infinitely transcends the finite being of which it is the ultimate source of meaning and power of being. In Tillich's dialectic the Divine Reality is present *paradoxically* in finite being.[21]

The affirmation of life and the importance of the "here and now"   Secular Humanism is concerned with this life and considers it highly unlikely that there is a future existence beyond the grave.[22] H. J. Blackham, an eloquent and dedicated spokesman for the Humanist movement in Great Britain, uses the formula "man is on his own and this life is all" to define one of the most basic Humanist tenets. The philosophical school in the United States that has been most directly allied with the Humanists is American Naturalism. John Dewey, Sidney Hook, Roy Wood Sellars, Irwin Edman, John H. Randall, Jr., Joseph L. Blau, and Corliss Lamont—all concerned and outspoken Humanists—have related philosophically to the school of Naturalism. Unfortunately, there is a frequent popular misconception about philosophic Naturalism. It is too often confused with nineteenth-century scientific materialism—a dogmatic "body of ideas founded on a reductive analysis of all processes to the motion of masses . . . to blind mechanical conjunctions of material entities" that were presumed to explain "all distinctively human values, moral, aesthetic, logical" by means of these motions and entities.[23] Yet once we deliver materialism from this crass and outdated interpretation, Naturalistic Humanism can be said to be materialistic, insofar as it is opposed to any treatment of spirit or spiritual goods that excludes nature and matter from its orbit of concern. "Humanism," states *Manifesto I,* "believes that man is a part of nature and that he has emerged as the result of a continuous process."[24]

Humanism, stated differently, is "this-worldly"; with Hume, it repudiates the "monkish virtues"—"It rules out the metaphysical dualisms which divide the universe into two separate realms, a material and a spiritual one; and which also divide man himself into two separate entities, hence making inevitable a dualistic psychology and a dualistic ethics."[25]

In this sense, Tillich's thought, too, must be considered essentially materialistic and this-worldly. This follows logically from his rejection of any supernatural order or purely sacred history. Tillich does not speak of "soul" but of "spirit," and spirit is for him an achievement and development of organic material existence. Tillich rejected all thinking in terms of separate levels or orders of reality, insofar as this denies in theory what we note in experience—an organic movement and interaction from one realm to another.

Modern biology and psychology have made us more aware of the influence of organic and even inorganic processes on man's intellectual and creative activities, in a word, on his spiritual life. When spirit is identified with mind or soul and seen as belonging to a superior level of life, Tillich claims that it is rightfully resented by the scientist as the establishment of a "separate substance exercising a particular causality," *interfering* in the biological and psychological process. Accordingly, Tillich speaks of "spirit" as a dimension of material organic life, which is present potentially even in the inorganic realm. The dimensions of life are unified in the life process and become actualized and distinct only when particular constellations occur in the lower dimension that supports them. In Volume 3 of the *Systematic*, Tillich distinguishes the following principal dimensions of life that increase in value from the lower to the higher, and yet interpenetrate each other at all times:

The Multidimensional Unity of Life

historical—the dimension under which new meaning is created; it presumes the development of the peculiarly human or "spiritual" dimension.

spiritual—the personal-communal realm that is proper to man; it can be actualized under special conditions of inner awareness in the organic dimension.

organic—to this dimension belongs the basic meaning of "life"; that which is organic is alive. Within this dimension appears "self-awareness," which is proper to animals.

inorganic—this is the basic dimension of existence, and the first condition for the actualization of every further dimension.[26]

Within the present context of the "affirmation of life," the spiritual dimension is for Tillich a development within the animal and psychological realm. It does not mean separated spirit or soul as opposed to body. Spirituality, in short, is a dimension of organic material reality. "Spirit" is defined by Tillich as the "unity of power and meaning." It presumes and is thoroughly grounded in material, organic life. Accordingly, Tillich's concept of "spirit" is diametrically opposed to Descartes' notion of the soul as a "ghost in a machine."

Tillich's opposition to supernaturalism is strongly implied in his doctrine of the multidimensional unity of life. With supernaturalism goes any literal interpretation of the biblical stories of the origins of life:

> These considerations reject implicitly the doctrine that at a precise moment of the evolutionary process God in a special act added an "immortal soul" to an otherwise complete human body, with this soul bearing the life of the spirit. This idea—in addition to being based on the metaphor "level" and a corresponding supranaturalistic doctrine of man—disrupts the multidimensional unity of life, especially the unity of the psychological and the spirit, thus making the dynamics of the human personality completely incomprehensible.[27]

For Tillich both the existence and the survival of disembodied spirits are outside the realm of theological interest and are best regarded as matters of empirical investigation for the anthropologists. He totally rejects a conceptual (as opposed to symbolic) understanding of "immortality" as "a continuation of the temporal life of an individual after death without a body."[28] He agrees with Hume's and Kant's attacks on immortality as the concept of a naturally immortal substance (the soul), and considers the Christian symbol of "resurrection of the body" as the more representative expression of Christian eschatological hope, especially when it is understood as including all dimensions of being. All traditional Christian emphasis on salvation of the soul, bodiless intermediary states, or "an unsymbolic application of measurable time to life beyond death"[29] is totally foreign and unaccepta-

ble to Tillich's theological perspective. If, then, by the term
materialist one understands simply the rejection of the notion
of an immaterial soul and the existence of a spirit realm apart
from concrete, material life, as we know it, then Tillich is
certainly a materialist.

Although Tillich's doctrine of "spirit" is clearly out of
harmony with the beliefs and attitudes of large numbers of the
Christian faithful, as expressed in many official church con-
fessions as well as in popular folk-beliefs, it finds much
support in the evidence of current New Testament research.
An ever-growing number of leading New Testament scholars
have accepted that the predominant early Christian conception of man was monistic. Man was understood as a unity of
matter and spirit; nature and matter were included within the
scope of the divine work of redemption.[30] Tillich's doctrine
of man, his emphasis on "resurrection" rather than immortality, his concept of the multidimensional unity of reality, and his preference for the term "centered self" or "personal center"[31] rather than "mind" or "soul" are reflective of
this New Testament perspective. It is unfortunate that in
attacking the Christian view of human destiny, Humanists
too often overlook these current theological developments,
and oppose their own views to the less critical and more
outmoded expressions of Christian belief.[32]

Although Tillich's doctrine of the unity of man and the
unity of reality are generally compatible with the humanist
outlook, Tillich also very seriously propounds the reality of
Eternal Life and the transcendent Kingdom of God. Even
though Tillich does not tire of reminding his readers of the
symbolic nature of such terms, a careful analysis of their
meaning in his system should easily prevent the error of
equating Tillich's view with the Secular Humanist conviction
that "this life is all and enough."[33] Although a detailed
analysis of these theological symbols is not possible within
this study, the following observations should sufficiently
indicate the gap that separates Tillich's thought from Secular
Humanism on this question.

1. The symbol of Eternal Life is for Tillich an aspect of his

fundamental ontological doctrine of the essential participation of finite being in the infinite, divine life: "The hope of eternal life is based not on a substantial quality of man's soul but on his participation in the eternity of the divine life."[34] Eternal life is not a time after time, but yet it is above time; it transcends time. It is the return to man's eternal Divine Ground that makes man eternal.

2. All of life in the state of existential estrangement is filled with ambiguity. Even the self-transcendence of life in religion cannot escape this essential ambiguity and finitude. Unambiguous life is received only by the power of God. The religious symbols for this gift of unambiguous Life are The Spirit of God, Kingdom of God, and Eternal Life.[35] "There is *one* power," wrote Tillich in one of his sermons, "that surpasses the all-consuming power of time—the eternal: He Who was and is to come, the beginning and the end . . . He gives us rest in His eternal Presence."[36]

3. Just as man in his spiritual dimension experiences the ambiguities of Life that call for the unambiguous Eternal Life, so also in the historical dimension, the only answer is the religious symbol "Kingdom of God." But the Kingdom of God "is the promise and expectation of the supra-historical fulfillment of history."[37] Although it does have an inner-historical as well as a trans-historical or transcendent aspect, the inner-historical power of the Kingdom is experienced only in a moment of *kairos* ("the breakthrough of the Eternal into historical time").

Despite the validity of these important distinctions, we must never undermine the force of Tillich's affirmation of material nature and the rejection of any body-soul dualism. Similarly, he shared with Secular Humanism an unflagging concern for the importance of the "here and now." We saw earlier that Tillich's experience in the trenches of France, his involvement in the subsequent social revolution, and his intellectual confrontation with the thought of Karl Marx brought him to a much more vivid historical awareness.[38] Tillich's early reflections on the pressing problem of the interpretation of history developed into a position he called

"historical realism" with its essential stress on contemporaneity—on the significance of the "here and now." Ever
alert to the religious dimension of reality, Tillich added
the notion of "kairos" and thereby transformed historical
realism into a "belief-ful realism"—one in which the ultimate
meaning of history could be discovered in decision and faith.
Humanists, such as Frankel, share Tillich's view on the great
importance of the interpretation of history in our cultural
situation,[39] but they certainly find little sympathy with his
concern for faith and divine breakthroughs. Like the
Humanists and unlike so much of traditional Christian
teaching, Tillich took time and the present with extreme
seriousness; he reproached our Western culture for its lack of
courage to accept the "present"; he reproved Christians for
their escape to the false consolations of "life after death."[40]

Still, Tillich's emphasis on the "here and now" was essentially tied to his notion of the breakthrough of the eternal that
gives meaning to the present moment. "There is no other way
of judging time than to see it in the light of the eternal."[41]
Furthermore, as we have seen in Tillich's doctrine of the
Kingdom of God, despite all the importance of contemporaneity, the decisive *telos* is yet to come; the *kairos* is not
the *eschaton*. "The fulfillment of history lies in the perma-
nently present end of history, which is the transcendent side
of the Kingdom of God: i.e., Eternal Life."[42] In his interpretation of history, then, Tillich maintains the inner tension,
characteristic of Christian eschatology, between the "here
and now" and the "not yet." This is hardly reconcilable with
the humanist notion of temporality. It is noteworthy,
nevertheless, that as long as the notion of "belief-ful realism"
remained a central concept in his system (i.e., during his
German period), Tillich's work was seriously engaged in the
concrete social and political issues of the time.

If we detect a certain uneasiness in Tillich's attempt to
balance in his theology of culture a "this-worldly" concern
with an equally emphatic insistence on a trans-historical
Kingdom of God, we cannot, nevertheless, conclude (with
Taubes) that this is to be attributed to Tillich's "Dionysiac

theology," which simply "does not lead to a 'beyond'," but signifies only an "intensity of the immanent."[43] The real cause of this tension and uneasiness is deeper; it is part of a fundamental ambiguity or paradox innate to the Gospel message, of which, after all, Tillich is a contemporary spokesman. Taubes, rather inconsistently, shows a clear awareness of the same root cause earlier in the same article:

> The Christian community was thrown into history against her expectations and against her will, and the hiatus between the eschatological symbols of faith and man's continuing existence in history is as old as the history of the Christian Church.[44]

Thus although there are some major aspects of agreement and emphasis between Tillich and Secular Humanism, these do not hide the equally fundamental differences, which also became apparent in the course of our analysis. We are reminded that Tillich's key concept of "theonomy" is the symbol of a religious Humanism, in the more confessional sense of that term. Theonomy is, after all, an attempt to offer an alternative for today's religious man, who is at the same time thoroughly imbued with the spirit of contemporary humanism. In this way, Tillich hoped to provide a bridge or point of contact between the serious-minded humanist and the humanistic Christian or Jew. He was neither openly promoting Secular Humanism as an alternative to biblical faith nor surreptitiously promulgating Humanist ideals under the protective camouflage of Christian symbols.

Despite Similarities Tillich Is Not a Humanist in Disguise

In brief, Tillich was a humanist but not a *secular* humanist of any form or variety. His 1958 address "Humanität und Religion"[45] can be seen as a formal declaration of the essential humanism of his thought. On the other hand, our analysis of the whole structure and development of Tillich's theology of culture has also drawn our attention to some notable and substantial differences between his outlook and that of the Secular Humanists. We contend that the more one explores the two positions in depth the less similar they begin to appear. Indeed, that which on the surface presents itself as a substantial point of agreement upon further inquiry vividly illustrates the root opposition between the two interpretations of culture. The outstanding case of this paradoxical situation is exemplified best by the notion of "revelation" as conceived by Tillich and by the "religious" Humanists.

Sir Julian Huxley, as well as a number of American Naturalists, have attributed some sort of objective reality to the notion of religious revelation. Randall, for example, maintains that there are "qualities of reality or of the world which act upon man, disclosing or revealing authentic powers in things."[46] Woodbridge, on his part, even uses the metaphor of *depth* to describe the existence of the supernatural in nature,[47] and Edman points out that the religions serve to draw attention to certain aspects of man's relation to nature which might otherwise be overlooked.[48] In short, revelation is by no means simply a question of projection or of creative imagination. It is not presented as a case of man speaking to himself—the way Tillich once described the humanist conception of revelation.

Our principal task at this point, then, is to show that despite these close affinities between Tillich's "depth theology" and the religious vision of these Humanists, the two views are, in the last analysis, even on this question of revelation, mutually incompatible. The following observations are intended to substantiate and clarify the most basic grounds of this incompatibility.

In the first place, the similarity we have encountered between Tillich's theonomy and the views of these American Naturalists represents only one side of the picture. The purely secular humanism of Russell, Hook, Edwards, Ayer, and many others is strongly opposed to attributing any kind of objective reality to the religious dimension. They would consider it either nonsense, fantasy, or the product of wishful thinking. In Tillich's terms they have simply lost the dimension of depth. We have already recognized that there are really two very different types of Secular Humanism, and that one of these, at least, stands irreconcilably opposed to Tillich's theology of culture. What all types of Secular Humanism share in common is only the most general humanistic attitude of "cherishing humanity" and recognizing the dignity and autonomy of human intelligence. Wheat, therefore, in attributing to Tillich a disguised secular humanism in which he is clandestinely declaring the divinity of mankind,[49] is guilty of overlooking the whole religious thrust of Tillich's thought. Wheat manages to do this by an incredibly selective and singularly arbitrary reading of Tillich's work.[50] That Wheat's conclusion is totally without foundation and contrary to the evidence of Tillich's own writings is not difficult to show. We need simply recall some of the most relevant conclusions that were previously established:

a. Unlike the Secular Humanists, Tillich's opposition to supernatural religion did not deny the reality of the Spiritual Presence or the Ground of Being. In fact, Tillich strongly opposed any merely "man-centered" theology. Theonomy, although preserving the dignity and autonomy of man's finite existence, sees his real value and worth as his participation in the Eternal Ground of his being, i.e., in Ultimate Reality.

b. The theological system of Tillich is thoroughly rooted in the ontology of Schelling, which is an attempt to explain the relationship between finite and infinite, between conditioned and Unconditioned Being. Schelling's system emphasized the "absolute break" between everything finite and its infinitely transcending creative Ground. Tillich, like his philosophical master, put great stress on the immanence of the divine, but like Schelling again, he also insisted that man cannot cross the infinite threshold that separates him from the divine Ground except by a free act of divine self-giving. The absolute transcendence of God is preserved.

Tillich had a very exalted view of the divine majesty, which was the very basis for his opposition to "Supranaturalism." To make God a being beside other beings, he insisted, is to take away the divinity of the divine. Although Tillich had his own (Schellingian) notion of transcendence, even in terms of the classical definition, i.e., that "God's being is essentially distinct and different—not separate—from all that is in the world,"[51] Tillich's God, without any doubt, absolutely transcends human nature. Wheat's attempt, therefore, to identify Tillich's Divine Ground of Being with humanity is a total distortion of Tillich's thought.

Theologians might question—and, indeed, a number have—whether the categories of romantic idealism, in general, and of Paul Tillich, in particular, are suitable for expressing the biblical concept of God. But there have been a number of different conceptions of God in the Judaeo-Christian tradition. Theologians will continue to dispute this issue in the future. What we can say for certain is that Tillich appealed to Schelling's ontology to defend the reality of the religious power that permeates man's total experience, but which cannot be derived therefrom. Man's religious experience, according to Schelling, derives from the depths of reality itself. In Tillich's understanding, the German idealists, in general, and especially Schelling, were really theologians at heart. Their philosophy represents a philosophical transformation of the traditional Christian symbols. Tillich's heavy and enduring debt to Schelling throughout his long career leaves little credibility to the charge that Tillich was a secular humanist in disguise.

c. Tillich's doctrine of the religious symbol, whatever might be its weaknesses and limitations, is fundamentally an attempt to speak meaningfully and intelligibly about God and the religious dimension, while preserving the infinite distance between God and man, between the Unconditioned Reality and conditioned finite being. That is why religious symbols must negate their own literal meaning and point beyond themselves to "the Holy-Itself, the ultimate power of being and meaning."[52] These symbols are *not* arbitrary, nor are they a substitute for a more honest, direct, and literal expression. Symbols are, indeed, the only proper and fitting language to express religious experience, for here we are dealing with the Ultimate Reality, which transcends by its very nature all objective, finite categories.

When Wheat complains that "Tillich is bluntly asserting that God is a symbol, nothing more,"[53] he reveals a blatant misunderstanding of Tillich's doctrine of the religious symbol. For Tillich fought during most of his career to combat the notion of a "mere" symbol. He insisted that a symbol is not less, but more than a literal assertion.[54] Finally, Wheat is seriously misinterpreting Tillich in maintaining that he simply equates "God" with a religious symbol. Tillich himself explicitly rejected this interpretation:

> . . . we cannot say that God is a symbol. We must always say two things about him: we must say that there is a non-symbolic element in our image of God—namely that he is ultimate reality, being itself, ground of being, power of being; and the other, that he is the highest being, in which everything that we have does exist in the most perfect way.[55]

d. Tillich's theonomous vision differs substantially even from that of "religious humanism," i.e., the more religiously oriented Secular Humanists. It is crucial to show this, for even Wheat cannot fail to notice the strong religious thrust that permeates all of Tillich's work. Wheat chalks this up to a kind of "religious humanism," which once having lost a genuine religious faith (for Wheat this means supernaturalism), turns to an ersatz faith and an ersatz god. Once again, the god to whom Tillich is supposed to have turned with all his religious dedication is "humanity."[56]

The kind of religious humanism that Wheat has in mind is far from being an obscure movement; it has been the object of scholarly study and has frequently boasted gifted and articulate spokesmen. These pioneers of contemporary Humanism who were a major driving force behind the *First Humanist Manifesto*[57] came primarily from the ranks of the Unitarian clergy, and include such notables as Curtis Reese, John H. Dietrich, and Charles Francis Potter. Their sermons and writings reveal not only a very interesting and very characteristically American brand of religion[58] but they also make clear the incompatibility of their stance with that of Tillich's humanistic theology.

It has already been pointed out that the Religious Humanists recognize and assert only the human qualities of religious experience. Religious humanism sacralizes that which is noblest and best in man, or to use Julian Huxley's phrase, "the fullest realization of his own inherent possibilities."[59] Religious humanism is secular in that it denies the validity of special revelation and the authority of the religious institutions whose teachings depend on such revelation. It is also secular, in the broader sense, in its thoroughgoing man-centeredness or anthropocentrism.

Randall, who has his own brand of religious humanism, which merits special attention, makes a very clear distinction between the religious humanism of Reese and the Unitarians, on the one hand, and Tillich's theonomous view of reality, on the other. Randall's explanation makes use of his own view of religion as an art—an art that has two essential ingredients: a human function and a divine action. The religious humanist, Randall maintains, stresses only one ingredient—the human function, i.e., the human discerning of what is revealed.[60] Tillich, on the other hand, continues Randall, puts far greater stress on the divine action; "Religion is the state of *being grasped* by an Ultimate Concern." This latter emphasis, according to Randall, is indicative of the attitude of humility that is characteristic of traditional biblical faith. Randall, who knows Tillich's thought far better than most critics of Tillich, had no difficulty in identifying the fundamental differences that separate Tillich's religious attitude from that of the Religious Humanists.

e. Tillich's theology of culture is, finally, not to be confused with any kind of religious naturalism, including that proposed by Randall and other American Naturalists. Randall, too, was a signer of both *Humanist Manifestoes;* he is secular in his rejection of the claims of biblical religion.[61] Furthermore, though Randall will not identify with the position of the Religious Humanists that has been discussed, he is a "religious humanist" in the sense that he insists that any view of man that neglects the religious dimension is seriously truncated.[62] It is Randall's naturalism that separates his thought from that of the Unitarians. Like Woodbridge and Edman, Randall sees the religious dimension as reflecting real powers in nature that are able to evoke religious vision in man. Is it possible that Wheat was correct after all? Is Tillich, in the last analysis, despite the great difference in language, a religious humanist of the naturalistic type? Can Tillich's theology, after all, be justly classified, as Taubes has suggested, as a kind of "ecstatic naturalism."[63]

For an answer to this question we do well to return to Randall's philosophy of religion, particularly as it is crystallized in the *Amherst Symposium* in 1958 at Amherst College, at which Tillich and Randall were the major participants.[64] Both of these scholars attempted to clarify their similarities and differences on the nature of religion. In a discussion that was in fact a continuation of many years of intellectual exchange at Columbia University, it readily became apparent to the audience that the agreements between the two far outweighed the differences. At times, the primarily youthful audience seemed to grow a bit impatient, having anticipated more of a head-on collision between a humanist and a Christian theologian. At one point in the symposium, when it came time for a response from Tillich to the positions outlined by Randall, Tillich had to admit that though he was listening, "he tried in vain to find points of attack."[65] Tillich, nevertheless, did proceed with his response, in order, as he said, "to clear up a few points," and only at this juncture in the otherwise extremely amicable discussion did the real differences between Randall's naturalistic humanism and Tillich's humanistic theology begin to emerge:

1. Randall sees religion as one of several important human arts and functions. It does not have for him the same kind of ultimacy that it has for Tillich. To highlight this difference, Randall purposely substituted the term "organizing concern" for Tillich's familiar "ultimate concern" as better representing his understanding of "the religious transaction."[66]

2. Although both Randall and Tillich agreed that a plurality of powers act upon man in his religious experience, and that religious vision serves to *unify* all this, together with our

secular dimensions of experience, the actual unification is for
Randall the work of the human mind and imagination,
whereas for Tillich there is an *antecedent unification*. This
consists in the actual unity of everything finite within the
Eternal Ground of Being: "The creative process of the divine
life precedes the differentiation between essences and exis-
tents."[67] Although we recognize how strongly opposed Tillich was to any supernaturalistic notion of God as a being
besides other beings, we must not forget that for him, the
authentic object of man's ultimate concern is not a
psychological, subjective creation of man, nor a unifying
vision of the forces that man encounters in nature, but only
and uniquely the Ultimate ontological Reality or Being-Itself.
These two positions, despite their many resemblances in
attitude, are radically different in substance.[68]

New Directions for Tillich's Theonomous Vision

Although we have unambiguously supported the validity of
Tillich's overall interpretation of culture and, in particular, of
his appraisal of secular humanism as an alternative for modern
man, a number of weaknesses do appear in the course of
scrutinizing his ideas. If the reader has begun to share our
high evaluation of Tillich's theology of culture as truly reflective of the human cultural situation and as potentially productive of a more authentically human society, we feel the need
of sharing with the reader our reflections on ways of overcoming these weaknesses. It is our contention that certain
correctives and new directions are required if there is to be
real and continuous progress toward achieving the goals and
ideals that Tillich has so carefully mapped out for us.

*A more accurate and detailed knowledge of cultural
movements*   In the American period of his career Tillich was
writing to an English-speaking audience, and though the
terms he often so ingeniously chose were English, the thought
behind them remained unmistakably German. Although Tillich does make many passing references in his work to

American philosophers, such as Dewey, James, and Wieman, the alert reader is not convinced that Tillich knows their thought in depth. Although the reader can certainly detect a touch of Heidegger and a careful sprinkling of psychoanalytic terminology in Tillich's writings, his idiom remains essentially that of nineteenth-century German romanticism.[69] This is evidently not what we should expect from a theologian who is trying to bridge the gap between Christian revelation and modern secular culture, especially in an American or British situation. Writing of Tillich's philosophical categories, Randall states that "This is all good Schelling . . ." but . . . "one wonders whether it is the thought form of contemporary culture."[70] The same difficulty prods Malcolm Diamond, despite his profound appreciation for Tillich's genius, to pose the sensible question: "Why talk Tillichese?"[71]

There can be no doubt that Tillich's interpretation of contemporary culture and secular humanism through the dialectical categories of heteronomy—autonomy—theonomy has a great deal of merit. It opens up important insights about the nature of religion, in general, and its relationship to secular culture, in particular. Like all idealist structures, however, it cannot by itself provide an adequate substitute for a detailed study of particular humanist philosophers and secular cultural movements. Tillich's categories for explaining secularity and humanism were already established by the time he arrived in America, as his early writings show. Unfortunately, his work in this country involved too much forcing of secular thought into this preestablished framework and too little reworking of the framework for the sake of accommodating the particulars of new information and new insights.

In short, although the insights of Tillich's theology of culture are profound, those who would follow up on these insights would do well to criticize, concretize and verify them through a much greater concern for the uniqueness and specificity of the phenomena under study. Certainly, they should acquire a far more precise and detailed knowledge of important contemporary cultural movements than their theological mentor appears to have done in respect to the Humanist movement in America.

Greater precision and responsibility in the use of language Tillich's thought, as has been suggested, could be greatly improved by a "translation" of his German romantic idiom into one that is more intelligible in an Anglo-Saxon culture. The highly poetic and fanciful nature of this romantic imagery runs sharply counter to the empirical orientation that dominates in English-speaking cultures. Although Tillich's language has been known to enthrall and mystify, a sense of responsibility for intelligibility would require that the meaning of the many metaphors and symbols he regularly employed should be more carefully explained and used with greater precision and consistency. Mystification and the power of language, though they have their proper place, are not the main criterion for acceptable philosophical or theological language. Intelligibility and clarity play at least equally important roles.

In countries like the United States, Canada, Australia, and Britain where a powerful and vital tradition of analytical and language philosophy has blossomed in this century, the followers of Tillich would hardly go wrong in attempting to subject Tillichian thought and expression to the rigors and discipline of this philosophy of precision. Clearly, there is a serious risk of losing the power of Tillich's thought in attempting so difficult a task, but in light of the very goals of his theology of culture it is a risk that must be taken.

In recommending a closer interplay with contemporary analytic philosophy, we are not suggesting that Tillichians abandon the language of depth. Recent linguistic philosophers, such as P. F. Strawson, Donald D. Evans, and David Pole, developing directions indicated especially by the later Wittgenstein,[72] have seen the necessity of drawing attention to certain kinds of depth-experience, and analyzing the kind of language that is used to express such experience. Strawson, in particular, has attempted to construct a new type of metaphysics that would uncover and describe the depth of structures and relations that lie beneath the surface of ordinary and scientific language. The disciples of Tillich should have a very special interest in the success of these projects, and would do well to pursue this kind of development themselves. Tillich, although he found analytic philosophy too narrow in its horizon of interests, insisted that "it could become useful if it increased in reach and acceptance of realities beyond the mere logical calculus."[73]

Continued close interaction with the findings of psychological research Tillich, especially in his American period, showed great sensitivity and familiarity with the insights and theories of depth psychology and psychoanalysis. Perhaps more than any other single element, this accounted for the tremendous power of Tillich's thought. This was the one science that Tillich knew well, and his theories are widely known and highly valued among many professional psychologists. Furthermore, our studies of the research of Maslow and Laski reveal that clinical psychological investigations can do much to complement Tillich's general theories, clarifying through concrete instances concepts that might otherwise remain vague or ambiguous in their abstractness. Humanistic psychology, with its emphasis on the hidden potential of the normal personality and the importance of values, provides a particularly important source for this kind of interchange. Unfortunately, to date there have been too few studies of the Maslow and Laski kind into the psychology of intense religious and ecstatic experience of "depth."[74] Theologians of "depth" should encourage and follow such studies with great interest. Our conclusions in this respect are fully supported by the Swiss analytic philosopher I. M. Bochenski, who maintains that a "fully developed philosophy of religion would have to use phenomenological and analytic methods, while relying at the same time on the results of psychology."[75] Bochenski's formula might well encourage us to explore more fully the resources of American naturalism, an indigenous philosophical school of still untapped wealth, which strongly supports and fully incorporates the input of the sciences, including psychology, into the very structure of its method.[76] In general, Tillich's philosophy of culture is strong and insightful in its psychological and existential analysis of experience. An ongoing dialogue with naturalism would continue to develop this strength, and hopefully begin to inject a terminology and style that is less foreign to an American audience. There is still another area, perhaps more important, where naturalism could enrich and enhance a Tillichian analysis of culture. We devote the next section to its serious consideration.

Philosophical naturalism and the need for empirical grounding   American Naturalism grew up in an atmosphere of enthusiasm for the potential of scientific method. It was inspired primarily by Dewey, who brought American philosophy into line with America's scientific and technological development. Although Naturalism is also concerned with precision of thought and language, it nevertheless escapes the arbitrary and restricting boundaries of mind and sense perception we too often encounter in current English philosophy, which continues to exert an unduly dominant influence on American academic philosophy. Naturalism, in a way that can serve to complement analytic and linguistic philosophy, leaves itself open to a far broader empiricism. As Roy Wood Sellars once put it, British philosophy of language has been too subjectivistic and tends to cut itself off from science, whereas in Naturalism the very mechanism of perception itself is to be scrutinized with careful attention to the findings of science.[77] For the Naturalist, sensations are not terminal. Like the scientist the Naturalist must strive to "penetrate into the intrinsic structures of the universe" in such a way that he finds himself "at grips with reality."[78]

Naturalistic philosophy can, in principle, neglect no aspect of human experience, including the religious dimension. Edman, Woodbridge, and Randall all locate man's religious experience in the encounter he has with nature. Blau argued specifically that the strength of the empirical evidence showing man's persistent belief in God makes it a proper subject matter for philosophical and humanistic investigation.[79]

All this suggests that for those who are impressed with Tillich's overall vision of life and culture, while at the same time feeling uncomfortable with his lack of empirical footing, might find in American Naturalism a good philosophical resource for providing Tillich's theology with a much needed grounding in the discoveries of science and an excellent check against unfolding a theology of culture that can only proceed at the expense of "by-passing the world around us."[80] When we consider the importance of "correlation" to Tillich's theological method, the potential advantages of dialogue with naturalism become even more apparent. Although Tillich was an undisputed master of existential analysis, what a boon it would be for his own goals if his disciples should learn to address more seriously our scientific discoveries about the natural world and the cosmos! Have not these discoveries captivated and fascinated the mind of contemporary man and to a great extent determined the questions he asks about the meaning of his existence?

A philosophy of being and "serving the logos"   Despite the strange sound of Tillichian language to the American ear, it has, nevertheless, the great merit of focusing our thought on the most crucial of all human concerns—the sense and meaning of our existence. It was the realization of this important feature that moved Randall, himself a metaphysician, to describe Tillich's philosophy as "a realistic interpretation of a world in which man can find a meaning for his life."[81] Despite the admitted vagueness and ambiguity in his philosophical language, Tillich, like so many of his nineteenth-century German predecessors, was dealing, as Randall acknowledges, with the important questions.[82]

Accordingly, we see great merit in retaining the language of "being," which characterizes Tillich's thought. Indeed, it would be quite impossible to dispense with it without abandoning the whole theological system, which is inextricably rooted in his philosophy of being. For Tillich, philosophy deals with the structure of being, whereas theology deals with the meaning of Being for us. The whole concept of theonomy and the root of Tillich's theology of culture depend upon his conception of God as Being-Itself. Rieunaud, author of a French commentary on Tillich's system, points out that "with the notion of theonomy, Tillich recaptures the royal road of German thought" and that "the secret of the depth of German philosophy is that is has never removed philosophical reflection from the problem of being, and that its great philosophers have never ceased to be, in a certain sense, theologians."[83] Tillich has successfully brought this rich tradition to the English-speaking world.

On the other hand, Tillich, also strongly insisted that theology must "serve the logos," i.e., it must assume intellectual responsibility for the intelligibility of its assertions. We have seen, however, that Tillich's language of being and its concomitant doctrine of symbols very often do not successfully serve the logos. For many humanists, in particular, Tillich's language is notoriously ambiguous if not fanciful. His own doctrine of symbolism, unfortunately, does not seem adequate as an explanation of the way his thought is related to reality.[84] The doctrine of symbolism remains far too vague; the content and meaning of the religious symbol is not very clear. His notion of symbol would fail to explain, for example, how the religious dimension and the religious vision in Tillich and Randall are substantially different. Tillichian metaphors, such as "depth," undoubtedly have their own power, but *alone* they are not sufficiently specific and precise to express a clear-cut intelligible meaning. To avoid the accusations of "pan-symbolism" or even "pan-fictionalism" the disciple of Tillich would do well to return to the *analogia entis,* which Tillich had abandoned too soon as an effective and responsible way of speaking about God or the religious dimension of culture, especially for those who are convinced they *must* approach reality through the philosophy of being. It has been widely recognized in recent philosophical developments that the notion of analogy can be recaptured today in a different framework, without the necessity of reaffirming a whole set of untenable medieval assumptions.[85]

In summary, we have found Tillich's overall theology of culture, with its critique of secular humanism and its outlines for a theonomous cultural situation, as essentially positive, profound, and filled with rich insights. In particular, we consider his notion of *theonomy* to be a very fertile philosophical concept, filled with important implications both for theology and for philosophy of culture. We agree with George Thomas' appraisal that "in general, Tillich's most distinctive and fruitful insights have been in the area of the relation of theology and culture."[86]

Conclusion

As we arrive at the end of our inquiry we can also reaffirm with greater confidence our complete concurrence with Paul Lehmann's judgment that no Protestant theologian "has addressed himself to the tremendous responsibility for culture . . . with the passion and persistence, the consecration and learning that marks Paul Tillich's life-long work."[87]

Although we have recognized the deficiencies in Tillich's system, we see them primarily as isolated and remediable items that do not substantially undermine the overall merit of Tillich's theology of culture as a whole. We have suggested specific directions that can be taken to help overcome these shortcomings and we are thoroughly convinced that with these guidelines and correctives, Tillich's theonomous outlook will continue to provide a reliable foundation as well as powerful motivation in the ongoing struggle for a truly human society.

From the point of view of personal and existential choices, Tillich's understanding of the relationship of our culture to its own spiritual depth provides the humanistic, secular-minded person with a real alternative between authoritarian religion, on the one hand, and shallow secularism, on the other. From the perspective of social and political concerns, Tillich's theonomous ideal offers a realistic vision to those who are actively committed to the search for justice and harmony in the public domain. From a specifically religious viewpoint, the Tillichian world view preserves a sensitivity to the New Testament hope in a coming *kairos* and helps create a greater openness and capacity to discern the breakthrough of the

196

Eternal into the situation of our time. By the same token, the paradigm of theonomy serves as a continual reminder that the joy of the Kingdom "is not to be reached by living on the surface," but only "by breaking through the surface, by penetrating the deep things of ourselves, of our world and of God."[88]

We recall that in his 1919 address on the theology of culture, Tillich had already laid out the principles and the program for his entire life project. To this program he remained faithfully committed to the end of his remarkable career. The vision of theonomy was conceived in his youth and never in Tillich's many years of scholarly growth and productivity did he ever swerve from his early conviction that the religious struggle of our time was not against the autonomy of contemporary culture, but rather against "the profanation, exhaustion and disintegration of culture in the latest epoch of mankind."[89]

It was for this reason that Tillich never tired of insisting that the struggle could only be successfully waged "under the banner of theonomy."[90]

List of Abbreviations

The following list of abbreviations covers two categories of works: (1) writings of Paul Tillich that are of particular importance to the theme of this book and (2) several key commentaries on Tillich's work that are referred to frequently in the course of this study.

Works by Tillich

CB   *The Courage to Be* (New Haven, Conn.: Yale University Press, 1952).

DF   *Dynamics of Faith* (New York: Harper & Row, 1957).

GW   *Gesammelte Werke,* Ed. Renate Albrecht. 14 vols. (Stuttgart: Evangelisches Verlagswerk, 1959–75). (For further details of publication, *see* Bibliography).

IH   *The Interpretation of History* (New York: Charles Scribner's Sons, 1936).

LL   "The Self-Understanding of Man in Contemporary Thought." The Lowell Lectures delivered at King's Chapel, Boston, 1958. Series of six lectures: (1) Art and Literature, (2) Philosophy and Science, (3) Religion and Theology, (4) Surface and Depth, (5) Thing and Self, and (6) Estrangement and Return.

OITC   "On the Idea of a Theology of Culture." In *What Is Religion?* Trans. and ed. James Luther Adams (New York: Harper & Row, 1969).

PE   *The Protestant Era* (Chicago: University of Chicago Press, 1948).

RS   *The Religious Situation* (New York: Meridian Books, 1956).

ST   *Systematic Theology,* 3 vols. (Chicago: University of Chicago Press, 1951–63).

TC   *Theology of Culture*, Ed. Robert C. Kimball. (New York: Oxford University Press, 1959).

Commentaries

JPG   Jean-Paul Gabus, *Introduction à la Théologie de la Culture de Paul Tillich* (Paris: Presses Universitaires de France, 1969).

K and B   *The Theology of Paul Tillich*, Ed. Charles W. Kegley and Robert W. Bretall (New York: Macmillan Publishing Co., 1964).

PCSR   James Luther Adams, *Paul Tillich's Philosophy of Culture, Science and Religion* (New York: Harper & Row, 1965).

Notes

Chapter 1

1. K and B, p. 161.
2. This expression was used independently as a description of Tillich's thought by John H. Randall, Jr., and Joseph L. Blau, both humanist philosophers, in personal interviews conducted by this writer (New York: Columbia University, November 1970; on tape).
3. Leonard F. Wheat, *Paul Tillich's Dialectical Humanism: Unmasking the God Above God* (Baltimore, Md.: The John Hopkins Press, 1970).
4. Paul Lehmann, "Review of Tillich's, *The Protestant Era*", *Union Theological Seminary Quarterly Review* 4, no. 2 (January 1949); reprinted in *Journal of Religion*, 46, no. 3 (April 1966, Paul Tillich: in Memoriam): 199.
5. TC, p. v.
6. *See* John Macquarrie, *God and Secularity, New Directions in Theology Today,* (Philadelphia: Westminster Press, 1967), vol. 3, p. 69, for a clear and succinct expression of the dialectical attitude of theology to the secular: "The church serves the world not by capitulating to it but by maintaining a dialectical attitude that both accepts and rejects, and in everything seeks to bring both church and world to deeper self-understanding."
7. *See* "Latin Vulgate Edition of the New Testament," *Novum Testamentum Graece et Latine,* ed. S. J. Augustinus Merk, 8th ed. (Rome: Pontifical Biblical Institute, 1957).
8. These few sample instances, showing the etymological development of the term *secular* are found in Charlton T. Lewis and Charles Short, *A Latin Dictionary* (Oxford: Clarendon Press, 1958), p. 1613.
9. *Hastings Encyclopedia of Religion and Ethics,* s.v. "Secularism."
10. Ibid.
11. Martin Marty, *The Modern Schism: Three Paths to the Secular* (New York: Harper & Row, 1969), p. 19.
12. *See* Alan Richardson, *Religion in Contemporary Debate* (London: SCM Press, 1966), p. 41.
13. Marty, *Modern Schism,* p. 95–108.
14. For a well-documented and illuminating development of this concept, *see:*

Robert N. Bellah, "Civil Religion in America," *Daedalus*, "Religion in America" issue 96 (Winter 1967): 1–21; Horace M. Kallen, *Secularism Is the Will of God: An Essay in the Social Philosophy of Democracy and Religion* (New York: Twayne Publishers, 1954); Robert Handy, *A Christian America* (New York: Oxford University Press, 1971); Sidney E. Mead, *The Lively Experiment: The Shaping of Christianity in America* (New York: Harper & Row, 1963).

15. Following are some of the key works dealing with this debate: Larry Shiner, "The Concept of Secularization in Empirical Research," *Journal for the Scientific Study of Religion* 6, no. 2 (Fall 1967): 207–20; Thomas O'Dea, "Secularism's Challenge" (Unpublished paper delivered at the Divinity School, Harvard University; at Colloquium on Judaism and Christianity, October 17–20, 1966); Arnold E. Van Loen, *Secularization*, trans. Margaret Kohn (London: SCM Press, 1967); Guy Swanson, "Modern Secularity," *The Religious Situation 1968*, ed. Donald R. Cutler (Boston: The Beacon Press, 1968), pp. 801–34; Huston Smith, "Secularization and the Sacred," *Religious Situation*, pp. 583–600; J. Milton Yinger, *The Scientific Study of Religion* (New York: The Macmillan Co., 1970), espec. pp. 490–94; Other appropriate references are found in the Bibliography.

16. Peter L. Berger, *The Sacred Canopy: Elements of a Sociological Theory of Religion* (Garden City, N. Y.: Doubleday & Company, Inc., 1967), p. 107.

17. Thus, for example, both O'Dea, "Secularism's Challenge," and Van Loen, *Secularization*, as well as Vernon Pratt, *Religion and Secularization* (London: Macmillan & Co., 1970), and Bernard Lonergan, "The Absence of God in Modern Culture," *The Presence and Absence of God*, ed. Christopher F. Mooney, S. J. (The Cardinal Bea Lectures; New York: Fordham University Press, 1969), pp. 164–78.

18. Peter McCaffery, "Secularization and Atheism," in *Talking with Unbelievers*, Part I, ed. Peter Hebblethwaite, S. J. (Douglas, Isle of Man: Month Publishers, 1970), p. 31.

19. The reality and seriousness of this crisis has been emphasized by O'Dea and Van Loen, as well as by René Dubos, *So Human an Animal* (New York: Charles Scribner's Sons, 1968), pp. 14–15, and S. S. Acquaviva, "The Psychology of Dechristianization in the Dynamics of Industrial Society," *Social Compass* 8 (1960): 219.

20. Macquarrie, *God and Secularity*, p. 20.

21. *See*, for example, Macquarrie, *God and Secularity*, pp. 43–49; also Langdon Gilkey, *Naming the Whirlwind: The Renewal of God Language* (New York: The Bobbs-Merrill Co., 1967) and John E. Smith, *Experience and God* (New York: Oxford University Press, 1968), pp. 180–205.

22. Roger L. Shinn, *Man: The New Humanism, New Directions in Theology Today*, (London: Lutterworth Press, 1968), vol. 6, p. 24.

23. Macquarrie, *God and Secularity*, p. 21.

24. *The Humanist*, the journal of the American Humanist Association and the American Ethical Union, gives a brief explanation of the humanism it professes on the introductory page of each issue. It states: "Humanism sees man as a product of this world—of evolution and human history—and acknowledges no supernatural purposes."

In the March/April, 1970, issue, the American Humanist Association ran an advertisement in which it stated that one of the aims of the association is "to help humanism continue to develop as a contemporary alternative to traditional religion and philosophy."

The 1967 policy statement of the British Humanist Association, "Humanists and Society," published by the BHA, London, begins with the general statement of belief, namely, that man "must face his problems with his own moral and intellectual resources, without looking for supernatural aid."

25. A clear and representative expression of this position is found in Corliss Lamont's work, *The Philosophy of Humanism*, 5th ed. (New York: Frederick Ungar Publishing Co., 1965), p. 14: "Humanism is the viewpoint . . . that the supernatural, usually conceived of in the form of heavenly gods or immortal heavens, does not exist; and that human beings, using their own intelligence and cooperating liberally with one another, can build an enduring citadel of peace and beauty upon this earth."

26. In his work *An Historian's Approach to Religion* (London: Oxford University Press, 1956), Arnold J. Toynbee gives extensive documentation to support the thesis that the rise of secularism in the West was primarily the result of a mounting impatience and disillusionment with the evil and destruction caused by the constant religious strife and controversy in Europe.

27. This position was very clearly expressed by A. J. Ayer, Oxford philosopher and former president of the British Humanist Association, in a personal interview at Oxford University (June 23, 1971). Ayer maintained that whereas it was philosophy and reason that required him to reject a religious world view, personal choice alone accounted for his election of a humanist outlook.

28. See, for example, John Dewey's classic work, *A Common Faith* (New Haven, Conn.: Yale University Press, 1934), and John Herman Randall, Jr.'s representative study, *The Meaning of Religion for Man* (New York: Macmillan Publishing Co., 1946). Other American naturalist philosophers, such as Roy Wood Sellars, Frederick Woodbridge, and Joseph Blau, write in a similar vein (*see* the Bibliography).

Although British humanists are ordinarily less than enthusiastic about such religious concerns, there are some outstanding exceptions in their ranks. One such exception is the British biologist Julian Huxley as evidenced in his own classic work *Religion Without Revelation* (London: C. A. Watts & Co., 1967). Huxley was a former president of the British Humanist Association.

29. Horace M. Kallen, *Secularism Is the Will of God: An Essay in the Social Philosophy of Democracy and Religion* (New York: Twayne Publishers, 1954), p. 209.

30. See Shinn, *Man: The New Humanism*, pp. 29–30.

31. This claim is commonly made today not only by various humanist writers, as might well be expected, but frequently also by theologians and representatives of the major religious creeds. Thus, for example, "Pastoral Constitution on the Church in the Modern World," *The Documents of Vatican II*, ed. Walter Abbott, S. J. (New York: Corpus Books, 1966), pp. 207–09 and Paul Tillich, *Religiöse Verwirklichung* (Berlin: Furche-Verlag, 1930), p. 195.

32. In the personal interview previously cited (note 27), A. J. Ayer complained that the humanist movement, as a movement and organization, had for this and other reasons become "old-fashioned and archaic."

33. Shinn, *Man: The New Humanism,* p. 24.

34. *See* pp. 35–38.

35. Our definition of secular humanism, therefore, makes this outlook to be incompatible with the creeds of the traditional biblical religions, both Christian and Jewish, but does not require that it be opposed to what we have called a religious orientation toward life in this world. When such a religious attitude is present among secular humanists, however, it is always anthropocentric—centered on humanity and faith in human ability. A number of contemporary authors understand "secular" humanism in this way, and the U. S. Supreme Court recognized "Secular Humanism" as one of several nontheistic religions in America (the *Torcaso* vs. *the State of Maryland* case cited by Corliss Lamont, *The Philosophy of Humanism,* p. 24).

36. This is essentially the way Tillich defines what he calls "God-centered" theology, which he opposes to "man-centered" (liberal humanist) theology, on the one hand, and "demon-centered" (nihilist and existentialist), on the other (*See* LL, no. 3).

37. Lamont, *Philosophy of Humanism,* p. 8.

Chapter 2

1. ST, 1: 65. Referring to liberal theology as "humanistic" in this sense, Tillich writes: "Questions and answers were put on the same level of human creativity. Everything was said by man, nothing to man. But revelation is 'spoken' to man, not by man to himself."

2. LL, no. 3, "Religion and Theology."

3. Paul Tillich, "Humanität und Religion," GW 9: (article first published in *Hansischer Goethe-Preis 1958*; [Hamburg: Stiftung F.V.S., 1958], pp. 25–30), 114: "Wo die Ehre Gottes mit der Entehrung des Menschen erkauft ist, da ist in Wahrheit Gottes Name entehrt." This article represents Tillich's address on the occasion of receiving the 1958 Hanse-Goethe Award for service to humanity.

4. ST, 3: 67: "In spite of these dangers, I suggest using the word 'humanity' in the sense of the fulfillment of man's inner aim with respect to himself and his personal relations, in co-ordination with justice as the fulfillment of the inner aim of social groups and their mutual relations."

5. H. Richard Niebuhr, Preface to Tillich's RS, p. 13.

6. This photograph and others, taken from various periods in Tillich's life, are preserved in the Paul Tillich Archives, Andover-Harvard Divinity School Library.

7. Paul Tillich, *On the Boundary: An Autobiographical Sketch* (New York: Charles Scribner's Sons, 1936), p. 95 and "Autobiographical Reflections," K and B, pp. 12–13: *See also* Wilhelm Pauck and Marion Pauck, *Paul Tillich: His Life and Thought,* 2 vols. (New York: Harper & Row, 1976), 1: 40–56.

8. *See,* for example: Tillich, "Religion und Kultur," GW, 9: 85 and Tillich, "Das Evangelium und der Staat," GW, 9: 196.

9. Tillich, "Mystik und Schuldbewusstsein in Schellings philosophischer Entwicklung," GW, 1:93: "Je tiefer und absoluter das Schuldbewusstsein, desto höher die Erfassung der wahren Identität."

10. Paul Tillich, "Autobiographical Reflections," K and B, p. 12.

Specific reference to the feeling of guilt and responsibility following the war, as well as to his very early consciousness of social guilt, is found in Paul Tillich, *On the Boundary: An Autobiographical Sketch* (New York: Charles Scribner's Sons, 1966), p. 20, p. 32.

11. Tillich, "Autobiographical Reflections," p. 13.

12. PE, pp. 48–49, 56. See also *On the Boundary*, pp. 76–77 and Pauck, *Paul Tillich*, p. 73.

13. PE, p. 85.

14. Ibid., p. 88.

15. Ibid., p. 89. In this autobiographical note Tillich cites his early work, *Die Sozialistische Entscheidung* (Potsdam: Alfred Protte, 1933), as a specific treatment of the positive and negative aspects in Marx, which he describes in terms of prophetic elements and rational-scientific terminology, respectively. This work has recently appeared in English translation by Franklin Sherman as *The Socialist Decision* (New York: Harper & Row, 1977).

16. Aside from the previously mentioned work, the number of other articles that Tillich wrote on this question is quite remarkable, so that the quantity of such studies alone reflects the importance with which Tillich viewed Marx's work. The following are but representative of Tillich's later works on this topic:

"Prophetische und marxistische Geschichtsdeutung," GW, 6: 97–108, (between 1934–1936).

"Der Mensch im Christentum und im Marxismus," GW, 3: 194–209 (1952).

"Christentum und Marxismus," GW, 3: 170–77 (1953).

17. *See*, for example, PE, p. xiv: "We have . . . learned more from Marx's dialectical analysis of bourgeois society than from any other analysis of our period. We have found in it an understanding of human nature and history which is much nearer to the classical Christian doctrine of man with its empirical pessimism and its eschatological hope than is the picture of man in idealistic theology."

18. IH, p. 65. *See also* "Autobiographical Reflections," p. 13.

19. Tillich, "Autobiographical Reflections," p. 8, and Pauck, *Paul Tillich*, pp. 10–14.

20. Tillich, "Autobiographical Reflections," p. 10.

21. Tillich, "Humanität und Religion," p. 119: "Die erste und immer bleibende Antwort auf die Frage nach Religion und Humanität ist das Gewahrwerden dessen, was in der Tiefe geschieht, im Kampf der Mächte, der in jedem Einzelnen und in der Menschheit als ganzer gekämpft wird. Hier liegen die religösen Wurzeln der Humanität, hier wird über die Möglichkeit des Menschseins entschieden."

22. Tillich's debt to Schelling is explicitly acknowledged in several places in Tillich's writings. *See*, for example: *On the Boundary*, pp. 51–52; "Schelling und die Anfänge des existentialistischen Protestes," GW, 4: 113.

For studies dealing with Tillich's dependence on Schelling, *see:* D. J. O'Hanlon, S. J., "The Influence of Schelling on the Thought of Paul Tillich" (Ph.D. Doctoral diss., Rome: Pontificia Universitas Gregoriana, 1958).

Kenan Osborne, *New Being: A Study on the Relationship Between Conditioned and Unconditioned Being According to Paul Tillich* (The Hague: Martinus Nijhoff, 1969), pp. 69–76.

23. *See* Bernard Martin, *The Existentialist Theology of Paul Tillich* (New York: Bookman Associates), 1963, p. 112. In this excellent short study of Tillich's doctrine of man, Martin makes a good case for this position.

24. PE, pp. x–xi. Tillich first developed this understanding of the doctrine of justification in a 1924 essay, entitled "Rechtfertigung und Zweifel," *Vorträge der theologischen Konferenz zu Giessen* (Giessen: Alfred Topelmann, 1924), p. 39. We discuss this work in the following chapter.

25. CB, p. 58.

26. Frederick Bolman, Jr., "Introduction," *The Ages of the World (Die Weltälter*, 1813, trans., also Bolman) (New York: Columbia University Press, 1942), p. 36. For Schelling's original German work, *see:* Friedrich Wilhelm Joseph von Schelling, *Sämmtliche Werke*, 14 vols. (Stuttgart and Augsburg: Cotta, 1856–1861), 4: 571–746. Henceforward this collection is cited as SW.

27. Bolman, "Introduction," *Ages of the World*, p. 25. Tillich made frequent use of this Schellingian formula in his own work whenever he sought to characterize the most basic philosophical question. *See,* for example, ST, 1: 163; PE, p. 85. The formula is not original with Schelling and goes back at least to Leibniz. *See* G. W. Leibniz, "Principles of Nature and of Grace, founded on Reason," in *The Monadology*, trans. and ed. A. Latta (Oxford: Oxford University Press: 1898), par. 7–8. The original was written in French in 1714.

28. Tillich, in his essay, "Schelling und die Anfänge des existenzialistischen Protestes," *Zeitschrift für philosophische Forschung* 9 (1955): 197–209, comments on this important aspect of Schelling's opposition to Hegel: "Schelling war auf dem Weg zu etwas, das Hegel verborgen blieb . . . Ihm blieb verborgen, dass das Nicht-Sein sich dialektisch nicht einfangen lässt" (GW, 4: 139).

29. Bolman "Introduction," *Ages of the World,* p. 25. Bolman is here citing Schelling's *"Kritische Fragmente"* of 1806.

30. That Tillich so understood the epistemological significance of Schelling's *Urgrund* can be seen in "Kairos und Logos: Eine Untersuchung zur Metaphysik des Erkennens," GW, 4:59.

31. Ibid.

32. *See* Osborne, *New Being*, p. 74. After reviewing Tillich's dependence on Schelling, the author concludes: "In Tillich's mind this is theonomy: the transcendent in the immanent, the divine process working within man's very essence and within his very history, not alongside of it."

33. Bolman, "Introduction," *Ages of the World*, p. 15. *See also* Paul Tillich, *The Construction of the History of Religion in Schelling's Positive Philosophy: Its Presuppositions and Principles*, trans. with an Introduction and Notes by Victor L. Nuovo (Lewisburg, Pa.: Bucknell University Press, 1974). This work is Tillich's doctoral dissertation in philosophy accepted by the University of Breslau in 1910. Herein Tillich argues that: "It is from the standpoint of the philosophy of identity that Schelling begins to draw the concept of God into his system. Hence, it can be seen from a more detailed discussion that as a consequence of equating God and identity, everything that holds true for the latter can be transferred to the concept of God" (p. 54). (This work henceforth is cited as *The Construction*).

34. This doctrine of the Fall was already present in Schelling's thought as early as his *Philosophie und Religion* (1804), but it became the decisive element in both his

break with the essentialism of Hegel and his progress from his negative philosophy
with the appearance of *Die Freiheitslehre* (1809). Obviously, for Tillich the transition
from the negative to positive philosophy constituted more of a continuity than a
revolution.

35. Osborne, *New Being*, p. 72.

36. *See* p. 51.

37. Osborne, *New Being*, p. 70.

38. In *The Construction* Tillich explains that for Schelling "sin" is identical with
affirming "particularity, selfhood and creaturehood" (p. 55).

39. The terms *Wille* and *Willkür* were already established by Kant as important
concepts in moral philosophy, as, for example, in *Religion Within the Limits of
Reason Alone* (1793). For Schelling they have more of an ontological than a moral
connotation.

40. Schelling, *Ages of the World*, pp. 153, 155.

41. ST, 1: 182–86.

42. *See* Tillich, "Reply to Interpretation and Criticism," in K and B, p. 343: "The
fall is the work of finite freedom, but it happened universally in everything finite, and
therefore unavoidably . . . The universality and consequently the unavoidability of
the fall is not derived from 'ontological speculation,' but from a realistic observation
of man, his heart, and his history."

43. Schelling, SW, 6: 38: "Nur durch den Abfall vom Urbild lässt Plato die Seele
von ihrer ersten Seligkeit herabsinken und in das zeitliche Universum geboren
werden, durch das sie von dem wahren losgerissen ist." In the context, he is
appealing to Plato in support of his own ontological theory of existence.

44. Schelling, SW, 6: 37: "The light of the divine essence has been refracted or
passed on to the Nothing, and from this encounter the material world came into
being."

45. Bolman, "Introduction," *Ages of the World,* p. 37.

46. Tillich, *The Construction*, p. 60.

47. Schelling, SW, 6: 41: "This Fall, furthermore, is as eternal (outside of all time)
as the Absolute Itself and as the World of Ideas."

48. For an excellent description of the thought process by which Schelling arrived
at his unusual doctrine of an irrational ground in God as well as in man, *see* Frederick
Copleston, S. J. *A History of Philosophy*, 7 vols. (Garden City, N.Y.: Doubleday &
Company; Image paperback, 1965), 7: Part 1, Fichte to Hegel, pp. 162–63.

49. Ibid. The clear implications for a religious interpretation of evolution contained in Schelling's ontology have been indicated by Ernst Benz, *Evolution and
Christian Hope*, trans. Heinz G. Frank (Garden City, N.Y.: Doubleday & Company, 1968). Benz rightly praises Schelling for his recognition of the importance of
the natural sciences and of the doctrine of evolution for religious philosophy, so far
ahead of his time. *See*, for example, pp. 171–72.

50. Tillich, "Reply to Interpretation and Criticism," K and B, p. 342. Responding
to his critics Daubney, Roberts and Niebuhr, Tillich frankly admits: . . . "the main
criticism of my doctrine of man comes from the theological side and is summed up in
the reproach that I identify finitude and evil."

51. *The Construction*, pp. 68–69: "God extricates being from the unconscious

blessedness of the substantial unity of the potencies and delivers it over to becoming and suffering, so that it may live with him in conscious and self-posited unity and blessedness." *See also* ST, 2: 44.

52. Schelling, SW, 7: 432: "Gott ist ein wirkliches Wesen, das aber nichts vor oder ausser sich hat. Alles, was er ist, ist er durch sich selbst; es geht von sich selbst aus, um zuletzt wieder auch rein in sich selbst zu endigen. Also mit Einem Wort: Gott macht sich selbst . . ."

53. Ibid.: "Um von Gott geschieden zu sein, müssen sie (die Dinge) in einem von ihm verschiedenen Grunde werden. Da aber doch nichts ausser Gott sein kann, so ist dieser Widerspruch nur dadurch auszulosen, dass die Dinge ihren Grund in dem haben, was in Gott selbst nicht ER SELBST IST, d.h. in dem, was Grund seiner Existenz ist." *See also*, Tillich, *The Construction*, pp. 48, 55.

54. Bolman, "Introduction," *Ages of the World*, p. 71. *See* Tillich, "Humanität und Religion," p. 111: "Der Kampf um den Menschen ist immer und überall ein Kampf dieser Mächte, was auch ihre Namen sein mögen: Götter oder Dämonen, Strukturen der Konstruktion oder der Destruktion, Ideen oder Illusionen im Sellischen wie im Sozialen . . . Der Mensch ist Mensch als Kampfplatz der Mächte, die in jeder Zelle seines Leibes und in jeder Bewegung seines Denkens für oder gegen sein Menschsein kämpfen."

55. David Hopper, *Tillich: A Theological Portrait* (New York: J. B. Lippincott Co., 1968), p. 102.

Chapter 3

1. PE, p. 49.
2. RS, "Introduction," p. 39. *See also* Chap. 2.
3. PE, p. 49.
4. *See* Chap. 2; K and B, p. 13; Tillich, *On the Boundary, An Autobiographical Sketch* (New York: Charles Scribner's Sons, 1936), p. 33; JPG, p. 19 and Wilhelm Pauck and Marion Pauck, *Paul Tillich; His Life and Thought*, 2 vols. (New York: Harper & Row, Publishers, Inc. 1976), pp. 67–75.
5. For Tillich's *logos* theory, *see* ST, 1: 77: "Subjective reason is the rational structure of the mind, while objective reason is the rational structure of reality which the mind can grasp and according to which it can shape reality . . . etc." *See also* PE, pp. 29–30, 90–91. As regards Tillich's application of this "logos" doctrine to the academic disciplines, *see* Adams, PCSR: "Every system of the sciences is of course an explication of a fundamental view of existence, of man and his world" (p. 124).
6. OITC, p. 179.
7. Ibid. *See* list of Abbreviations and Bibliography for details of publication.
8. JPG, p. 24.
9. OITC, p. 157.
10. Tillich, "The Philosophy of Religion," *What Is Religion?* trans. with Introduction by James Luther Adams (New York: Harper & Row, 1969), p. 27. The original German essay was first published in 1925.
11. Ibid., p. 30.
12. Ibid., p. 32.

13. Ibid., p. 31.

14. Ibid., p. 105. *See also* PE, p. xxii, in which Tillich discusses his early understanding of the relationship of theology to the other disciplines, as contained in *Das System der Wissenschaften nach Gegenständen und Methoden* (1923): "Theology is defined as 'theonomous metaphysics,' a definition that was a first and rather insufficient step toward what I now call the "method of correlation."

15. Among Tillich's more important works dealing specifically with the relationship of religion to secular culture, we might mention: *Die religiöse Lage der Gegenwart* (1926), *Religiöse Verwirklichung* (1929), *The Protestant Era* (1948), *The Courage to Be* (1952) and *Theology of Culture* (1959). (Details of publication are available in the Bibliography). It will also be a major point of the present work to demonstrate that Tillich's entire theological enterprise and, in particular, his *Systematic* is fundamentally a theology of culture.

16. John Herman Randall, Jr., "The Ontology of Paul Tillich," in K and B, p. 136. *See also* ST, 1: 110–13. For Tillich's criticism of Kant, Hegel and Schleiermacher on this issue, see OITC, p. 160.

17. PE, p. 57. The essential doctrine of this formula was already present even in the earliest Tillichian efforts at a theological interpretation of culture, thus: OITC, p. 166 and Tillich, "The Philosophy of Religion," p. 73.

18. OITC, p. 164.

19. *See* ST, 1: 201: also "The Philosophy of Religion," pp. 56–67; Commenting on Tillich's early work in his Introduction to *What Is Religion?*, James Luther Adams remarks: "Tillich's philosophy of religion then, is a philosophy of meaning, and of relatedness to the Unconditional in terms of meaning" (p. 19).

20. Tillich, "The Philosophy of Religion," p. 57.

21. *See* Chap. 1, n. 19 and Adams, "Introduction" to *What Is Religion?*, p. 19.

22. OITC, p. 164.

23. Tillich, *On the Boundary*, p. 70.

24. Tillich, "The Philosophy of Religion," p. 74.

25. OITC, p. 167.

26. Ibid.

27. Ibid., p. 161.

28. This allegation, which we have already mentioned in the Introduction, deserves serious consideration, and is, accordingly, taken up in some detail later in the book.

29. OITC, p. 175: "a universal profanation and desecration of life would be inevitable if no sphere of holiness existed to oppose and contradict it."

30. Ibid., p. 176.

31. Tillich, "The Philosophy of Religion," p. 117.

32. Ibid., p. 107. In ST, 1: 211, Tillich argues the same point in terms of his later concept of "ultimate concern": "It is impossible to be concerned about something which cannot be encountered concretely."

33. OITC, p. 178.

34. Ibid., p. 177.

35. At this point, it is clear that "proper functioning" of the theological faculties is synonymous with their directedness toward a theonomous fulfillment of culture, "in

which the entire cultural movement is filled by a homogeneous substance, a directly spiritual material, which turns it into the expression of an all-embracing religious spirit whose continuity is one with that of culture itself" (OITC, p. 178).

36. *See* Bibliography for publication details. The first and last of these works, together with the article, "Über die Idee einer Theologie der Kultur" (OITC), comprise the contents of James Luther Adams' collection, *What Is Religion?*

37. PCSR, pp. 178–79.

38. Tillich, "The Philosophy of Religion," p. 53.

39. Ibid., p. 54.

40. *See* GW, 6: 1ff; IH, pp. 219–41 and JPG, p. 26: "Tillich insiste ici—et c'est l'élément nouveau apporté par cet article—sur le fait que la théonomie ne saurait résulter d'un effort et d'une oeuvre de l'homme, mais seulement d'un acte divin."

41. In RS, p. 115, Tillich admits that his early thought on theonomy was too much influenced by "unrealistic enthusiasm" and romanticism. He goes on to explain that "there are societies which are turned toward the eternal and which express in their forms the judgment which they have experienced as proceeding from it. But there are no societies which possess the eternal" (p. 176).

42. PE, p. xiii. Tillich's concern for the meaning of history is evidenced in articles written during this period (1926–1930), especially "Kairos: Ideen zur Geisteslage der Gegenwart" (1926), "Kairos und Logos: Eine Untersuchung zur Metaphysik des Erkennens" (1926), "Eschatologie und Geschichte" (1927), and "Christologie und Geschichtsdeutung" (1930).

43. *See* Chap. 2. Tillich borrowed the word *kairos* from the New Testament where it signified qualitative and fulfilled time, as opposed to *chronos*, which meant simple duration. It became a key concept for his interpretation of history.

44. JPG, p. 27.

45. Ibid.; *see also* GW, 6: 83–96.

46. JPG, p. 30.

47. Tillich, "Autobiographical Reflections," K and B, p. 5. *See also* PCSR, pp. 85–86.

48. ST, 2: 125–26.

49. Ibid., 1: 218.

50. Jean-Paul Gabus, "Introduction à la Traduction Francaise," *Théologie de la Culture* (Paris: Editions Planète, 1968), pp. 23–23. This French translation with brief introduction by Gabus must not be confused with his own excellent commentary (1969), which we designate by the abbreviation JPG.

51. Tillich, *On the Boundary*, pp. 60–61.

52. Christoph Rhein, *Paul Tillich: Philosoph und Theolog* (Stuttgart: Evangelisches Verlagswerk, 1957), p. 12.

53. *See*, for example, Wilhelm Hartmann, "Die Methode der Korrelation von philosophischen Fragen und theologischen Antworten bei Paul Tillich" (Ph.D. diss. Göttingen; Georg August University 1954). A hectograph copy at P. Tillich Archives, Göttingen.

54. ST, 1: 8.

55. PE, p. xxii.

56. See Kenan Osborne, *New Being: A Study on the Relationship Between*

Conditioned and Unconditioned Being According to Paul Tillich (The Hague: Martinus Nijhoff, 1969), p. 20, n. 58 for a list of some of the more important works on the subject.
  57. ST, 1: 64.
  58. See Osborne, *New Being*, pp. 20–24, but especially Tillich's own admonition on the subject in ST, 2: 13–16.
  59. ST, 1: 64.
  60. Ibid.: 7–8.
  61. TC, p. v.

Chapter 4

  1. See GW, 14: 339–40. The term is used abundantly throughout volumes 1, 2, 6, 7, 9–13.
  2. s.v. "Theonomie," 2nd ed. (hereafter cited as RGG).
  3. Ibid.: ". . . die Zerbrechung der selbstgesetzlichen Formen menschlichen Denkens und Handelns durch ein dem Geiste fremdes und äusserliches Gesetz."
  4. Tillich, "Der Begriff des Dämonischen und seine Bedeutung für die systematische Theologie," *Theologische Blätter* 5 (1926): 32, cited by Adams in PCSR, p. 229: "The profane and the secular can be only an inchoate tendency within the Sacred (which is all-embracing), and culture can be only a form that is substantially religious. . ." *See also* PE, p. 59, where Tillich maintains that the greatest proof for the fallen state of the world is the existence of "a religious culture beside a secular culture."
  5. ST, 1:85. *See also* PE pp. 56–57: "Theonomy asserts that the superior law is, at the same time, the innermost law of man himself . . ."
  6. PE, xii and ST, 1: 86.
  7. "Theonomie", RGG: "Über die sich selbst überlassene Autonomie führt zur Entleerung und—da es auch im Geistigen nichts Leeres gibt—zur Erfüllung durch dämonisch-zerstörerische Kräfte." Trans. Adams, PCSR, p. 61.
  8. Paul Tillich, *Christianity and the Encounter of World Religions* (New York: Columbia University Press, 1963), p. 5.
  9. Ibid., p. 14: ". . . in the depth of technical creativity, as well as in the structure of the secular mind, there are religious elements which have come to the fore when the traditional religions have lost their power."
  10. Paul Tillich, "Humanität und Religion," GW, 9: 113 and ST, 3: 85. *See also* PCSR, p. 54: Adams quotes Tillich as maintaining that the religious background of secular humanism is that "of fighting the religious demonry and trying to protect human nature as such."
  11. ST, 1: 86. *See,* PSCR, pp. 50–53.
  12. *See* John Macquarrie, *God and Secularity. New Directions in Theology Today* (Philadelphia. The Westminster Press, 1967), vol. 3. p. 101.
  13. PE, p. 57.
  14. *See* Chap. 1, p. 40.
  15. Paul Tillich, "Autobiographical Reflections," K and B, pp. 9–10.

16. ST, 3: 250.

17. Paul Tillich, *On the Boundary: An Autobiographical Sketch* (New York: Charles Scribner's Sons, 1936), pp. 47–48.

18. John Dillenberger, "Paul Tillich: Theologian of Culture," *Paul Tillich Retrospect and Future*, ed. Nels F. S. Ferre et al. (Nashville, Tenn: Abingdon Press, 1966), p. 34.

19. ST, 3: 67.

20. Tillich, "Humanität und Religion," GW, 9: 113: "Durch die dämonischen Verzerrungen, denen die Religionen unterliegen, verzerren und verderben sie die von ihnen geschaffene Humanität. Die Religionen sind beides: Stätten der Menschwerdungen und Stätten der Menschenopfer."

21. ST, 3: 358.

22. PCSR, p. 172, and p. 214: ". . . this principle of theonomy represents more an attitude than a material principle."

23. Such as, "depth," "infinity," "Abyss," "boundary-situation," "kairos," "ontic shock," and "demonic," to name a few typical terms. For the variety of concepts formulated from meditation on the sea, *see* Tillich's *On the Boundary*, p. 18.

24. Ibid., p. 28.

25. JPG, p. 17. Tillich is not, however, equating artistic and religious symbols, for the artistic symbol may open up a dimension other than that of religious "depth".

26. Paul Tillich, *Masse und Geist: Studien zür Philosophie der Masse* (Berlin: Verlag der Arbeitsgemeinschaft), 1922, pp. 1–3, 5–7, 9–12; reprinted in GW, 2: 70–90. Cited by Adams in PCSR, p. 90.

27. Tillich, *On the Boundary*, p. 26.

28. *See* Chap. 3.

29. RS, pp. 86–87.

30. André Malraux, *The Voices of Silence*, trans. Stuart Gilbert (New York: Doubleday & Co., 1953), p. 120.

31. RS, p. 86.

32. Tillich, *Religiöse Verwirklichung* (Berlin: Furche-Verlag, 1929), p. 65. Cited By Adams, PSRC, p. 112.

33. PSRC, p. 113.

34. "Theonomie," RGG.

35. ST, 1: 85 and OITC, p. 164.

36. OITC, p. 162. *See also* PSRC, pp. 112–13.

37. ST, 1: 85.

38. *See* Chap. 3.

39. "Theonomie," RGG.

40. Although Tillich speaks frequently of the influence of the aesthetic experience in molding his thought, the reader must not forget Tillich's philosophical indebtedness to Schelling, who had developed a very intricate philosophy of aesthetics in which he considered art the door to reality. Only a very careful study of Schelling's philosophy of art would reveal the degree of originality in Tillich's artistic-philosophical vision. *See*, for example, Schelling's *System of Transcendental Idealism*, trans. Peter Heath (Charlottesville: University Press of Virginia, 1978);

Bruno: Über das göttliche und natürliche Prinzip der Dinge (Munich: Rupprechtpresse, 1928 and *Schriften zur Philosophie der Kunst,* ed. Otto Weiss (Leipzig: F. Meiner, 1911).
  41. RS, pp. 90–91.
  42. *See* Chap. 2.
  43. IH, p. 219 and PE, p. 70.
  44. H. Richard Niebuhr, Translator's Preface to RS, p. 17.
  45. PE, p. 72.
  46. Ibid., pp. 71–72 and RS, p. 17.
  47. PE, p. 71.
  48. Ibid., p. 64.
  49. John Herman Randall, Jr., "The Philosophical Legacy of Paul Tillich," in *The Intellectual Legacy of Paul Tillich,* ed. James R. Lyons (Detroit, Mich.: Wayne State University Press, 1969), p. 40.
  50. Tillich, *On the Boundary,* p. 31.
  51. Ibid., pp. 32–33.
  52. PE, p. 76.
  53. "Belief-ful realism" is Tillich's earlier term found in his 1927 essay, "Gläubiger Realismus." This article was included in his collection, *Religiöse Verwirklichung.* When Tillich revised and lengthened the essay for PE in 1948, he substituted the term "self-transcending realism."
  54. PE, p. 76.
  55. H. Richard Niebuhr, Preface to RS, p. 13.
  56. IH, p. 256.
  57. ST, 1: 103.
  58. DF, pp. 76–77.
  59. JPG, p. 98. *See also,* Tillich, "History as the Problem of our Period," *Review of Religion* 3, no. 3 (March 1939): 255.
  60. Tillich, "The Philosophy of Religion," *What Is Religion?*, p. 78.
  61. Tillich, *On the Boundary,* pp. 49–50.
  62. Immanuel Kant, *Groundwork of the Metaphysics of Morals,* trans. with an introduction by H. J. Paton (London: 1950). Found *also* in Immanuel Kant, *Gesammelte Schriften,* ed. Royal Prussian Academy of Sciences, 22 vols. (Berlin: George Reimer, 1902–42), vol. 4.
  63. *See* Chap. 3.
  64. ST, 1: 75.
  65. ST, 3: 58.
  66. ST, 3: 250–65.

Chapter 5

  1. ST, 1: 72–73.
  2. *See* Chap. 4.
  3. ST, 1: 73.
  4. RS, p. 47.
  5. PCSR, p. 50.

6. Tillich, *Saturday Evening Post* (June 14, 1958), pp. 29, 76, 78, 79. *See also* GW, 5: 43–50.

7. ST, 1: 79.

8. TC, p. 43.

9. Tillich, "The Philosophy of Religion," *What Is Religion?*, trans., ed. and with an introduction by James Luther Adams (New York: Harper & Row, Publishers, 1969), pp. 56–67.

10. CB, pp. 46–51.

11. ST, 1: 102.

12. Joseph Haroutunian, "The Question Tillich Left Us," *Tillich: Retrospect and Future*, p. 58.

13. CB, pp. 36–39.

14. JPG, p. 54: ". . . les processus techniques peuvent devenir eux-mêmes théonomes, et s'ouvrir à un sens ultime." Tillich expresses this hope for a humanizing theonomy within technological culture in a number of places in his writing, particularly in Vol. 3 of the *Systematic*. See, for example, Tillich, ST, 3: 61–62, 72–74, 258–60. At ST, 3: 259, Tillich explains that "the divine Spirit, cutting out of the vertical direction to resist an unlimited running-ahead in the horizontal line, drives toward a technical production that is subjected to the ultimate end of all life processes—Eternal Life."

15. Tillich, "The Philosophy of Religion," p. 74. *See also* Paul Tillich, *Religiöse Verwirklichung* (Berlin: Furche-Verlag, 1930), p. 195 and PCSR, p. 53.

16. IH, p. 227.

17. ST, 1: 86.

18. TC, p. 43.

19. Ibid., p. 44.

20. Ibid., pp. 45–47.

21. Tillich, "The Philosophy of Religion," pp. 116–17.

22. *See* Chap. 4.

23. PE, p. 74.

24. Ibid., pp. 69–70.

25. ST, 3: 102.

26. Ibid., 87.

27. Ibid., 249.

28. PE, p. 46.

29. Paul Tillich, *Christianity and the Encounter of World Religions* (New York: Columbia University Press, 1963), p. 5.

30. ST, 3: 85.

31. PE, p. 68.

32. This appraisal of secular humanism as an "idealism" is found in various places in Tillich's work, extending from his earliest to his most recent writings. See, for example, ST, 1: 112 and ST, 3: 86; but also in "The Philosophy of Religion," (1925) and PE, pp. 67–68 (Chapter 5, "Realism and Faith" in this latter work dates from 1929).

33. TC, p. 44.

34. DF, p. 12.

35. PE, p. 68.
36. *See* Chap. 3.
37. PSCR, p. 51; *see also* ST, 3: 247.
38. ST, 3: 86.
39. *See* Chap. 4 and TC, p. 136.
40. PE, pp. 28–29.
41. ST, 3: 249
42. Ibid., 3: 86.
43. PE, p. 78.
44. ST, 1: 26.
45. Ibid., 1: 102.
46. Paul Tillich, *Love, Power and Justice* (New York: Oxford University Press, 1954), p. 24. To get the full sense of Tillich's suggestion, we do well to cite the expression in context:

> Is there a way of verifying ontological judgments? There is certainly not an experimental way, but there is an experiential way. It is the way of an intelligent recognition of the basic ontological structures within the encountered reality, including the process of encountering itself. The only answer, but a sufficient answer, which can be given to the question of ontological verification is the appeal to intelligent recognition.

47. *See* for example, Thomas S. Kuhn, *The Structure of Scientific Revolutions* (Chicago: University of Chicago Press, 1962); Michael Polanyi, *Personal Knowledge* (Chicago: University of Chicago Press, 1958); Ian Barbour, *Myths, Models and Paradigms* (New York: Harper & Row, 1974) and N. R. Hanson, *Patterns of Discovery* (Cambridge: Cambridge University Press, 1958).
48. Barbour, *Myths*, p. 146.

Chapter 6

1. Paul Edwards, "Professor Tillich's Confusions," *Mind: A Quarterly Review of Psychology and Philosophy* 74, no. 294 (April 1965): 199–200. Edwards rejects Tillich's whole system of symbols on positivist grounds, classifying them as "irreducible metaphors," and, therefore, as inauthentic assertions.
2. *See also* TC, pp. 43 ff. and Tillich, "The Person in a Technical Society," in *Christian Faith and Social Action* (New York: Charles Scribner's Sons, 1953). In both places, Tillich describes the existentialist movement as a cultural protest against the depersonalizing forces of technical society.
3. LL, no. 1, "Art and Literature."
4. Ibid.
5. LL, no. 4, "Surface and Depth."
6. LL, no. 1, "Art and Literature."
7. LL, no. 2, "Philosophy and Science."
8. Ibid.
9. Ibid.
10. *See*, for example, Theodore Roszak, *The Making of a Counter Culture:*

Reflections on the Technocratic Society and Its Youthful Opposition (New York: Doubleday & Company, 1969) and his *Where the Wasteland Ends* (New York: Doubleday & Company, 1972). Likewise, *see* Carlos Castaneda, *The Teachings of Don Juan: A Yaqui Way of Knowledge* (Berkeley, Cal.: University of California Press, 1968).

11. LL, no. 2, "Philosophy and Science."
12. LL, no. 3, "Religion and Theology."
13. LL, no. 4, "Surface and Depth."
14. LL, no. 5, "Thing and Self."
15. LL, no. 6, "Estrangement and Return."
16. Ibid.
17. For examples of Tillich's influence, *see:* Maslow, *Religions, Values, and Peak Experiences* (New York: The Viking Press, 1970), p. 31; Erich Fromm, *Man for Himself* (New York: Holt, Rinehart and Winston, Inc., 1947), pp. 58, 78, 200–201, and 251 and Rollo May, *Man's Search for Himself* (New York: W. W. Norton & Co., 1953), pp. 20, 61, 143, 180, 190, and 203. May has also done a recent study of Tillich's life from a psychological perspective: Rollo May, *Paulus: Reminiscences of a Friendship* (New York: Harper & Row, 1973).
18. *See,* for example, Abraham Maslow, *Religions,* pp. 19, 31, 32, 47 and Maslow, *Toward a Psychology of Being* (New York: Van Nostrand Reinhold Company, 1968), pp. 73, 74, 77.

A complete bibliography of Maslow's studies on trancendent or "peak" experiences can be found in *The Farther Reaches of Human Nature,* edited posthumously by Bertha Maslow and Miles Vich (New York: The Viking Press, 1971).
19. This is made very clear in Maslow's introduction to *Religions* (pp. 3–10). Maslow was a regular contributor to *The Humanist* magazine and a one-time recipient of the "Humanist of the Year" award.
20. Maslow, *Religions,* p. 61.
21. Ibid., pp. 25–26.
22. Ibid., pp. 54–58.
23. It is for this reason that Maslow dedicated a good deal of effort toward analyzing and clarifying the effects of nineteenth-century positivistic science on contemporary culture and attitudes. See Maslow, *Religions,* pp. 37–38 and *The Psychology of Science: A Reconnaissance* (New York: Harper & Row, 1966).
24. Maslow, *Religions,* p. 56.
25. PE, p. x–xi. *See* Chap. 2.
26. Maslow, *Religions,* p. 56.
27. Maslow, *Psychology of Being,* p. 76.
28. Maslow, *Religions,* p. 45: ". . . if, as actually happened on one platform, Paul Tillich defined religion as 'concern with ultimate concerns,' and I then defined humanistic psychology in the same way, then what is the difference between a supernaturalist and a humanist?" Tillich, of course, would, in fact, have objected to being classified as a "supernaturalist."
29. *See* Chap. 5.
30. CB, p. 180.
31. Maslow, *Religions,* p. xiv. Although there has not been a lack of inquiry into

religious or transcendent experience prior to Maslow's work, previous studies were done either from the presuppositions of supernatural intervention or from those of pathological morbidity.

32. Ibid., p. 61.
33. Ibid., p. 65.
34. ST, 1: 76.
35. Maslow, *Psychology of Being*, p. 74.
36. *See* Chap. 5.
37. *See* Chap. 4.
38. JPG, p. 17. *See* Chap. 4, n. 25.
39. Maslow, *Religions*, p. xv: "Peak experiences are also epistemological and ontopsychological. They have to do with the nature of reality, of man's relation to it, of knowledge of it, and of the values inherent in it. They can be trans-moral, transcending distinctions between good and evil."
40. Maslow, "Peak Experiences in Education and Art," *The Humanist* 30 (September/October, 1970): 31.
41. *See*, for example, Bertrand Russell, *New Hopes for a Changing World* (New York: Simon and Schuster, 1952), p. 164 and John Dewey, "Philosophy Is Education," in *John Dewey, His Contribution to the American Tradition*, ed. Irwin Edman (New York: Greenwood Press, 1968), p. 100.
42. ST, 3: 86.
43. Ibid.
44. ST, 3: 249.
45. Marghanita Laski, *Ectasy: A Study of Some Secular and Religious Experiences* (New York: Greenwood Press, 1968).
46. Ibid., p. 373–74.
47. Maslow, *Toward a Psychology of Being*, p. 89 and 106. Laski, *Ecstasy*, p. 20.
48. The term *secular humanism* can refer both to a general cultural outlook as well as to a specific movement, especially known in the United States and Britain. The movement includes such organizations as the Humanist Association and the Ethical Union in both countries. In this country, the tenets of humanism have been explicitly spelled out in two noteworthy manifestoes, one published in 1933 and the other in 1973 (see Bibliography for further details).

Lower-case letters are used when referring to the outlook or viewpoint, and capital letters are used when referring to the movement. If both meanings are present, the choice will depend on the emphasis.
49. Tillich's awareness of the more open-minded and religiously oriented humanism is reflected in statements such as the following: "This does not mean that Humanism ignores 'religion.' Ordinarily, though not always, it subsumes religion under the cultural creation" (Tillich, ST, 3: 85). *See also* ST, 1: 65. It is typical of Tillich's style that he frequently makes reference to ideas or theories that are unmistakably related to certain authors or schools, without citing the authors or authorities by name.
50. *See* Chap. 5.
51. Maslow, *Psychology of Being*, p. 87.
52. *See* Chap. 1.

53. Charles Frankel, *The Case for Modern Man* (Boston: The Beacon Press, 1955).

54. Ibid., p. 2. *See also* Sidney Hook, "The New Failure of Nerve," in *The Quest for Being and Other Studies in Naturalism and Humanism* (New York: Dell Publishing Co., Delta Book, 1934). "A failure of nerve," a term derived from Gilbert Murray's characterization of the decline of Greek culture and the rise of Christianity *(Four Stages of Greek Religion)* is frequently used as a polemical term by Humanists. It serves to counter a kind of religious apologetic that appeals to the crisis and disappointments of contemporary civilization as the basis for a return to faith and religious absolutes.

55. Frankel, *Modern Man*, p. 2.

56. Ibid., pp. 39–40.

57. Ibid., pp. 205–6.

58. Maslow, *Religions*, p. 67.

59. *See* n. 53 and Hook, "The Atheism of Paul Tillich," in *Religious Experience and Truth,* ed. Sidney Hook (New York: New York University Press, 1961), pp. 59–64, for representative works of Hook on this issue.

60. Hook, "The New Failure of Nerve," pp. 81–82.

61. Maslow, *Religions,* p. 47.

62. Ibid., p. 43.

63. Gerhard Szezesny, *The Future of Unbelief,* trans. from the German by Edward B. Garside (New York: George Braziller, 1961), pp. 11–12.

64. Ibid., p. 25.

65. Tillich's term is either "shallow secularism" or "mere humanism"; *see* Chap. 5 and Chap. 6.

66. Hook, "The New Failure of Nerve," p. 87.

67. Leonard Wheat, *Tillich's Dialectical Humanism* (Baltimore, Md.: The John Hopkins Press, 1970), p. 254. Wheat's argument in this instance is derived from Walter Kaufmann, *The Faith of a Heretic* (Garden City, N.Y.: Doubleday & Company, 1961), pp. 95–97.

68. Wheat, *Tillich's Dialectical Humanism,* p. 255.

69. ST, 1: 11. Tillich is citing Mark 12: 29 (RSV).

70. Corliss Lamont, *The Philosophy of Humanism* (New York: Frederick Ungar Publishing Co., 1965) and Harold John Blackham, *Humanism* (Baltimore, Md.: Penguin Books, 1968).

71. ST, 3: 87. Cf. also Tillich, ST, 3: 98: "Religion is the highest expression of the greatness and dignity of life; in it the greatness of life becomes holiness. Yet religion is also the most radical refutation of the greatness and dignity of life; in it the great becomes most profanized; the holy most desecrated."

72. *See,* for example, ST, 3: 99–100; "The Conquest of the Concept of Religion in the Philosophy of Religion," in *"What Is Religion?"* trans., ed., and with an Intro by James Luther Adams (New York: Harper & Row, Publishers, 1969), p. 145 and PE, p. 183.

73. Bertrand Russell, *New Hopes for a Changing World* (New York: Simon and Schuster, 1952), p. 155.

74. *See* Chap. 5., pp. 115–16.

75. *See* Chap. 3, p. 76.

76. Julian Huxley, *Religion Without Revelation* (London: C. A. Watts & Co., Ltd., 1967), p. 189.

77. Ibid., p. 172.

78. Ibid., p. 160.

79. OITC, pp. 173–174.

80. *See* Chap. 5.

81. *See* above, pp. 140–45. *See also* Maslow, *Religions,* p. 18: ". . . what the more sophisticated scientist is now in the process of learning is that though he must disagree with most of the answers to the religious questions which have been given by organized religion, it is increasingly clear that the religious questions themselves—and religious quests, the religious yearnings, the religious needs themselves—are perfectly respectable scientifically, that they are rooted deep in human nature, that they can be studied, described, examined in a scientific way, and that the churches were trying to answer perfectly sound human questions."

82. We have already seen clear evidence of Maslow's and Huxley's views on this issue. Laski's own detailed study of the religious experience, characterized by thorough seriousness and scientific objectivity, is the best evidence that she shared this same outlook. Laski also explicitly states in the conclusion of her book: "I do not think it sensible to ignore, as most rationalists have done, ecstatic experiences and the emotions and ideas to which they give rise. To ignore or to deny the importance of ecstatic experiences is to leave to the irrational the interpretation of what many people believe to be of supreme value, etc." *(Ecstasy,* p. 373).

83. Blackham, *Humanism,* p. 199.

84. Lamont, *Philosophy of Humanism,* p. 192.

85. Ibid., Foreword by Edwin Wilson, pp. viii–ix.

86. Roy Wood Sellars, *Reflections on American Philosophy from Within* (Notre Dame, Ind.: Notre Dame University Press, 1969), p. 165.

87. Ibid., p. 162; Hook, *Quest for Being,* p. 157. Hook, in a manner reminiscent of A. J. Ayer, maintains that Tillich was deceived by grammar in his understanding of "Being-Itself."

88. *See* p. 155.

89. *See* Chap. 5.

90. Lamont, *Philosophy of Humanism,* p. 64; H. J. Blackham, *Objections to Humanism,* ed. H. J. Blackham (Philadelphia: J. B. Lippincott Co., 1963), p. 21.

91. John H. Randall, Jr., *The Meaning of Religion for Man* (New York: Harper & Row, 1946), p. 30.

92. John Dewey, *A Common Faith* (New Haven, Conn.: Yale University Press, 1934), p. 46.

93. John H. Randall, Jr., *The Meaning of Religion for Man* (New York: Macmillan Publishing Co., 1946), pp. 25–35; Horace L. Friess, "Functioning Religiously," in *Naturalism and Historical Understanding: Essays on the Philosophy of John Herman Randall, Jr.* (Albany, N.Y.: State University of New York Press, 1967), p. 244. William James, *Varieties of Religious Experience* (New York: Longmans, Green & Co., 1902); Curtis W. Reese, *Humanism* (Chicago: The Open Court Publishing Company, 1926), p. 18.

94. Frederick J. E. Woodbridge, *An Essay on Nature* (New York: Columbia University Press, 1940), p. 307. Irwin Edman, "Religion Without Tears," in *The Uses of Philosophy: An Irwin Edman Reader*, ed. Charles Frankel (New York: Greenwood Press, 1968), pp. 183 ff. Joseph L. Blau, "God and the Philosophers," in *The Idea of God: Philosophical Perspectives*, ed. E. H. Madden, R. Handy, and M. Farber (Springfield, Ill.: Charles C. Thomas, 1968), p. 157.

95. *See* p. 155, and Huxley, *Religion Without Revelation*, p. 201.

96. John H. Randall, Jr., "Towards a Functional Naturalism," in *Contemporary American Philosophy*, 2nd Series, ed. John E. Smith (New York: Humanities Press, 1970), p. 56.

97. *See*, for example, "Is Religion a Human Art or a Divine Revelation?", *A Symposium and Discussion: Paul Tillich and John H. Randall, Jr.* (Amherst College, 1958), on tape: private archives of Rev. Peter John, United Methodist Church, Rockland, Mass. (Hereafter cited as *Amherst Symposium*).

98. Personal interview with John H. Randall, Jr., New York (on tape), November, 1970.

99. Tillich, "The Philosophy of Religion," *What Is Religion?* p. 97.

100. OITC, p. 163. Tillich here attempts to show that the conflict between the special fields of culture with the religious realm is overcome in the "theonomy of a fundamental religious experience."

101. Maslow, *Religions*, p. 68.

102. DF, p. 76.

103. *See* Chap. 1; also Harvey Cox, *The Feast of Fools* (Cambridge, Mass.: Harvard University Press, 1969) and Peter Berger, *A Rumor of Angels* (Garden City, N.Y.: Doubleday & Co., 1969). For a critique of secular theologies along these lines, *see* Andrew Greeley, *Unsecular Man* (New York: Schocken Books, 1972).

104. *See* "The Conversion of a Square," review of Roszak's *Where the Wasteland Ends* in *The New York Times Book Review*, Sept. 24, 1972, pp. 28, 30.

105. Ibid., p. 28.

106. Maslow, *Religions*, p. 47.

107. Ibid.

108. *See* Chap. 5.

Chapter 7

1. Leonard Wheat, *Paul Tillich's Dialectical Humanism* (Baltimore: The Johns Hopkins Press, 1970), p. 236.

2. PE, p. xv.

3. *See* Chap. 2.

4. *See* Chap. 3.

5. Paul Tillich, "The Philosophy of Religion," *What Is Religion?*, trans., ed., and with an Introduction by James Luther Adams (New York: Harper & Row, 1969), pp. 75–76.

6. ST, 3: 247: "The principle of the 'consecration of the secular' applies as well to movements, groups and individuals who are not only on the secular pole of the

ambiguities of religion but who are openly hostile to the Churches and beyond this to religion itself in all its forms, including Christianity. In this way the Spiritual Presence has used anti-religious media to transform not only a secular culture but also the churches."

7. "A Humanist Manifesto," in Corliss Lamont, *The Philosophy of Humanism*, 5th ed. (New York: Frederick Ungar Publishing Co., 1965), p. 287. The document was originally published in *The New Humanist* 6, no. 3 (1933).

8. Sidney Hook *The Quest for Being and Other Studies in Naturalism and Humanism* (New York: Dell Publishing Co., Delta Book, 1934), p. 100.

9. See, for example, Cornelio Fabro, *God in Exile*, trans. and ed. Arthur Gibson (Westminster, Md.: Newman Press, 1968), pp. 1003–4.

10. Jacob Taubes, "On the Nature of the Theological Method: Some Reflections on the Methodology Principles of Tillich's Theology," *The Journal of Religion* 34 (January, 1954): 21.

11. ST, 1: 237.

12. Taubes, "Nature of Theological Method," p. 21.

13. Paul Tillich, *Perspectives on Nineteenth and Twentieth Century Protestant Theology*, ed. and with an Introduction by Carl E. Braaten (New York: Harper & Row, 1967), p. 118.

14. Ibid., p. 123. *See also* Chap. 2.

15. Tillich, in *Philosophical Interrogations*, ed. Sydney Rome and Beatrice Rome with Introduction (New York: Holt, Rinehart and Winston, 1964), p. 360.

16. *See* Chap. 2.

17. Kenan Osborne, *New Being: A Study on the Relationship Between Conditioned and Unconditioned Being According to Paul Tillich* (The Hague: Martinus Nijhoff, 1969), p. 80.

18. Daniel Day Williams, *What Present Day Theologians Are Thinking* (New York: Harper & Row, 1959), p. 86.

19. ST, 3: 112–13.

20. Ibid.: 263.

21. Ibid. 150–51; Tillich, "Philosophy of Religion," p. 98; ST, 3: 190.

22. Lamont, *Philosophy of Humanism*, p. 115: ". . . the value of man's happiness and achievement is not to be measured in terms of infinite duration. The philosophy of Humanism, with its conscious limitation of the human enterprise to this existence, sets us free to concentrate our entire energies, without distraction by either hopes or fears of individual immortality, on that building of the good society." Lamont dedicates an entire chapter to the theme that "This Life Is All and Enough" (pp. 81–115). Lamont has also authored a book entitled *The Illusion of Immortality* (New York: Philosophical Library, 1952).

23. John H. Randall, Jr., "The Nature of Naturalism," in *Naturalism and the Human Spirit*, ed. Yervant H. Krikorian (New York: Columbia University Press, 1944), p. 360.

24. Lamont, "A Humanist Manifesto" p. 286, no. 2.

25. Lamont, *Philosophy of Humanism*, p. 131.

26. ST, 3: 17–30.

27. Ibid., 26.

28. Ibid., 409.

29. Ibid., 418.

30. *See,* for example, John A. Robinson, *The Body: A Study in Pauline Theology* (London: SCM Press, 1952).

31. ST, 3: 27. *See also* DF, pp. 4–8.

32. One could find an abundance of examples in Humanist authors, such as Antony Flew, Hector Hawton, Corliss Lamont, and Sidney Hook. *See,* for example, Antony Flew, *God and Philosophy* (New York: Dell Publishing Co., Delta book, 1966). Flew has recourse to *The Book of Common Prayer* to find a definition of God he will refute, and to the 1922 Commission on *Doctrine in the Church of England* for the notion of sin that he sees implied in the traditional doctrine of God (pp. 28–29).

33. See n. 22.

34. ST, 1: 276.

35. Ibid., 3: 107.

36. Paul Tillich, "The Eternal Now," in collection *The Eternal Now* (New York: Charles Scribner's Sons, 1963), p. 132. Once again we see that for Tillich the transcendence of God is essentially related to the pure gratuitousness of His gift.

37. Paul Tillich, "The Kingdom of God and History," *Church Community and State* (London: 1937 Oxford Conference, 1938—), 3: 141.

38. *See* Chap. 2.

39. Charles Frankel, *The Case for Modern Man* (Boston: The Beacon Press, 1955), p. 5.

40. Tillich, "Eternal Now," pp. 125, 131.

41. Ibid., p. 123.

42. ST, 3: 396.

43. Taubes, "Nature of Theological Method," p. 21.

44. Ibid., p. 13.

45. *See* Chap. 2, n. 3.

46. *A Symposium and Discussion: Paul Tillich and John H. Randall, Jr.* (Amherst College, 1958).

47. Frederick J. E. Woodbridge, *An Essay on Nature* (New York: Columbia University Press, 1969), p. 307: "The existence of the supernatural in Nature may be likened to the existence of depth in a mirror and be named a 'perspective' in accord with a philosophical usage having some present currency."

48. Irwin Edman, "The Vision of Naturalism," in *The Uses of Philosophy: An Irwin Edman Reader* (New York: Greenwood Press, 1968), p. 209: "The religious traditions have formulated certain aspects of man's relation to nature which naturalists themselves do ill to forget or ignore."

49. Wheat, *Tillich's Dialectical Humanism,* p. 233.

50. Wheat maintains, for example, that Tillich's sermon "The Eternal Now" marks the moment of Tillich's loss of faith. The passage that Wheat quotes is a typical Tillichian expression of the dialectical absence of God in contemporary secular culture. In order to press his thesis, Wheat uses this passage, while completely ignoring its original context (pp. 26–27).

51. *Sacramentum Mundi,* ed. Karl Rahner, et al., s.v. "Transcendence."

52. Paul Tillich, "The Meaning and Justification of the Religious Symbol," *Religious Experience and Truth*, ed. Sidney Hook (New York: New York University Press, 1961), p. 10.

53. Wheat, *Tillich's Dialectical Humanism*, p. 39.

54. TC, p. 64.

55. Ibid., p. 61.

56. Wheat, *Tillich's Dialectical Humanism*, p. 258.

57. See Lamont, *Philosophy of Humanism*, p. 24.

58. *See*, for example, Curtis W. Reese, *Humanism* (Chicago: The Open Court Publishing Co., 1926) and *Humanist Sermons*, ed. Curtis W. Reese (Chicago: The Open Court Publishing Co., 1927).

59. Julian Huxley, *Religion Without Revelation* (London: C. A. Watts & Co., Ltd., 1967), p. 166.

60. *Amherst Symposium.*

61. In his response to Tillich's address, Randall made it clear that in his judgment Tillich's thought was more determined by Christian theology than by philosophy. For his part, Randall was not interested in defending Christian theology and was "ready to let it go by the boards . . . rather than preserve it by double talk."

62. *See* Chap. 6.

63. Jacob Taubes, "Nature of Theological Method," p. 21.

64. *See* Chap. 6, n. 96.

65. *Amherst Symposium.*

66. Ibid.

67. ST, 1: 255. *See also* ST, 1: 237: ". . . everything finite participates in being-itself and in its infinity. Otherwise it would not have the power of being."

68. We should also add, more from a theological perspective, that Randall, like all Secular Humanists is a nontheist. Although Tillich often launched severe attacks against (See, e.g., *The Courage to Be*) theism, these attacks must be understood as an objection to "supernaturalistic" forms of theism. Tillich's doctrine of the Ground of Being is an attempt to rescue and preserve the validity of the Christian doctrine of God. For Tillich, God is Ultimate Realty; for Randall, God is a symbol that serves as a unifying concept.

69. *See*, however, Thomas O'Meara's article, "Tillich and Heidegger: A Structural Relationship," *Harvard Theological Review* 60 (1968): 249–61, in which the author argues for a much more central and significant influence of Heidegger's thought on Tillich.

70. John H. Randall, Jr., "Review of Tillich's *Systematic Theology*," *The Journal of Religion* 46, no. 2 (January 1966): 42.

71. Malcolm L. Diamond, *Contemporary Philosophy and Religious Thought: An Introduction to the Philosophy of Religion* (New York: McGraw-Hill Book Co., 1974), p. 375.

72. P. F. Strawson, *Individuals* (London, Methuen & Co., 1961). Donald D. Evans, "Differences Between Scientific and Religious Assertions," *Science and Religion*, ed. Ian G. Barbour (New York: Harper & Row, 1968). David Pole, "Breadth and Depth in Language," *Philosophy* (Spring 1971).

73. Tillich, "The Nature of Religious Language," TC, p. 53.

74. Walter H. Clark, "Intense Religious Experience," *Research on Religious Development: A Comprehensive Handbook,* ed. Merton P. Strommen, under direction of the Religious Education Association (New York: Hawthorn Books, 1971), p. 525; Referring to Laski's book, Clark states:

"The only general study of the types and conditions of mystical experiences—if we except the studies of Maslow (1962, 1964) of peak experiences—is not the product of a social scientist, but of a novelist who wished to procure more exact information on ecstasies, of which she had written in one of her novels."

More recently, there has been an increase of good, scientific studies of intense religious experience. *See,* for example, Ralph W. Hood, Jr., "Psychological Strength and the Report of Intense Religious Experience," *Journal for the Scientific Study of Religion* 13, no. 1 (March 1974): 65–72.

75. Innocentius M. Bochenski, "The Logic of Religious Language," *Religious Experience and Truth,* p. 41.

76. Roy Wood Sellars, *Reflections on American Philosophy from Within* (Notre Dame, Ind.: Notre Dame University Press, 1969), pp. 5, 60.

77. Roy Wood Sellars, "American Critical Realism and British Theories of Sense-Perception: Part I," *Estratto Rivista Methodos* 14 (1962): 74.

78. Thomas F. Torrance, "Determinism and Free Creation according to the Theologians" (Paper delivered at Joint Meeting of the *Académie Internationale des Sciences Religieuses and the Académie Internationale de Philosophie des Sciences,* St. John's University, New York, July, 1977), p. 1.

79. Joseph L. Blau, "God and the Philosophers," *The Idea of God: Philosophical Perspectives* ed. E. H. Madden, R. Handy, and M. Farber (Springfield, Ill.: Charles C. Thomas, 1968), p. 157.

80. Sellars, *American Philosophy from Within,* p. 165.

81. John H. Randall, Jr., "The Philosophical Legacy of Paul Tillich," in *The Intellectual Legacy of Paul Tillich,* ed. James R. Lyons (Detroit: Wayne State University Press, 1969), p. 36.

82. Ibid., p. 22.

83. Jean Rieunaud, *Paul Tillich, Philosophe et Théologien* (Paris: Éditions Fleuris, 1969), p. 92.

84. This point is well made by J. Heywood Thomas, a reliable and generally sympathetic interpreter of Tillich's thought. *See* his *Paul Tillich: An Appraisal* (Philadelphia: The Westminster Press, 1963), p. 195.

85. *See* for example, Donald Evans, "Preller's Analogy of 'Being'," *New Scholasticism* 14 (1971) and David Stagaman, S. J., " 'God' in Analytic Philosophy," *God in Contemporary Thought,* ed. Sebastian A. Matczak (New York: Learned Publications, Inc., 1977), espec. pp. 831–38.

86. George Thomas, *Religious Philosophies of the West* (New York: Charles Scribner's Sons, 1965), p. 422.

87. *See* Chap. 1. Paul Lehmann, "Review of Tillich's *The Protestant Era,*" *Union Theological Seminary Quarterly Review* 4, no. 2 (January 1949).

88. Paul Tillich, *The Shaking of the Foundations* (New York: Charles Scribner's Sons, 1948), p. 63.

89. OITC, p. 181.

90. Ibid., p. 180.

Bibliography

Works Pertaining to Tillich's Theology of Culture

Works by Tillich

Books

Biblical Religion and the Search for Ultimate Reality. Chicago: University of Chicago Press, 1955.

Christianity and the Encounter of the World Religions. (No. 14 of "The Bampton Lectures in America," delivered at Columbia University in 1961.) New York: Columbia University Press, 1963.

The Courage to Be. New Haven, Conn.: Yale University Press, 1952.

Dynamics of Faith. New York: Harper & Row, 1957.

The Eternal Now. New York: Charles Scribner's, Sons, 1963.

The Future of Religions. Edited by Jerald C. Brauer. New York: Harper & Row, 1965.

The Interpretation of History. Translated by N. A. Rasetzki (Part I) and Elsa L. Talmey (Parts II, III, IV). New York: Charles Scribner's Sons, 1936.

Love, Power and Justice. New York: Oxford University Press, 1954.

Masse und Geist: Studien zur Philosophie der Masse. Berlin: Verlag der Arbeitsgemeinschaft, 1922.

Morality and Beyond. New York: Harper & Row, 1963.

My Search for Absolutes. New York: Simon and Schuster, 1967.

The New Being. New York: Charles Scribner's Sons, 1955.

226   A BLUEPRINT FOR HUMANITY

On the Boundary: An Autobiographical Sketch. New York: Charles Scribner's Sons, 1966.

Paul Tillich: Gesammelte Werke. Edited by Renate Albrecht. 14 vols. Stuttgart: Evangelisches Verlagswerk, vol. 1, 1959; vol. 2, 1962; vol. 3, 1966; vol. 4, 1961; vol. 5, 1964; vol. 6, 1963; vol. 7, 1962; vol. 8, 1969; vol. 9, 1967; vol. 10, 1968; vol. 11, 1969; vol. 12, 1971; vol. 13, 1972 and vol. 14 (index), 1975.

Perspectives on Nineteenth and Twentieth Century Protestant Theology. Edited with an Introduction by Carl E. Braaten. New York: Harper & Row, 1967.

Political Expectation. New York: Harper & Row, 1971.

The Protestant Era. Chicago: University of Chicago Press, 1948.

Religiöse Verwirklichung. Berlin: Furche-Verlag, 1930.

The Religious Situation. New York: Meridian Books, 1956 (originally published in Berlin, 1926, as *Die Religiöse Lage der Gegenwart*).

The Socialist Decision. Translated by Franklin Sherman with an introduction by John Stumme. New York: Harper & Row, 1977. (Original German work: *Die Sozialistische Entscheidung.* Potsdam: Alfred Protte, 1933).

Systematic Theology. 3 vols. Chicago: University of Chicago Press, vol. 1, 1951; vol. 2, 1957; vol. 3, 1963.

Theology of Culture. Edited by Robert C. Kimball. New York: Oxford University Press, 1959.

What Is Religion? Translated with an introduction by James Luther Adams. New York: Harper & Row, 1969. (Contains translations of Tillich's German articles: "Religionsphilosophie," "Die Überwindung des Religionsbegriffs in der Religionsphilosophie," and "Über die Idee einer Theologie der Kultur," q.v., below).

Articles

"Christian Criteria for Our Culture." *Criterion* (Journal of Yale University Christian Association) 1 (1952): 1–4.

"Depth." *Christendom* 9 (1944): 317–25.

"Der Begriff des Dämonischen und seine Bedeutung für die systematische Theologie." *Theologische Blätter* 5 (1926): 32–35.

"History as the Problem of our Period." *Review of Religion* 3 (March 1939): 255–64.

"Interrogation of Paul Tillich." In *Philosophical Interrogations.* Edited by Sydney Rome and Beatrice Rome, pp. 355–409. New York: Holt, Rinehart and Winston, 1964.

"Lost Dimension in Religion." *Saturday Evening Post,* 14 June 1958, p. 29.

"The Meaning and Justification of the Religious Symbol." In *Religious Experience and Truth.* Edited by Sidney Hook, pp. 3–11. New York: New York University Press, 1961.

"The Nature of Man." *Journal of Philosophy* 43 (1946): 675–77.

"Rechtfertigung und Zweifel." In *Vorträge der theologischen Konferenz zu Giessen,* pp. 19–32. Giessen: Topelmann, 1924. See GW 8: 85–100.

"Religion and Secular Culture." *Journal of Religion* 26 (1946): 79–86.

"The Religious Symbol." *Journal of Liberal Religion* 2 (1940): 13–33.

"Schelling und die Anfänge des existentialistischen Protestes." *Zeitschrift für Philosophische Forschung* 9 (1955): 197–208. See GW 4: 133–44.

"Theonomie." In RGG. Vol. 5. 2d ed., pp. 1128–29. Tübingen: Mohr, 1931. See GW 2: 159–74.

"Über die Idee einer Theologie der Kultur." In *Religionsphilosophie der Kultur: Zwei Entwürfe von Gustav Radbruch und Paul Tillich.* Edited by G. Radbruch and P. Tillich, pp. 28–52. Berlin: Reuther und Reichard, 1919. Also published in *Philosophische Vorträge der Kant-Gesellschaft,* no. 24. Berlin: Pan-Verlag, 1921. See GW 9: 13–31 and List of Abbreviations, OITC.

Works on Tillich

Books

Adams, James Luther. *Paul Tillich's Philosophy of Culture, Science and Religion.* New York: Harper & Row, 1965.

Adorno, Theodor, ed. *Werk und Wirken Paul Tillichs.* Stuttgart: Evangelisches Verlagswerk, 1967.

Amelung, Eberhard. *Die Gestalt der Liebe: Paul Tillichs Theologie der Kultur.* Gerd Mohn: Gütersloher Verlagshaus, 1972.

Benktson, Benot-Erik. *Christus und die Religion: Der Religions-*

begriff bei Barth, Bonhoeffer und Tillich. Stuttgart: Calwer Verlag, 1967.

Ferré, Nels F. S. *Paul Tillich: Retrospect and Future.* Nashville: Abingdon Press, 1967.

Gabus, Jean-Paul. *Introduction à la Théologie de la Culture de Paul Tillich.* Paris: Presses Universitaires de France, 1969.

Hamilton, Kenneth. *The System and the Gospel: A Critique of Paul Tillich.* London: The Library of Philosophy and Theology, SCM Press, 1963.

Hopper, David. *Tillich: A Theological Portrait.* Philadelphia: J. B. Lippincott Co., 1968.

Kegley, Charles W., and Bretall, Robert W., eds. *The Theology of Paul Tillich.* New York: Macmillan Publishing Co., 1964.

Kuhlman, Gerhardt. *Brumstad und Tillich zum Problem einer Theonomie der Kultur.* (Series: Philosophie und Geschichte, ed. Joachim Wach, no. 18). Tübingen: Mohr, 1928.

Leibrecht, Walter, ed. *Religion and Culture: Essays in honor of Paul Tillich.* New York: Harper & Row, 1957.

Lyons, James R., ed. *The Intellectual Legacy of Paul Tillich.* Detroit, Mich.: Wayne State University Press, 1969.

Mahan, Wayne W. *Tillich's System.* San Antonio, Tex.: Trinity University Press, 1974.

Martin, Bernard. *The Existentialist Theology of Paul Tillich.* New York: Bookman Associates, 1963.

May, Rollo. *Paulus: Reminiscences of a Friendship.* New York: Harper & Row, 1973.

Osborne, Kenan B., *New Being: A Study on the Relationship Between Conditioned and Unconditioned Being According to Paul Tillich.* The Hague: Martinus Nijhoff, 1969.

Pauck, Wilhelm, and Pauck, Marion. *Paul Tillich: His Life and Thought.* Vol. 1. New York: Harper & Row, 1976.

Petit, Jean-Claude. *La Philosophie de la Religion de Paul Tillich: Genèse et Evolution: La Période Allemande 1919–1933.* Montréal: Fides, 1974.

Rhein, Christoph. *Paul Tillich: Philosoph und Theologe.* Stuttgart, Germany: Evangelisches Verlagswerk, 1957.

Rieunaud, Jean. *Paul Tillich, Philosophe et Théologien.* Paris: Editions Fleuris, 1969.

Rowe, William L. *Religious Symbols and God: A Philosophical Study of Tillich's Theology.* Chicago: University of Chicago Press, 1968.

Scabini, Eugenia. *Il Pensiero di Paul Tillich.* Milan: Vita e Pensiero, 1967.

Scharlemann, Robert. *Reflection and Doubt in the Thought of Paul Tillich.* New Haven, Conn.: Yale University Press, 1969.

Thatcher, Adrian. *The Ontology of Paul Tillich.* London: Oxford University Press, 1978.

Thomas, J. Heywood. *Paul Tillich: An Appraisal.* Philadelphia: The Westminster Press, 1963.

Tillich, Hannah. *From Time to Time.* New York: Stein & Day, 1973.

Wheat, Leonard F. *Paul Tillich's Dialectical Humanism: Unmasking the God Above God.* Baltimore, Md.: The John Hopkins Press, 1970.

Articles

Adams, James Luther. "Theology and Modern Culture: Paul Tillich." In *On Being Human Religiously.* Edited by Max L. Stackhouse, pp. 225–54. Boston: Beacon Press, 1976 (originally published in Tillich's *The Protestant Era.* Chicago: University of Chicago Press, 1948).

Dillenberger, John. "Paul Tillich: Theologian of Culture." In *Paul Tillich: Retrospect and Future.* Edited by Nels Ferre et al. Nashville, Tenn.: Abingdon Press, 1966.

Doe, H. "Paul Tillich's Doctrine of Man." *Pastoral Psychology* 3 (1952): 18–24.

Edwards, Paul. "Professor Tillich's Confusions." *Mind: A Quarterly Review of Psychology and Philosophy* 74 (1965): 192–214.

Fabro, Cornelio. "Existential Reason Dissolved into Atheism (Tillich)." In *God in Exile: Modern Atheism.* Translated and edited by Arthur Gibson, pp. 1003–13. Westminster, Md.: Newman Press, 1968.

Ferré, Nels F. S. "Tillich and the Nature of Transcendence." In *Paul Tillich: Retrospect and Future.* Edited by Nels F. S. Ferré, pp. 7–18. Nashville, Tenn.: Abingdon Press, 1967.

Gabus, Jean-Paul. Introduction to *Théologie de la Culture,* French translation by Gabus of Tillich's TC. Paris: Éditions Planète, 1968.

Hook, Sidney. "The Atheism of Paul Tillich." In *Religious Experience and Truth*. Edited by Sidney Hook. New York: New York University Press, 1961, pp. 59–64.

Kattenbusch, Ferdinand. "Das Unbedingte und der Unbegreifbare." *Theologische Studien und Kritiken* 99 (1926): 319–422.

Lehmann, Paul. Review of Tillich's *The Protestant Era, Union Theological Seminary Quarterly Review* 4 (1949): 142–45.

Meland, Bernard E. "The Significance of Paul Tillich." *Christian Register* 92 (1933): 41–50.

Niebuhr, Reinhold. "The Contribution of Paul Tillich." *Religion in Life* 6 (1937): 574–81.

O'Meara, Thomas F., O. P. "Tillich and Heidegger: A Structural Relationship." *Harvard Theological Review* 51 (1968): 249–61.

Randall, John Herman, Jr. "The Ontology of Paul Tillich." In *The Theology of Paul Tillich*. Edited by C. Kegley and R. W. Bretall. New York: Macmillan Publishing Co., 1964, pp. 132–61.

————. Review of Tillich's *Systematic Theology,* vol. 1. *The Journal of Religion* 46 (1966): 208–10.

————. "The Philosophical Legacy of Paul Tillich." In *The Intellectual Legacy of Paul Tillich*. Edited by James R. Lyons. Detroit: Wayne State University Press, 1969, pp. 21–51.

Urban, Wilbur M. "Reply to Paul Tillich." *Journal of Liberal Religion* 2 (1940): 34–36.

Williams, Daniel Day. "Tillich's Doctrine of God." *Philosophical Forum* 18 (1960–61): 40–50.

Works Representing Secular Humanism

Books

Ayer, A. J., ed. *The Humanist Outlook*. London: Pemberton, 1968.

Blackham, H. J. *Objections to Humanism*. Philadelphia: J. B. Lippincott Co., 1963.

————. *Humanism*. Baltimore, Md.: Penguin Books, 1968.

Dewey, John. *A Common Faith*. New Haven, Conn.: Yale University Press, 1934.

Flew, Antony. *God and Philosophy*. New York: Dell Publishing Co., 1966.

Frankel, Charles. *The Case for Modern Man*. Boston: The Beacon Press, 1955.

———. ed. *The Uses of Philosophy: An Irwin Edman Reader*. New York: Greenwood Press, 1968.

Hook, Sidney. *The Quest for Being and Other Studies in Naturalism and Humanism*. New York: Dell Publishing Co., Delta Book, 1934.

Huxley, Julian, ed. *The Humanist Frame: The Modern Humanist Vision of Life*. New York: Harper & Row, 1961.

———. *Religion Without Revelation*. London: C. A. Watts & Co., 1967.

Krikorian, Yervant H., ed. *Naturalism and the Human Spirit*. New York: Columbia University Press, 1944.

Lamont, Corliss. *The Illusion of Immortality*. New York: Philosophical Library, 1952.

———. *The Philosophy of Humanism*. New York: Frederick Ungar Publishing Co., 1965.

Murray, Gilbert. *Five Stages of Greek Religion*. Garden City, N. Y.: Doubleday & Co., 1955.

Reese, Curtis W. *Humanism*. Chicago: The Open Court Publishing Co., 1926.

———. ed. *Humanist Sermons*. Chicago: The Open Court Publishing Co., 1927.

Randall, John H., Jr. *The Meaning of Religion for Man*. New York: Macmillan Publishing Co., 1946.

Russell, Bertrand. *New Hopes for a Changing World*. New York: Simon and Schuster, 1952.

Sellars, Roy Wood. *Reflections on American Philosophy from Within*. Notre Dame, Ind.: Notre Dame University Press, 1969.

Szezsny, Gerhard. *The Future of Unbelief*. Translated by Edward B. Garside. New York: George Braziller, 1961.

Woodbridge, Frederick J. E. *An Essay on Nature*. New York: Columbia University Press, 1969.

Articles

Blau, Joseph L. "God and the Philosophers." In *The Idea of God: Philosophical Perspectives.* Edited by E. H. Madden, R. Handy, and M. Farber, pp. 139–63. Springfield, Ill.: Charles C. Thomas 1968.

Dewey, John. "Philosophy Is Education." In *John Dewey: His Contribution to the American Tradition.* Edited by Irwin Edman, pp. 90–210. New York: Greenwood Press, 1968.

Edman, Irwin. "Religion Without Tears." In *The Uses of Philosophy: An Irwin Edman Reader.* Edited by Charles Frankel, pp. 177–87. New York: Simon and Schuster, 1955.

Kurtz, Paul. "Humanism and the Freedom of the Individual." *The Humanist* 30 (1969): 14–19.

————. "What Is Humanism." In *Moral Problems in Contemporary Society: Essays in Humanistic Ethics.* Edited by Paul Kurtz, pp. 1–14. Englewood Cliffs, N. J.: Prentice Hall, 1969.

Randall, John H., Jr. "What Is the Temper of Humanism?" In *The Humanist* 30 (1970): 34–35.

Wilson, Edwin H. "Humanism's Many Dimensions." *The Humanist* 30 (1970): 35–36.

Documents

British Humanist Association. *Humanists and Society: A General Statement of Policy, 1967.* (Issued by BHA, 13 Prince of Wales Terrace, London W8).

"A Humanist Manifesto." First published in *The New Humanist* 6 (1933); reprinted in Corliss Lamont, *The Philosophy of Humanism,* New York: Frederick Ungar Publishing Co., 1949, pp. 285–89.

"Humanist Manifesto II." *The Humanist* 33 (1973): 4–9.

Other Related Works

Books

Barbour, Ian. *Myths, Models and Paradigms.* New York: Harper & Row, 1974.

Barthel, Pierre. *Interprétation du Language Mythique et Théologie Biblique.* Leiden: E. J. Brill, 1967.

Berger, Peter. *The Sacred Canopy: Elements of a Sociological Theory of Religion.* Garden City, N. Y.: Doubleday & Co., 1967.

———. *A Rumor of Angels.* Garden City, N. Y.: Doubleday & Co., 1969.

Castaneda, Carlos. *The Teachings of Don Juan: A Yaqui Way of Knowledge.* Berkeley, Cal.: University of California Press, 1968.

Cox, Harvey. *The Secular City.* New York: Macmillan Publishing Co., 1965.

———. *The Feast of Fools.* Cambridge, Mass.: Harvard University Press, 1969.

Diamond, Malcolm L. *Contemporary Philosophy and Religious Thought.* New York: McGraw Hill Book Co., 1974.

Dubos, René. *So Human an Animal.* New York: Charles Scribner's Sons, 1968.

Fabro, Cornelio. *God in Exile: Modern Atheism.* Translated and edited by Arthur Gibson. Westminster, Md.: Newman Press, 1968.

Fromm, Erich. *Man for Himself.* New York: Holt, Rinehart and Winston, 1947.

Greeley, Andrew. *Unsecular Man.* New York: Schocken Books, 1972.

Hook, Sidney, ed. *Religious Experience and Truth.* New York: New York University Press, 1961.

Kallen, Horace M. *Secularism Is the Will of God: An Essay in the Social Philosophy of Democracy and Religion.* New York: Twayne Publishers, 1954.

Kant, Immanuel. *Groundwork of the Metaphysics of Morals.* Translated with an introduction by H. J. Paton. New York: Harper & Row, 1964.

Malraux, André. *The Voices of Silence.* Translated by Stuart Gilbert. Garden City, N. Y.: Doubleday & Co., 1953.

Macquarrie, John. *God and Secularity. New Directions in Theology Today,* Philadelphia: The Westminster Press, vol. 3, 1967.

Martin, James Alfred, Jr. *The New Dialogue Between Philosophy and Theology.* New York: The Seabury Press, 1966.

Marty, Martin. *The Modern Schism: Three Paths to the Secular.* New York: Harper & Row, 1969.

Maslow, Abraham. *Motivation and Personality.* New York: Harper & Row, 1954.

———. *The Psychology of Science: A Reconnaissance.* New York: Harper & Row, 1966.

———. *Religions, Values and Peak Experiences.* New York: The Viking Press, 1970.

———. *Toward a Psychology of Being.* New York: Van Nostrand Reinhold Co., 1968.

———. *The Farther Reaches of Human Nature.* Edited by Bertha Maslow and Miles Vich, New York: The Viking Press, 1971.

Matczak, Sebastian A., ed. *God in Contemporary Thought.* New York: Learned Publications, 1977.

McReady, William C., and Greeley, Andrew M. *The Ultimate Values of the American Population.* Beverly Hills, Cal.: Sage Publications, 1976.

Pratt, Vernon. *Religion and Secularization.* London: Macmillan & Co. 1970.

Richardson, Alan. *Religion in Contemporary Debate.* London: SCM Press, 1966.

Rome, Sydney and Rome, Beatrice, eds. *Philosophical Interrogations.* New York: Holt, Rinehart and Winston, 1964.

Roszak, Theodore. *The Making of a Counter Culture.* Garden City, N. Y.: Doubleday & Co., 1968.

Schelling, Friedrich Wilhelm Joseph, von. *The Ages of the World.* Translated with an introduction by Frederick Bolman, Jr. New York: Columbia University Press, 1942.

———. *Sämmtliche Werke.* Edited by K. Schelling. 14 Vols. Stuttgard and Augsburg: Cotta, 1856–61.

Shinn, Roger L. *Man: The New Humanism,* Vol. 6 of *New Directions in Theology Today.* Edited by William Hordern. London: Lutterworth Press, 1968.

Strawson, P. F. *Individuals.* London: Methuen & Co., 1961.

Thomas, George. *Religious Philosophies of the West.* New York: Charles Scribners Sons, 1965.

Toynbee, Arnold J. *An Historian's Approach to Religion.* London: Oxford University Press, 1956.

Williams, Daniel Day. *What Present-Day Theologians Are Thinking.* New York: Harper & Row, 1959.

Articles

Bellah, Robert. "Civil Religion in America." *Daedalus: Religion in America Issue* 96 (Winter 1967): 1–21.

Bochenski, Innocentius M. "Some Problems for a Philosophy of Religion." In *Religious Experience and Truth*. Edited by Sidney Hook. New York: New York University Press, 1961, pp. 39–47.

Clark, Walter H. "Intense Religious Experience." In *Research on Religious Development: A Comprehensive Handbook*. Edited by Merton P. Strommen, pp. 521–50. New York: Hawthorn Books, 1971.

Evans, Donald. "Preller's Analogy of 'Being'." *New Scholasticism* 45 (1971): 1–37.

Hood, Ralph W., Jr. "Psychological Strength and the Report of Intense Religious Experience." *Journal for the Scientific Study of Religion* 13 (March 1974): 65–72.

Lonergan, Bernard. "The Absence of God in Modern Culture." In *The Presence and Absence of God*. Edited by Christopher F. Mooney, S. J., pp. 164–78. New York: Fordham University Press, 1969.

Pole, David. "Breadth and Depth in Language." *Philosophy: The Journal of the Royal Institute of Philosophy* 46 (April 1971): 109–19.

Shiner, Larry. "The Concept of Secularization in Empirical Research." *Journal for the Scientific Study of Religion* 6 (Fall 1967): 207–220.

Smith, Huston. "Secularization and the Sacred." In *The Religious Situation 1968*. Edited by Donald R. Cutler. Boston: The Beacon Press, 1968, pp. 583–600.

Stagaman, David. " 'God' in Analytic Philosophy." In *God in Contemporary Thought*. Edited by Sebastian A. Matczak. New York: Learned Publications, 1977, pp. 813–49.

Swanson, Guy. "Modern Secularity." In *The Religious Situation 1968*. Edited by Donald R. Cutler, Boston: Beacon Press, 1968, pp. 810–34.

Unpublished Material

Mueller, Philip J. "The Centrality and Significance of the Concept of Ecstasy in the Theology of Paul Tillich." Ph.D. dissertation, Fordham University, 1971.

O'Dea, Thomas. "Secularism's Challenge." Paper read at Colloquium on Judaism and Christianity, 17–20 October 1966, at Harvard Divinity School. Mimeographed.

O'Hanlon, D. J. "The Influence of Schelling on the Thought of Paul Tillich." S. T. D. dissertation, Pontifical Gregorian University, Rome, 1958.

Randall, John H., Jr., and Tillich, Paul. "Is Religion a Human Art or a Divine Revelation?" Symposium and Discussion, Amherst College, 1958. On tape.

Sommer, Günther F. "The Significance of the Late Philosophy of Schelling for the Formation and Interpretation of the Thought of Paul Tillich." Ph.D. dissertation, Duke University, 1960.

Tillich, Paul. "Frontier Between Religion and Culture." Lecture delivered at Brandeis University, 1956. On tape.

———. "The Doctrine of Man and the Scientific Knowledge of Today." Four Lectures. Mimeographed.

———. "Religious and Secular Bases of Culture and Politics." Lecture delivered at the Spring Retreat of Christian Action, n.d. Mimeographed.

———. "The Self-Understanding of Man in Contemporary Thought." The Lowell Lectures delivered at King's Chapel, Boston, 1958. On tape.*

Torrance, Thomas F. "Determinism and Free Creation According to the Theologians." Lecture delivered at the Joint Meeting of the *Académie Internationale des Sciences Religieuses* and the *Académie Internationale de Philosophie des Sciences,* July 5–9, 1977, at St. John's University, New York. Mimeographed.

*The above-mentioned unpublished materials of Paul Tillich as well as the tape for the Amherst Symposium with Randall are part of the holdings of the Paul Tillich Archives, Andover-Harvard Divinity School Library, Cambridge, Massachusetts.

Index